Praise for *Ruptured Bodies*

The division of the churches may be long and ugly, but Schlesinger's book is beautiful, elegant, full of grace and insight—and even short.

—Eugene Rogers, professor of religious studies,
University of North Carolina Greensboro

Ruptured Bodies is an achievement both practical and theoretical. It is a work that theologically wrestles with the problem of ecclesial disunity in the midnight of Christian sin, particularly Christian sins in their racial, gendered, and sexual apertures. In writing that is at once urgent and informative, Schlesinger authors a compelling argument for how essential the issue of ecclesial unity remains to Christian coherence, and for how our sin threatens the integrity of our communities and our theologies. *Ruptured Bodies* offers a hope braced by the cross, and indeed makes the case that no other hope can meet Christians as they in fact are in history.

—Anne M. Carpenter, PhD, Danforth Chair in
Theological Studies, Saint Louis University

This is ecumenism at its finest: a historically and theologically honest appraisal of the problem and possibilities of church division. Centering his proposal on Vatican II catholicity with an Anglican corrective, Schlesinger argues that we must neither shut our eyes to the empirical reality of a divided church, nor stop at that division and so miss the mysterious unity that rests in the love of God revealed in Christ's cross.

—Anthony D. Baker, professor of systematic theology,
Seminary of the Southwest

RUPTURED BODIES

RUPTURED BODIES

BODIES

A

THEOLOGY

OF THE

CHURCH

DIVIDED

EUGENE R. SCHLESINGER

FORTRESS PRESS
MINNEAPOLIS

Library of Congress Cataloging-in-Publication Data

Names: Schlesinger, Eugene R., author.
Title: Ruptured bodies : a theology of the church divided / Eugene R. Schlesinger.
Description: Minneapolis : Fortress Press, [2024] | Includes bibliographical
    references and index.
Identifiers: LCCN 2023040102 (print) | LCCN 2023040103 (ebook) | ISBN
    9781506489674 (print) | ISBN 9781506489681 (ebook)
Subjects: LCSH: Church—Unity.
Classification: LCC BV601.5 .S36 2024 (print) | LCC BV601.5 (ebook) | DDC
    262/.72—dc23/eng/20231102
LC record available at https://lccn.loc.gov/2023040102
LC ebook record available at https://lccn.loc.gov/2023040103

Cover design and image: L. Whitt

Print ISBN: 978-1-5064-8967-4
eBook ISBN: 978-1-5064-8968-1

To Susan K. Wood, SCL
With affection, and in honor of her tireless work for the church's unity.

Ad maioram Dei gloriam

Contents

Acknowledgments

This book matters more to me than anything else I've ever written, and its writing has been an intensely personal and deeply transformative exercise. I had no idea when I first conceived it that it would turn out as it has, but now that I've written it, I can't imagine it unfolding differently. I've frequently had the sense of working without a net, as I've ventured into previously unexplored discourses, and staked out positions beyond the safe, comfortable, or familiar. And for precisely this reason, I'm profoundly grateful for the support I've received from various quarters.

Ryan Hemmer has accompanied this project from nearly the beginning, working with me to give it a home at Fortress Press. Whenever I needed an editorial consultation, he made himself available, always offering incisive and insightful counsel, which allowed me to clarify what I really wanted to do, rather than getting bogged down with things I thought I needed to do, but which weren't actually what this project was about. Without him this would have been a very different, much more boring book.

Along with Ryan, Anne Carpenter, Jonathan Heaps, and Jakob Rinderknecht have been frequent interlocutors. All of us, in our various ways, are trying to figure out how to proceed when we recognize that the master's house must be dismantled, and that we have to commence with the tools actually at our disposal, sometimes even the master's own. We've supported each other in trying out ideas, but more importantly, in celebrating life's triumphs, lamenting its disappointments, and maintaining hope amid its uncertainties.

Along with Jakob, Brianne Jacobs and Kelli Joyce have been kind enough to read drafts of various chapters, and have offered helpful advice, not all of which have I taken (which means that any shortcomings remain very much my own). I've also benefited from conversations with Luke Togni, Shaun Blanchard, Sarah Coakley, Neil Dhingra, Elyse Raby, Zack Guiliano, and my parents, Lou Schlesinger and Paula Savich.

In a variety of ways, Santa Clara University has left its mark on this project. Working here has brought me face-to-face with the legacy of colonialism and the complex ways it intersects with the beauty and the deformity of the church's history. This is the first book I've written that has been noticeably influenced by my teaching, and so I owe my students a debt of gratitude for allowing me to think through many of these ideas with them. Our wonderful library staff kept me well provisioned in the resources I needed, to the point that I'm convinced I'd not have had an easier time even at an R1 institution. Particularly worthy of mention is Sarah Smith, who, as my research for the project was winding down, was frequently disappointed if I was only picking up one or two books rather than a whole cart's worth.

The deeper I get into my career the more grateful I am for my family. I love my work, but it doesn't and can't love me back. My family does. I thank my children, Joann and Evelyn, for supporting my work and being periodically interested in it, but not really caring what I do. Without a doubt, the best part of my life is my marriage to Loren, which is nearly coextensive with my adult life. "Of making many books there is no end, and much study is a weariness of the flesh" (Eccl 12:12), but time spent with her is always refreshing, something of which I never tire, and never intend to.

Finally, I've learned the most about theology, and ecclesiology in particular, from Susan K. Wood, SCL. I'm grateful for her mentorship as my career got started and for her friendship as it's continued. While I hope that this book will be of use to those engaged in ecumenism, it is not itself an ecumenical work, but rather a speculative elaboration of what we can mean by the one church, given its divisions. Susan, though, has been tirelessly engaged in the actual work of pursuing the church's unity for decades. In view of these efforts and to honor them to what extent I'm able, I dedicate this book to her with great joy and affection.

Eugene R. Schlesinger
Feast of the Visitation of the Blessed Virgin Mary, 2023

Abbreviations

ARCIC	Anglican–Roman Catholic International Consultation
ATR	*Anglican Theological Review*
bapt.	*De baptismo* [Baptism][1]
BCP	*Book of Common Prayer*
c. ep. Parm.	*Contra epistulam Parmeniani* [Answer to the Letter of Parmenian]
c. Faust	*Contra Faustum manicheum* [Answer to Faustus, a Manichean]
c. litt ep.	*Contra litteras Petiliani* [Against the Writings of Petilian]
cath. Fr.	*Epistula ad Catholicos de secta Donatistarum* [Letter to Catholics on the Sect of the Donatists]
CDF	Congregation for the Doctrine of the Faith
ciu.	*De civitate Dei* [The City of God]
conf.	*Confessiones* [The Confessions]
CWBL	Collected Works of Bernard Lonergan
doctr. chr.	*De doctrina christiana* [Teaching Christianity]
DV	Dogmatic Constitution on Divine Revelation, *Dei Verbum*
GS	Pastoral Constitution on the Church in the Modern World, *Gaudium et Spes*
Io. eu. tr.	*In Iohannis evangelium tractatus* [Homilies on the Gospel of John]
JAS	*Journal of Anglican Studies*
JDDJ	*Joint Declaration on the Doctrine of Justification*
LG	Dogmatic Constitution on the Church, *Lumen Gentium*

---

1 I follow the standard scholarly conventions for citing Augustine's works (giving abbreviated Latin titles). However, for the ease of readers, I will always refer to the appropriate pages of English translations of his works. Where possible, I utilize the WSA, and, hence, follow their English titles.

ps. c. Don.	*Psalmus contra partem Donati* [Psalm against the Party of Donatus]
Tanner	Norman P. Tanner, ed., *Decrees of the Ecumenical Councils*
trin.	*De Trinitate* [The Trinity]
TS	*Theological Studies*
UR	Decree on Ecumenism, *Unitatis Redintegratio*
WCC	World Council of Churches
WSA	The Works of Saint Augustine: A Translation for the 21st Century

Introduction

Awash in a Sea of Division

I ask not only on behalf of these, but also on behalf of those who will believe in me through their word, that they may all be one . . . so that the world may believe that you have sent me.

— *John 17:20–21*

*When you come together as a church, I hear that there are divisions [*schismata*] among you; and to some extent I believe it. Indeed, there have to be factions [*haireseis*] among you.*

— *1 Corinthians 11:18–19*

Never has any organization been so content to act against the express wishes and instruction of its founder as the Christian church. Any number of books could be written about any number of failures of the Christian community to be what it says it is supposed to be. This book is focused on one, which, apparently, has beleaguered the church since its inception—the reality of Christians divided. If Jesus intends the church to be one, if upon this unity hinges the credibility of the Christian message, and if the churches are content to exist without full visible unity, then that existence is a performative contradiction, one that threatens the entire basis of the Christian faith.

And yet, this incongruity hardly seems to register within Christian consciousness. Our divisions are acknowledged, even lamented, but they persist. Ecumenical dialogues, which aim at the proximate end of differentiated consensus in the service of the eventual end of reunion, continue, issuing joint documents and celebrating new convergences, but reunion always eludes our grasp, receding away from us like the horizon. Even as certain doctrinal issues are determined to be no longer church dividing, the churches remain divided. And despite this scandal, the churches continue with business as usual. Division may be regrettable, but it hardly constitutes a crisis. Or so it would seem.

The problem, though, is that continuing with business as usual allows us to imagine the church as existing with integrity, when in reality, the churches are sick unto death.[1] The problem of division is not simply a failure to live up to our best ideals, nor a mere inconvenience or embarrassment, not a disjunction between theory and practice. It is, instead, an existential crisis, sabotaging Christian faithfulness in and to the world.

SICKNESS UNTO DEATH, THE WOUNDS OF DIVISION

That divided Christians cannot be faithful is a strident and stringent claim, one that in polite company would call for countless qualifications and exceptions. We might assert some notion of relative faithfulness. We might call attention to the ambiguity of how best to proceed in an already-established state of division. Even if the divisions we have inherited were inexcusable, isn't it better to carry on with what faithfulness we can, rather than resign ourselves to abject infidelity? Yet here I resist those qualifications. Not because they are not valid, but because they are all too readily available, and because we can ill afford to blunt the force of squarely facing the wounds of our divisions. Christians are well aware of the relative fidelity they can enact. The problem is that its *relative* character is not clearly evident because the damage wrought by division is glossed over. More needs to be said than that division precludes fidelity, but not at the expense of saying less. The problem is that so often in our desire to say the more we do indeed say less. We point to the favorable

---

1 This is compounded in ecumenical contexts where, rightly, the churches learn to recognize one another as church, and to celebrate the ways that God is at work in those communities with whom they are not in full communion. The ecumenical task could hardly proceed if our starting point were to note all the ways that our dialogue partners have gotten it wrong and are distorted. As chapter 5 will show, it was not until this lens was put away and replaced by one of mutual recognition that division could be seen as the problem that it is and reunion become a goal.

cholesterol levels in a body ravaged by cancer and celebrate that body's "relative" health.

The Word Made Trivial

By their divided existence, the Christian churches trivialize the Christian faith. The entire witness of the New Testament assumes the unity of the church, where it does not command it. Paul exhorts the churches to unity (e.g., Rom 12:3–21; 1 Cor 1:10–17; 12:1–31; 2 Cor 13:11; Phil 2:1–4; 4:1–3; Eph 4:1–13). The other epistles and the Apocalypse presume such unity, with no imaginative space for division. No Christian can claim fidelity to Scripture's authority while flouting its call to unity. This injunction is especially pertinent because so many of the church's divisions have occurred and continue to be tolerated in the name of biblical fidelity. My own Anglican Communion is currently being rent by divisions, and while the presenting issue is the full inclusion of LGBTQ persons and couples, schismatic Anglicans will insist that the true conflict is not over sexuality, but biblical authority. And yet by breaking away, they abandon the authority of Scripture, which proscribes division.

The Nicene-Constantinopolitan Creed stresses the unity of the church as an article of faith (along with its sanctity, catholicity, and apostolicity). To confess the Nicene Creed in a state of division, then, is to contradict the creed. One cannot be doctrinally orthodox in a divided church, because one's very existence-in-division is a denial of credal faith.

Of course, not all Christians accept the authority of Nicaea and its creed. (Some will affirm its trinitarian affirmations, but on a basis other than the authority of a general council, others would eschew credal formulae altogether.) Similarly, not all Christians understand Scripture or its authority in the same manner. But Jesus, in the words quoted in the epigraph of this introduction, indicates his desire that the church be one. Questions about the role of Scripture and creed in Christian life notwithstanding, how can one plausibly claim to follow Jesus while ignoring, even flouting, his express wishes? What could it possibly mean to be his disciples, or to confess him as Lord when his desires mean so little to those making that confession?

The problem compounds, though, for its effects extend beyond individual or even corporate faithfulness. If the teachings of Scripture, creed, and Savior have become optional, then they are also trivial. What does it matter how the church preaches and teaches, or how Christian people order their lives, when so basic a matter is dispensable? The risen Christ commissions his apostles: "Make disciples of all nations . . . teaching them to obey everything that I have commanded you" (Matt 28:19–20). On what basis can an invitation to become Jesus's disciple be extended when following his commands is flagrantly rendered trivial?

In a state of division, the churches are reduced to one option among many. Would-be followers of Christ must then select among the offerings, leaving the churches to squabble over market share. Brand awareness and niche appeal come to overshadow the gospel message or conviction. Even in the emerging postdenominational Christianity, or in earlier eras of evangelistic cooperation or missionary comity agreements, the need to select one church among many perdures. And if one's joining a church is a matter of selection among options, then the church itself is also reduced to one option among others: a matter of preference, rather than of principle.

An Uncertain Sound

Beyond its trivialized message, the divided church cannot speak with one voice on any number of issues, which, once more, affects both intra- and extraecclesial matters. Here, I do not mean simply that Christians disagree, even, at times, upon matters of great import. To my mind, this is hardly a pressing issue—there is nothing wrong with disagreement on a whole host of matters— and disagreement is not at all incompatible with full visible unity. There is a broad consensus on such basics as "Scripture is, somehow, authoritative for the Christian community," or "Jesus is Lord," or "God is the Trinity," or "salvation is by grace." On the most fundamental matters, Christians are in relative agreement. Rather, the problem is with a divided external witness and a short-circuited internal forum of discernment. I'll begin with the latter.

History is real, and is a product of human activity and especially of human meaning making. Because human beings are living and dynamic organisms, we change with time. Shared cultural meanings shift and develop. To revert to or insist on some cultural arrangement from the past without considering how it ought to change in order to meet the present, is to insist on a subhuman set of values. The church is a human reality—more than this, to be sure, but also never less. Hence, the church must also change and develop as history progresses and new cultural forms emerge.

Because the way forward is not always clear, and, indeed, because Christians acting in good faith sometimes reach divergent conclusions, if this change and development is to be authentic and faithful, the church must engage in discernment. To take a no-longer controversial matter, the earliest Christians faced the quandary of whether gentile converts were to be circumcised in accordance with the Mosaic law. In order to become Christians, did they also have to be Jews? Sharp disagreement and vigorous debate ensued, until at the Council of Jerusalem a consensus emerged—gentile Christians were not bound by the Mosaic law, but were also instructed to abstain from certain behaviors that might provoke scandal among their Jewish elder siblings (Acts 15). The conciliar decree did not simply end debate either, as Paul's Letter to the Galatians attests. For some time thereafter, both positions were found within the Christian churches, and only over time was the Council's decision received as settled and consistently practiced among the churches.

To move toward the still controversial, for several decades now, the churches have sought to reckon with the sea change brought about by newly emergent understandings of gender and sexuality. While, like the cultural matrices that generated them, the biblical witness and the subsequent theological tradition have been more or less unreflexively heteronormative and patriarchal, we have reached a new stage of how the meaning of gender and sexuality are constructed within our cultures.

While hardly actually implemented, it is generally accepted that women ought to have access to opportunities and responsibilities equal to those of men, that far from being deficient men, they are, in all ways, the equals of men. With the advent of reliable artificial contraception, sexual activity and procreation can be effectively decoupled in a way that they never could before. Research into sexual reproduction has moved us beyond an outdated Aristotelian view wherein women were simply passive recipients of male seed, but rather equally active in the process of conception. The category of sexual orientation, and the recognition that a nonnegligible portion of the population has a persistent sexual orientation to their own sex; or that sexuality exists on a spectrum, wherein the binary of hetero- and homosexuality are hardly the only options, has raised the question of how folks with nonheterosexual orientations can most faithfully live out their sexuality.[2] The recognition that gender is a social construction, performed differently between and within cultures, and the experience of trans and nonbinary persons has disrupted long-standing anthropological assumptions (theological and otherwise), and raised the question of how LGBTQ experience fits within the life of the church.

The answers to these developments' implicit questions are not straight-forward, and different churches have engaged in their own discernment and made their own decisions according to that discernment. Some, in view of the newly recognized equality of women with men, have admitted women into holy orders. Others have resisted this, whether insisting that fidelity to Scripture and tradition demands otherwise, or simply declaring it an impossibility. Some have opened marriage or marriage-like unions to couples of the same-sex or ordained ministers who are in same-sex unions. Others have insisted that marriage is reserved for a man and a woman or that its validity depends upon an openness to procreation, ruling out same-sex couples, and, by implication, clergy in same-sex unions (as well as heterosexual couples who use birth control).

That Scripture and the tradition reflect heteronormative patriarchy is incontestable, but this alone does not resolve the question. While Scripture and tradition are also more than simply products of human meaning-construction, they are not less. Recognizing a biblical, or patristic, or medieval, or early modern figure's patriarchal or heteronormative assumptions does not necessarily mean that they are binding as divinely revealed. But it also does not rule out this possibility. Careful discernment is needed to disentangle what is bindingly authoritative and what is a reflection of a cultural matrix that no longer obtains.

The point of all this is not to rehearse any of these debates, but to highlight how a state of division robs the church of its capacity for discernment. As

2 The terms *homosexual* and *heterosexual* are largely regarded as outdated, impersonal, overly clinical. While I avoid using the former term throughout this book, I have decided to retain the latter, because while LGBTQ functions as a substitute for the one, there is not a handy substitute for the other. *Straight*, for instance, implies a rectitude and normativity that I wish to avoid. On that note, I recognize that *queer* is a fraught term, one that some but not all members of the LGBTQ community have claimed as their own. I utilize this term as a synonym for *LGBTQ* in contexts where *LGBTQ* would not suffice. I don't necessarily imply transgression in this usage (nor do I exclude those who understand themselves and their sexuality in this transgressive sense), nor do I impose this label on LGBTQ people who do not apply this term to themselves.

those churches who still do not ordain women and who still prohibit same-sex unions deliberate and demur, they do so without the full complement of Christian people, notably those churches who have found women's ordination and LGBTQ affirmation to be deeply compatible with if not entailed by the gospel. Meanwhile, those latter churches have moved forward by their best lights, but these are matters that affect the church as a whole and that must ultimately be decided and received by the church as a whole.[3]

The point here is not to argue for one position or another on the questions of women's ordination or gay marriage (or, for that matter, contraception), though I am convinced that the most viable way forward is for the churches to thread the needle of affirming women's ordination and LGBTQ identity and sexuality while also upholding fulsome and traditional positions on biblical authority and doctrinal orthodoxy. Instead, the point is that the churches lack any way of resolving the issues so long as they remain divided, and that this cuts both ways. The churches who have revised their positions can only do so on a tentative, provisional basis, while they await the developments' reception by the church as a whole. The churches who have not are incapable of discerning a final no to the question, so long as the full complement of the *catholica* is not part of the deliberations. And as we wait, stymied in our attempts at discernment, women and LGBTQ folks are left in the lurch. The best anyone can do is muddle their way forward.

Meanwhile, humanity faces unprecedented crises, ranging from climate change to a resurgence of far-right authoritarian forces in government. While, historically, the churches' divisions fell along doctrinal lines, in the past century or so, political and ideological divisions have tended to be more prominent. While the former has its own problems, the latter leaves the churches susceptible to political co-optation. So long as a church contains a broad representation of political conviction, it resists being simply assimilated to some point along the political spectrum (usually one of the polar wings).

---

3 At times "conservatives" within these churches protest that only by a new general council could these issues truly be resolved or authentic developments be enacted. On the one hand, this is correct and is precisely the point I am arguing. But in this context, it is disingenuous special pleading to name an impossible condition for the possibility of this development, while remaining content to carry on with the life of the church in other areas. Suddenly, when the well-being of vulnerable populations is on the line, we must defer to the counsels of the wider church, even though these wider counsels do not stand in our way at any other time.

This has been driven home to me as, steadily since the 1980s, conservative white Christians in America have become essentially a proxy to the Republican Party and eventually Trumpist authoritarianism. While I find the policies pursued by the Trump administration and the post-Trump Republican Party odious, the problem here would exist even if the GOP had not been swept up in the MAGA wave. The problem isn't that political co-optation leads them to support bad policies—though it often does—but that it confuses the ultimate ends of the Christian faith with the immanent ends of the modern nation-state, bastardizing the gospel, and undermining the unique allegiance owed by Christians to the one God by substituting an allegiance to a contingent political order. And, while I occupy the political left, and, so see more readily the failings of the right, I am under no illusions that the same dangers do not also exist for "liberal" and "progressive" Christians. Hence, while existential threats mount, the divided church can only offer mealy-mouthed guidance, despite the bold vocality of its various factions. In a state of division, no one can really know what the Christian church stands for. "And if the bugle gives an indistinct sound, who will get ready for battle?" (1 Cor 14:8).

Deadly Feasting

Jesus's dying bequest to the church is the eucharistic banquet, which remains a feature of the common life of all mainstream Christians, though with differences in emphasis, frequency, understanding, and practice. Dom Gregory Dix's *The Shape of the Liturgy* famously ends with a meditation on how faithfully Christian communities have carried out the injunction "Do this in remembrance of me." Whatever else we might do, or neglect, we keep the eucharistic feast. Our divided state, though, risks transforming the medicine of immortality into deadly poison.

From Henri de Lubac's *Corpus Mysticum* onward, it has been well-established that the primary referent of the eucharistic "body of Christ" is not the real presence but the church, and that this ecclesial dimension of the sacrament was occluded as debates over the manner in which Christ is present in the sacrament constricted theological focus to the elements. Though the meaning—or, in some quarters, the truth—of the real presence has been and remains a site of controversy, we need not delve into it here, for Paul's injunction to the Corinthians, while compatible with—and gesturing toward and assuming—a theology of eucharistic presence, does not depend on one.

Writing to the Corinthians, Paul laments that their eucharistic assemblies have nothing to commend, because they do more harm than good. Divided as the Corinthian church is by factions, they cannot even really be said to be eating the Lord's supper (1 Cor 11:17–20). By celebrating the Eucharist in a state of mutual disregard, the Christians of Corinth eat and drink unworthily, and, so, are "answerable for the body and blood of the Lord" (1 Cor 11:27). To participate in the meal "without discerning the body," is to "eat and drink judgment against" oneself and can lead to illness and death (1 Cor 11:29–30). The context demands an ecclesial referent to the warning about discerning the body. A chapter earlier, Paul had written that the community is "one body" because all eat of the "one bread" (1 Cor 10:17), and, of course, the present instructions turn upon the problem of factional and exclusionary practices within the community's celebration.

Christians divided among themselves court divine judgment when they celebrate the sacrament, and for several related reasons. Such celebrations contradict the meaning of the meal, which is the unity of Christ's body. The Eucharist is meant to effect ecclesial unity (1 Cor 10:17), so a celebratory context of willful division falsifies and resists the divine initiative for it. Similarly, the Eucharist commemorates the death of Christ, by which he reconciled divided humanity to one another and to God (John 11:52; Eph 2:11–22). A divided Eucharist, then, makes of the death whereby humanity has been redeemed a mockery. How shall we escape the dread judgment when we are "crucifying again the Son of God and are holding him up to contempt" (Heb 6:6)?

Once more, the dissonance barely seems to register, much less the grievous danger facing the church. Division is not merely embarrassing or inconvenient, but blasphemous and deadly. Perhaps in our division, fasting and lament ought to be the order of the day, though this seems to be a prospect no one can quite countenance. Similarly, churches will pronounce upon the validity of their separated siblings' sacraments, but the possibility that none of our Eucharists are valid is too threatening to stomach. Yet, given the Pauline injunction, it might be better if our Eucharists *were* invalid, for at least then the deadly effects might be ameliorated.

But it is the position of this book that, for the most part at least, our Eucharists *are* valid, and that this ought to fill us with foreboding and dread. For in a divided church, it is impossible to receive the bread of heaven and the cup of salvation without in that very act eating and drinking judgment upon oneself. And does not the sorry state of the church present its own empirical verification of the Pauline warning? We are sick unto death, and, in some quarters, nigh "falling asleep."

If the Foundations Be Destroyed . . . ?

Whether dismissed as irrelevant, or wracked with sexual abuse scandals or a reckoning for its legacies of harm (colonialism, patriarchy, the oppression of the LGBTQ community), or its co-optation by nationalism or calls for a renewed integralism that would eschew liberal values and forge alliances with authoritarians, despite pockets of vitality, the church's overall trajectory is decline. To take but one striking example, the figures for my own Episcopal Church suggest that if present trends continue, it will be dead in under thirty years. (That this is not how statistics work notwithstanding, it is nevertheless a sobering realization.)

While I do not intend to, nor do I think I could demonstrate causation, I cannot help but suspect that the church's sorry state, its sickness unto death, derives from the upstream pollutant of our division. Yes, in many cases, we can point to rather specific causes for our decline. Folks who depart from the Christian faith (or at least from association with any Christian church) might cite disgust over abuse, or the descent into MAGA, or their own exclusion on the basis of their sexuality or gender identity, or their solidarity with those so excluded, or so on. But I've yet to encounter someone who attributes their decision to disaffiliate to ecclesial division, nor is it likely to appear very high (or, really, at all) on the list of reasons nonbelievers would give for not becoming Christians. But, as I've argued above, the more proximate reasons for decline are downstream from and compounded by the church's divided state.

To be sure, we cannot know whether the counterfactual of a united church would have avoided these issues that have led to decline. And it is certainly not as though a united church is incapable of perpetrating harm. Chapter 3 will explore the ways in which unity can be weaponized for inflicting further injury, especially upon vulnerable communities. In fact, many of the legacies of harm with which we are presently reckoning have their roots in times of greater unity. But even so, most of the church's history has been one of division. From 1054 onward, there has been no united church of which to speak, and that leaves unaddressed whether smaller-scale schisms, such as Donatism and Novatianism, or even Corinthian fractiousness, falsify the church's unity.

So, while a direct line of causation between division and decline cannot be drawn, it strikes me that with our decline, we are witnessing a fulfillment of Paul's warning to the Corinthians. By our divided Eucharists we invite divine judgment, and as a result, our churches are deformed and nearing death. A sickened Corinthian could probably receive a medical diagnosis, but that finding would not preclude a eucharistic etiology for the disease.

By our own actions, as well as, perhaps because of, cultural factors beyond our control, many find the church's proclamation of Jesus Christ crucified and raised to be in-credible. In view of this, we must attend once more to the words of the Johannine Jesus:

> I ask not only on behalf of these, but also on behalf of those who will believe in me through their word, that they may all be one. As you, Father, are in me and I am in you, may they also be in us, so that the world may believe that you have sent me. The glory that you have given me I have given them, so that they may be one, as we are one, I in them and you in me, that they may become completely one, so that the world may know that you have sent me and have loved them even as you have loved me. (John 17:20–23)

Christ insists that the credibility of the gospel message will hinge upon the unity of his followers. There is a causal relationship between the church's unity and the credibility of its proclamation of Jesus Christ as sent by God and of God's love for us in him. Is it any wonder then if the divided church finds its message(s) unheeded and itself in decline? By our divisions, we undermine the foundations of our faith.

I do not suggest that if the churches put aside our differences and found our way to full visible unity that the scandals would disappear and decline would reverse. But if the church believes that its foundation lies in Jesus Christ as the one sent from the Father, and if that same Jesus Christ prays for the church's unity and suggests that upon that unity hinges the credibility of that foundation, I fail to see how any reversal of present decline could possibly occur apart from the restoration of unity. While I do not offer a program for church reunion in these pages, this book is offered in the service of addressing this crisis. Its contribution is to attempt something that, on its surface, should be impossible: a systematic ecclesiology of the divided church, but apart from such an account, attempts at reunion will devolve into groping about in the dark.

THE SEEMING IMPOSSIBILITY
OF THIS WORK

A divided church presents at least two challenges to a would-be systematic ecclesiology. First, ecclesiology is, by its very nature, particular. It attempts to describe and understand an actual community, not simply the idea of one. Therefore, ecclesiological reflection must be rooted within the context of a particular Christian church, lest it be fiction rather than theology, aiming to describe "the church," but actually describing no church. And yet, an ecclesiology that concerns itself with only one church tradition to the exclusion of others, while it might gain a certain coherence, can only be partial, incomplete, provincial, falling short of the catholic reality affirmed in the creed.

Ecclesiology must unfold with reference to a particular community, but it must also transcend that community. Such transcendence cannot come at the cost of particularity, though, lest the result be merely idealistic and overly "thin," an ecclesiology of the lowest common denominator, speaking merely to those aspects shared in common by all the churches. Such an account, useful as it might be in ecumenical statements, lacks the specificity and richness of any of the particular communities from which it is distilled. The choice between specificity and comprehensiveness dogs the ecclesiological enterprise.

The second difficulty stems from the nature of division. It is an article of faith, confessed weekly by those churches that utilize the Nicene-Constantinopolitan Creed in their liturgies, that the church is one (and holy, and catholic, and apostolic). Yet, while the mainstream Christian tradition confesses these classical Nicene *notae ecclesiae*, empirical reality seems to contradict most, if not all of them. The church is manifestly divided and has been for some time, and despite the concerted efforts of the twentieth and early-twenty-first centuries, these divisions persist. We might add the reckoning currently underway for the churches' legacies of harm, which militate against claims of sanctity; or their often-provincial lack of openness to the whole of humanity (e.g., the tendency for white, male, heterosexual, Anglo-European voices to be privileged at the expense and exclusion of BIPOC, API, female, LGBTQ perspectives and experience). The churches also regularly contest one another's apostolicity, though that particular note is more difficult to assess empirically, because the contestation is bound up with decisions about what apostolicity means and how it is manifested and measured. While the first of these contradictions, the lack of unity, is the most germane for our purposes here, the others, particularly the lack of holiness and of catholicity, will also inform our considerations, for so often they lay at the heart of the churches' decisions to divide.

Assuming that the Nicene-Constantinopolitan confession of one, holy, catholic, and apostolic church is indeed an article of faith; assuming that the Johannine Jesus's prayer that his followers all be one represents the divine will for the church; assuming that Pauline admonitions toward unity are morally incumbent upon Christians, a divided church is not simply an unfortunate, regrettable mishap. It is sinful. Because being is good and intelligible, and because sin is a decision contrary to this intelligibility, which is to say, fundamentally irrational, a divided church is a departure from intelligibility, an absurdity. This presents its own challenge to the theological task, which seeks understanding. It would seem that a systematic ecclesiology is impossible if the church is divided.

Understanding what I mean by that stems from the notion of systematic theology that informs this work. Obviously, there are multiple, competing notions of systematic theology available. Adjudicating between them is a matter of fundamental theology or theological method, which I will not undertake here. It would take another work entirely to establish my understanding of systematics, so rather than do that, I will simply provide an account of how I understand the task.

Systematic theology is one functional specialization within the overall theological task. Its particular mandate is to provide a coherent articulation of the church's faith, as expressed in the doctrines taught by the church. Systematic theology operates, then, in a speculative mode. It does not aim to establish the truth of church teaching, which depends upon divine revelation. Nor does it even aim to establish what the teaching of the church is, which is the provenance of the magisterium, and, in a derivative sense, of the functional specialization Bernard Lonergan called "doctrines," the task of which is to articulate what the magisterium has taught and in what manner it has taught it (e.g., definitively, or in some other manner). Instead, systematics receives the teachings of the church, which are believed to be true because divinely revealed, and seeks to understand them. The questions systematic theology asks and attempts to answer are not questions of truth (*Is this so?*), but rather questions for understanding (*How? Why? What?*).

Systematic theology trades in intelligibilities. Church division, though, presents not an intelligibility, but a surd. Despite whatever reasons might lead up to them, divisions are, in the end, irrational. They defy intelligence not because they are superior to it, but because there is nothing intelligible to grasp. Obviously, this is a strong claim, demanding more nuanced treatment, but given the strong impetus toward unity found in the New Testament documents and the credal confession of the church's unity, then it would seem that a divided church is a contradiction in terms. But if there is a surd ensconced amid the data to be understood, then it would seem that a systematic ecclesiology is impossible when the church is divided.

This book attempts to address the second of these challenges and to operate with an awareness of and to attempt to minimize the liabilities of the first. Only if the second is addressed can any headway be made on the first. It is written by an Anglican, though with primary reference to the Catholic Church, for reasons that will become clear in due course. While this does not lead to a fully comprehensive account, it does (1) locate the work within a particular community, two in fact, and (2) avoid the chauvinism or myopia of preoccupation with a single tradition. Other perspectives, particularly those of the Orthodox and of the united churches, further inform the outlook.

Addressing this second difficulty depends on recognizing that ecclesiology under the conditions of division is an amalgamation of two mysteries, each of which, in inverse ways, defy our comprehension. On the one hand, there is the *mysterium redemptionis*, by which God has done something new through the missions of the Word and the Holy Spirit, regathering a renewed humanity into one in what some have called the mystical body of Christ. This mystery defies our comprehension through a surplus of meaning, though such mysteries admit of a partial, though most fruitful understanding. On the other hand, we have the *mysterium iniquitatis*, by which humanity, irrationally, acts against our own best interests. Assuming that being is both intelligible and good, then sin is simply irrational. And so this mystery defies our understanding because there is nothing to understand. Both of these mysteries frustrate our attempts to understand the church when Christians are divided from each other.

And yet, crucially, the *mysterium redemptionis* is enacted precisely to counteract and heal the effects of the *mysterium iniquitatis*. Of course, this redemption occurs not by mere cancelation, as if the absurd can simply become the intelligible, but it is theologically important to insist that the balance falls on the side of redemption, rather than of sin. The Good is infinite and eternal, while evil is privation and shall not endure forever, even if it will not be fully eradicated within history's bounds. Nevertheless, we must also reckon with how ecclesial division represents a postredemption development. It is a regression into absurdity, and so its unintelligibility is perhaps compounded.

One might, of course, adjust their understanding of the theological task, abandoning the goal of systematic coherence, and opting instead for a merely "constructive" theology, one that will, in the end, involve aporiae and perhaps even contradictions. While I have sympathy for this approach, and have more or less operated according to it in my previous forays into the question of the church and especially its divisions, it is not the one I undertake here, because I am persuaded that a systematic ecclesiology remains desirable, and not only desirable but also possible, and this last adjective for a specific reason: because the one church of Jesus Christ subsists in the Catholic Church.[4]

For a Catholic to claim *Lumen Gentium*'s *subsitit in* would be somewhat pedestrian, a matter of course. For an Episcopalian to do so is perhaps perplexing, and, in my experience, based on others' reactions, apparently irksome, but there is a venerable, if small, tradition of Anglo-Papalism, and Episcopalians have a well-established penchant for idiosyncrasy. So, a few eyebrows may be raised in response, but little else. I aim beyond the idiosyncratic or the pedestrian, though, and argue that all Christians have a stake in affirming the *subsistit in*, and in insisting that this is not the sole and final word to be spoken. In other words, no reverse chauvinism or Roman triumphalism informs the present argument. Important perspectives and resources from my own Anglican tradition will complement this Catholic claim and do so in such a way as to invite the other churches to make their own contributions.

THE ROAD AHEAD

This theology of the divided church unfolds over five chapters, which range from the church's foundation to its future, from origins to prospects. Throughout I shall be animated with a conviction that we must take the church as it is, not as we think it should be, nor as we might wish it were instead. This outlook will factor prominently in chapter 1—which considers the extent to which there has ever actually been a united church—and chapter 5—which considers the ways in which the churches must face one another and forge

---

4 *LG*, no. 8 [Tanner, 2:854].

new paths if they will ever find true unity. I shall be concerned to relate ideal statements of ecclesial identity and vocation to the empirical reality of the churches as they actually are.

A particular metaphor, which Bernard Lonergan utilized in developing his theology of history, has been particularly instructive for me in this regard. He writes,

> Newton's planetary theory had a first approximation in the first law of motion: bodies move in a straight line with constant velocity unless some other force intervenes. There was a second approximation when the addition of the law of gravity between the sun and the planet yielded an elliptical orbit for the planet. A third approximation was reached when the influence of the gravity of the planets on one another is taken into account to reveal the perturbed ellipses in which the planets actually move. The point to this model is, of course, that in the intellectual construction of reality it is not any of the earlier stages of the construction but only the final product that actually exists. Planets do not move in straight lines nor in properly elliptical orbits; but these are needed to arrive at the perturbed ellipses in which they actually do move.[5]

Just as the ideal and the empirical must complement each other in order to understand planetary orbits, so it is with the church. Both are vital in grasping the reality, and both exert a certain control upon our affirmations of the church. The ideal allows us to affirm that there is more to Christian community than meets the eye, while the empirical rules out naïve assertions of the ideal. This insight shall be borne out in due course, and will hopefully become clearer as we progress.

Chapter 1 challenges the notion that there was some original united church that was subsequently rent by divisions. From the earliest days, the Christian movement has been pluriform, fractious, and a site of contestation. Recognizing this fact releases us from the quixotic task of a primitivism whereby we might try to recover a lost unity that never actually existed. It, moreover, prompts us to reconsider what the church's unity is. It is an article of faith that the church is one, so empirical reality leads us not to deny the ideal (nor does the ideal lead us to deny what is evident to observation), but rather to adopt a more adequate understanding of it. We shall note that the church's unity encompasses a wide diversity, and not merely a friendly diversity, but

---

5 Bernard J. F. Lonergan, "Insight Revisited," in *A Second Collection*, ed. Robert M. Doran and John D. Dadosky, CWBL 13 (Toronto: University of Toronto Press, 2016), 228.

one that goes so far as enmity, agonism, and strife. In its original enactment, the church's unity is a union of enemies.

This consideration of enmity leads naturally to chapter 2, which considers the centrality of love in ecclesial unity. The church is founded on the love of God enacted in the life of Christ, and especially his self-bestowal upon the cross. The law of the cross (to use a phrase drawn from Lonergan) is the church's deepest meaning, is the force that binds the church in unity, and is enacted in every eucharistic celebration. A central conviction of this study emerges in chapter 2, one drawn from Augustine of Hippo's anti-Donatist writings: church division always stems from a refusal of love. It is a repudiation of the law of the cross. Moving beyond the Donatist controversy, forays into two major divisions—the East-West schism, and the divisions of the Western church during the sixteenth-century reformations, bear out the thesis that no division is inevitable. They are all a matter of love and love's refusal.

The first two chapters more or less treat division as inexcusable and unity as an unquestioned good. Chapter 3 provides an important corrective and challenge to that outlook, by considering the ways in which the churches have weaponized unity as a tool of oppression. Such a unity, which I call crucifying unity, is its own refusal of love, a parody of the law of the cross, for rather than freeing us to give to and for one another in charity, this law demands that some must give through the compulsory instruments of legislation and enforcement. It insists that the ongoing crucifixion of some is the price that must be paid for unity of all. Divisions over race and sexuality are the particular focus here.

By recognizing the problem of crucifying unities, we are primed to sketch the contours and potential of unity, for now we know what sort of unity we must avoid. This is the task of chapter 4, which places Anglican and Catholic accounts of unity into mutually corrective dialogue. The Anglican tradition has consistently recognized that we are but a portion of the church as a whole, and has insisted that any unity falling short of the union of all the baptized with one another in Christ will be incomplete. But while Anglicans have recognized the inadequacy of a merely invisible unity, we lack the resources to affirm that the church God intends can be found here and now. The Catholic Church, on the other hand, affirms that the one church subsists in its communion. I argue that this self-understanding actually provides what's missing from the Anglican conception and provides an ecumenically and ecclesiologically necessary piece of the puzzle. But I argue further that it needs to be chastened by the Anglican commitment to the full unity of all the baptized. The Catholic Church needs to recognize its own incompleteness apart from the rest of us.

The final chapter considers the weight of history, recognizing that while unity and division are principally matters of the will, our wills are also constrained by our histories, and that these represent the greatest barrier to reunion. We have all walked different, sometimes incompatible paths with the Lord in our sojourns. Our ways forward must not involve repudiations of ourselves or our histories (these would be crucifying unities), because this would be a repudiation of our very walks with the Lord, betrayals of the gospel and of our salvation by it. We must forge new paths together, taking each other as we are, not as we might prefer one another to be. Ecumenically vexing matters such as the papacy, women's ordination, and LGBTQ affirmation receive particular attention here, and I argue that the church's eventual full visible unity will include them all.

Beyond the ideal and our failure to attain it, there is also grace and redemption. The final word belongs not to human failure or infidelity, but to divine mercy and grace. For, while the division of Christians from each other is an evil, the existence of the churches is a good, and through them God continues to carry out the divine redemptive purpose. Through the churches in all their woundedness, God draws people back to Godself. Moreover, while division represents a failure of charity, in the end, it is the love of God that binds together the church. Even when the church is faithless, God remains faithful. Salvation occurs not by any merely human achievement, but by divine grace. Our failures to live up to that grace, while not excusable, are also not ultimately fatal. Were they able to thwart divine grace, salvation would be an impossibility from the outset. Since this is not the case, it follows that the last word, granted to divine mercy, must be the decisive one.

CHAPTER ONE

Divided from the Beginning?

But now in Christ Jesus you who once were far off have been brought near by the blood of Christ. For he is our peace; in his flesh he has made both groups into one and has broken down the dividing wall, that is, the hostility between us . . . that he might create in himself one new humanity in place of the two, thus making peace, and might reconcile both groups to God in one body through the cross, thus putting to death that hostility through it.

Ephesians 2:13–17

Now I appeal to you, [siblings], by the name of our Lord Jesus Christ, that all of you be in agreement and that there be no divisions among you, but that you be united in the same mind and the same purpose. For it has been reported to me by Chloe's people that there are quarrels among you, my [siblings].[1]

1 Corinthians 1:10–11

Ecclesiology must take the church as it is, not as we think it should be or wish that it were instead. To do otherwise is to engage in fiction, not theology. This impetus is keenly apparent when we consider the church's original unity.

---

1 Throughout this text, I utilize the New Revised Standard Version of the Bible. True to its aim of inclusive language, I also correct its constructions to avoid the gender binary. I do so similarly with translations of other texts, considering such constructions a translation decision, rather than necessarily authorial intent. Otherwise, though, I leave sources as they are. The historical record is what it is, and I won't retroactively copyedit. My aim is to be inclusive in my work at the present, not dictate what others should have been doing.

Conventional wisdom suggests that church unity is primarily a matter of agreement; that once upon the time the church was united as it ought to be and that along the way this unity was tragically lost. While there is a kernel of truth to this viewpoint, one to which we shall return, it is, in the end, "a fond thing, vainly invented."[2] True, creeds, doctrinal pronouncements and their theological explanations, and even the preponderance of statements about the church in the New Testament describe the Christian community as an integral and united reality, the result of the redemptive mission of the one Christ, who, sent by the one God in the power of the one Holy Spirit, has gathered and reconstituted a new humanity,[3] but we must reckon with the fact that there has never been a time when the community called forth by the gospel in this manner has existed in this ideal form.

That this ideal unity has never obtained is a strong claim, no doubt shocking, at least in some quarters. Paul Avis articulates the conundrum well, writing, "It would be straining faith to say, 'I believe (*Credo*) in the unity of the church, though I recognize that it has never actually been united,'" leading him to pursue an account of an "original" and "essential" unity of the church.[4] And yet, Avis's insistence on an original and essential church unity is not naïve. He dismisses the "superficially attractive notion of 'the undivided church'" as so much "romantic illusion," and notes that "the quest for the historical 'one church' is just as problematic as the quest for the historical Jesus—it never quite reaches its goal."[5] No matter how far back we push, this ideal unity recedes ever further, eluding our grasp.

The Pauline and deutero-Pauline epistles are all addressed to churches in turmoil. The Corinthians are riven by factionalism and moral failure. The Galatians and Colossians face serious doctrinal divergences, while the Romans seek to navigate a cleavage between Jewish and gentile Christians. The Ephesians and Philippians face interpersonal strife, perhaps overlaid with doctrinal divergences, while the pastoral epistles address similar situations of doctrinal, moral, interpersonal, and factional errors. The ideal of ecclesial unity found so often on the Pauline pen is evoked in order to counteract a state of affairs that has diverged from that ideal.

---

2 This phrase is used by the Anglican Thirty-Nine Articles of Religion with reference to purgatory and the intercession of the saints (Article XXII).

3 This basic narrative is well-articulated by the *LG*, nos. 1–8 [Tanner, 2:859–55].

4 Paul Avis, *Reconciling Theology* (London: SCM, 2022), 148.

5 Avis, *Reconciling Theology*, 149.

Similarly, while the Acts of the Apostles contains quite a few statements to the effect that the Christian community was operating "in one accord" (Acts 1:14; 2:46; 4:24; 5:12; 7:57; 8:6; 12:20; 15:25; 18:12; 19:29), with attendant descriptions of a community marked by mutuality and unity (Acts 2:42–47; 4:32–37), these are generally regarded as idealized depictions rather than as straightforward factual description.[6] Moreover, by the time we reach the seventh chapter, factions between Greek-speaking and Aramaic-speaking Christians lead to a crisis point that results in the creation of, if not the diaconate, properly speaking, its precursor to address it (Acts 6:1–6),[7] and from then on disputes mar the community's ostensible unity (Acts 9:26; 11:1–18; 15:1–21) at times leading even erstwhile collaborators to part ways (Acts 15:36–41).

Even at the very founding event of the church—Jesus's death and resurrection—the disciples are not united. They are scattered (Matt 26:56; Mark 14:51). The resurrection appearances, by and large, are not to a unified community. Matthew records that at the time of the Great Commission, some disciples worshiped the risen Jesus, while some doubted (Matt 28:17). The Lucan narrative finds the initial reports of Jesus's resurrection by the women to be dismissed as idle speech, while Cleopas and his companion's heart-burning conversion on the road to Emmaus occurs in isolation from the rest of the company of disciples (Luke 24:1–35). The Johannine Jesus must repeat his initial appearance because, at the first, Thomas was absent and he found the report of his apostolic colleagues incredible (John 20:24–29). Meanwhile, Peter, having been recommissioned as the head of the apostolic college after denying Jesus in his hour of need and having—after the postresurrection

---

6 In the end, Avis suggests Pentecost as something of a historical singularity at which the church existed in an original, essential, and integral unity. And this notion of singularity is taken in its full force. As a singularity lacks all dimensiveness, so this posited original unity is a mere "pinpoint in time" (*Reconciling Theology*, 150). Furthermore, singularities do not actually exist as anything other than mathematical phenomena, artifacts of our incomplete knowledge (I owe this insight to Ryan Hemmer). Avis goes so far as to liken it to the primeval Edenic prehistory or the resurrection of Christ, events that cannot be located in history per se, but that nevertheless found histories, and inaugurate historical processes. Avis is quick to affirm the resurrection as historical, even if also "trans-historical," and on this I concur with him. Nevertheless, I don't believe that an original ecclesial unity must be posited, at least not as an attribute of the community, nor do I believe it can be historically substantiated, in view of all the foregoing. I shall return to this question below, but we must first survey several other matters.

7 Thus, at least one of the three offices of the churches' ministerial structure has its origin in an experience of intrachurch divisiveness.

appearances, apparently—determined to return to his former occupation as a fisherman (John 21:1–19), immediately resumes his rivalry with the beloved disciple. The risen Jesus has told Peter that he will die a martyr's death, provoking him to engage in a "whataboutism" regarding John (John 21:20–22). None of this bespeaks the ideal ecclesial unity we tend to project upon the earliest Christians.

From the standpoint of a systematic theology, none of these observations necessarily falsify the ideal of ecclesial unity. As divinely revealed, this unity is a given. Instead, they raise the question of how that ideal relates to the empirical reality of the church that it purports to describe theologically. It raises the question of *how* it is true, given the fact that no community that embodies this ideal can now be said to exist, or to have existed at some point in the past. The church's unity is not a concept already out there now, into which the church's empirical reality must be assimilated. Instead, to affirm the church's unity is an act of judgment, a matter of the meaning we attribute to the reality that is the church.[8] To return to the orbital metaphor introduced in the introduction, neither the straight-lined motion nor perfectly elliptical orbits that we use to arrive at an understanding of orbital paths exist, only the perturbed ellipses along which celestial bodies actually travel in their orbits do. In constructing an account of the church's unity, ideal statements might be helpful, even necessary, but they are a starting point, not a conclusion. Our notion of unity must correspond to reality.

Among other things, our recognition that such ideal unity never actually obtained removes from serious consideration the siren song of an ecclesiological primitivism, as if, faced with the reality of division, we could simply retreat into a bygone era of pristine unity, whether to reconstruct it or to lament its loss. Such an endeavor would be doubly quixotic, running afoul of both historical and empirical reality. Primitivism is a losing task because, as Michael Ramsey repeatedly asserts in his classic work *The Gospel and the Catholic Church*, ecclesiology is not a matter of archaeology, whether of the New Testament—which evinces multiple manners of organizing Christian

---

8 My positions here depend upon Bernard J. F. Lonergan, *Insight: A Study of Human Understanding*, ed. Frederick E. Crowe and Robert M. Doran, CWBL 3 (Toronto: University of Toronto Press, 1992), chap. 12; *Verbum: Word and Idea in Aquinas*, ed. Frederick E. Crowe and Robert M. Doran, CWBL 2 (Toronto: University of Toronto Press, 1997), 194–96.

communities—or any other time period.[9] Ramsey's observation is borne out by the way that primitivist impulses to recreate a "New Testament ecclesiology" have yielded different, mutually incompatible, results (e.g., Presbyterianism, congregationalism, plural and single-pastor leadership within congregations). History only moves in one direction. We cannot excavate the past in order to resurrect it like so many dinosaurs' DNA conveniently preserved in amber-encased mosquitos. And rather than be so preoccupied with whether we could (we cannot), we should also stop to ask if we should do so (we should not).

It has become popular in the past several decades to engage in a sort of primitivism, labeling it *ressourcement*, in imitation of the mainly French renewal movement in early-twentieth-century Catholicism, known for its turn to Scripture, patristics, and the liturgy as theological sources.[10] However, few things could be farther from the motivations of authentic *ressourcement*, which recognizes that the past is irretrievably gone, and so seeks not to repristinate or recover it, but to inhabit the fundamental sources of the faith so that one might respond authentically to the challenges of the times and circumstances in which we actually live.[11] An authentic ecclesiology suited for a different cultural matrix than our own would be wholly inadequate for the present day, and not through any fault of its own.[12] Time moves on, and with it the church must change. This change can be faithful or unfaithful, but the attempt to recreate the forms of a bygone era virtually guarantee that the

---

9 Michael Ramsey, *The Gospel and the Catholic Church* (Cambridge: Cowley, 1990), 68–69. Some of the most recent scholarship on the question may be found in Alistair C. Stewart, *The Original Bishops: Office and Order in the First Christian Communities* (Grand Rapids: Baker, 2014).

10 The classic programmatic statement is Jean Daniélou, "Les orientations présentes de la pensée religieuse," *Études* 249 (1946): 5–21. See further the essays gathered in Gabriel Flynn and Paul D. Murray, eds., *Ressourcement: A Movement for Renewal In Twentieth-Century Catholic Theology* (Oxford: Oxford University Press, 2014).

11 E.g., Henri de Lubac, *The Splendor of the Church*, trans. Michael Mason, 2nd ed. (San Francisco: Ignatius, 1999), 21, 241–57; *Medieval Exegesis: The Four Senses of Scripture*, 3 vols. (Grand Rapids: Eerdmans, 1998–2009), 1:xix–xxi; 3:98; *History and Spirit: The Understanding of Scripture According to Origen*, trans. Anne Englund Nash (San Francisco: Ignatius, 2007), 14, 491–93. I have recently argued this at length with reference to de Lubac's thought. *Salvation in Henri de Lubac: Divine Grace, Human Nature, and the Mystery of the Cross* (Notre Dame: University of Notre Dame Press, 2023). See also the historically grounded theology of tradition articulated in Anne M. Carpenter, *Nothing Gained Is Eternal: A Theology of Tradition* (Minneapolis: Fortress Press, 2022).

12 Avis, *Reconciling Theology*, 123.

changes will not be carried out in fidelity, because they will not be carried out attentively, intelligently, reflectively, and responsibly, but haphazardly and unwittingly.[13] We shall return to these matters in chapter 5.

The second way primitivism falters is simpler to state: there is no unified church that we can go back in time to reconstruct. Even if we could revert to the New Testament reality, what we would find would be the tumultuous, factionalized communities whose disorder led the apostles to describe their ecclesiologies in these idealized forms in order to correct concrete problems. In this way, we see that, while primitivism is no answer to the quandary of the church's divisions, the New Testament remains instructive for our attempt to grapple with the relationship between unity and division. Among other things, it invites us to recognize that our understandings of unity and of division need to be considerably refined. If Paul appeals to this ideal ecclesiological statement in addressing divided communities, it follows that he does not view its performative contradiction as a falsification, per se. The church's unity, it would seem, is rather more capacious than we tend to give it credit for, capable of embracing a rather wide array of diversity, and not just diversity, but disagreement, even enmity. Considering this capacity is our task in this chapter.

DIVERSITY AS ORIGINAL GOODNESS

Like all things, the church's unity and diversity has its basis in God, for all things that exist do so either because they are God or because God has created them. God is one. This fundamental conviction, shared by the three Abrahamic faiths, must be asserted before all else. Indeed, as Katherine Sonderegger has argued, the divine unity ought to be our starting point more fundamentally than it often is.[14] (Trendy appeals to the Cappadocian Fathers, who ostensibly began with the three hypostases who are God, in contrast to a Latin tradition, exemplified by Augustine, who allegedly began with the

---

13 Bernard J. F. Lonergan, *Method in Theology*, ed. Robert Doran and John Dadosky, CWBL 14 (Toronto: University of Toronto Press, 2017), 3, 7–27, 82–95; "The Transition from a Classicist World-View to Historical-Mindedness," in *A Second Collection*, 3–10.

14 Katherine Sonderegger, *Systematic Theology*, 2 vols. (Minneapolis: Fortress Press, 2015–20).

unity of the divine substance, notwithstanding.)[15] Among other things, this theological taxonomy of Eastern versus Latin trinitarian theologies, largely stemming from the work of Theodore de Regnon,[16] lacks a solid historical basis. The Pro-Nicene theological tradition is remarkably consistent in both its Eastern and Western expressions, which is not to suggest that there are no differences among theologians, but rather to challenge this handy bifurcation.[17]

God is one and eternally simple.[18] Were this not so, then God would not be God, at least not in the way that the monotheistic traditions understand God: the absolute origin of all that is not God. Were there any composition in God, then God would be somehow derivative. Yet the one God's simplicity is not undifferentiated, for the one God is also the Trinity.[19] The Father, the Son, and the Holy Spirit are the one God, and yet not each other. The most fundamental reality, then, is both one and diverse, there is no incompatibility between the two. Recently Linn Marie Tonstad has challenged the impulse to find in the Trinity a basis for affirming difference and diversity, noting especially how reading sexual difference into or out of the Trinity leads necessarily to discourses of subjugation of women and LGBTQ folks.[20] Incisive as her critique is, I do not believe it applies to the argument I advance here, which makes no statements about sex or gender, per se, and does not turn upon any ostensible subordination, but instead on the rather more modest observation that the trinitarian persons are not each other.

---

15 This claim is frequently repeated. See, e.g., and variously, Catherine Mowry LaCugna, *God for Us: The Trinity and Christian Life* (San Francisco, HarperSanFrancisco, 1991); John D. Zizioulas, *Being as Communion: Studies in Personhood and the Church* (Crestwood, NY: St. Vladimir's Seminary Press, 1997); Karl Rahner, *The Trinity* (New York: Continuum, 2001); Colin E. Gunton, *Father, Son, and Holy Spirit: Toward a Fully Trinitarian Theology* (London: T&T Clark, 2003).

16 Théodore de Régnon, *Études de théologie positive sur la Sainte Trinité*, 3 vols. (Paris: Retaux, 1892).

17 Michel René Barnes, "De Régnon Reconsidered," *Augustinian Studies* 26 (1995): 51–79; "Augustine in Contemporary Trinitarian Theology," *TS* 56, no. 2 (1995): 237–50; Lewis Ayres, *Nicaea and Its Legacy: An Approach to Fourth-Century Trinitarian Theology* (Oxford: Oxford University Press, 2004); *Augustine and the Trinity* (Cambridge: Cambridge University Press, 2010).

18 Thomas Aquinas, *Summa Theologiæ* 1.3.1–8; 1.9.1–10.6. See also D. Stephen Long, *The Perfectly Simple Triune God: Aquinas and His Legacy* (Minneapolis: Fortress Press, 2016).

19 See Khaled Anatolios, *Retrieving Nicaea: The Development and Meaning of Trinitarian Doctrine* (Grand Rapids: Baker, 2011).

20 Linn Marie Tonstad, *God and Difference: The Trinity, Sexuality, and the Transformation of Finitude* (London: Routledge, 2017).

While the Trinity alone is necessary—God could have been the same God and Being would have been no less rich and good if only God had been[21]—God has also willed that there be beings that are not God, and so there is a creation, which introduces further diversity, first by the sheer fact of its existence as not God, but also by virtue of the intracreation diversity that characterizes it. The creation narrative of Genesis 1 depicts the one God, by their Word and Spirit—which later the Prologue of John and the development of trinitarian doctrine will clarify are not simply divine speech and wind, but divine hypostases—bringing forth the rich variety of created beings, and noting at every turn that all this is good.

The biblical narrative soon introduces discord into the picture as the result of human sin, but the original state of the creation is a diverse and harmonious relationship between the world and its creator. The infinite difference between creator and creature is good, as are the finite differences between various creatures. Diversity, then, is both necessary (because God is diverse) and chosen (because God wills that there be even further diversity than what is necessary). This latter point is especially pertinent: God wills diversity and its proliferation. There is no incompatibility between diversity and unity. Hence, from the outset, we must resist any tendency to view unity and diversity as opposed or existing on a spectrum, such that as unity increases diversity decreases or vice versa.

From Diversity to Enmity

The advent of sin brings about a diversity lived as enmity. The human family is riven as Adam recriminates Eve and the curse of male domination of women is introduced. Such discord proves to be congenital as sibling rivalry and murder follow on the heels of the primordial sin. Humans are alienated from the earth, which now gives its fruit only grudgingly. The seed of the woman and the seed of the serpent will now have mutual enmity, striking at head and heel, respectively. Humans are alienated from God, who now calls out, "Adam, where are you?"

---

21 Excellent statements of this principle are available in Erich Przywara, Analogia Entis: *Metaphysics: Universal Structure and Universal Rhythm*, trans. John R. Betz and David Bentley Hart (Grand Rapids: Eerdmans, 2014); Robert Sokolowski, *The God of Faith and Reason: Foundations of Christian Theology* (Washington, DC: CUA Press, 1995); Kathryn Tanner, *God and Creation in Christian Theology: Tyranny or Empowerment?* (Minneapolis: Fortress, 2005).

This picture is complicated by our current scientific understanding that death did not enter the world with sin, but preexists humanity by eons, and is a major component of the mechanism whereby humans have emerged through the process of natural selection.[22] But this recognition is far less disruptive to the fundamental theological affirmation than fundamentalists of either Christian or scientific persuasion assume. An ecosystem is an orderly, harmonious whole, and though death is hardly to be enjoyed, neither is the agonism of predator and prey nor the striving of life anything to abhor.

This realization can yield dividends for how we conceptualize diversity and conflict within the life of the church. We tend to associate agonism with enmity and assume that unity will involve concord. This conceptualist mindset runs afoul of empirical verification, and may be among the greatest barriers to ecclesial unity because it commits us to a definition of unity at odds with reality. The natural order is shot through with agonism that is not simply due to sin. Scripture, too, is replete with conflictual relations, some of which are cast in rather positive light. Jacob, on the eve of his reunion with his estranged brother Esau, spends a night wrestling with an enigmatic heavenly figure, from whom he eventually wrests a blessing. This figure is, apparently, God, for at the end of the episode, Jacob is renamed Israel, for he strives with God, a designation presented in a positive light. The figure of striving with God in prayer until the blessing is bestowed has been a mainstay of devotional exhortations ever since, and is, perhaps echoed in the prophetic injunction, "You who remind the Lord, take no rest, and give him no rest until he establishes Jerusalem and makes it renowned throughout the earth" (Isa 62:6–7).

The fullest expression of this dynamic comes in Christ's passion narrative. In Gethsemane, Jesus prays in bloody anguish that the cup might pass from him, even as he acquiesces to the divine will. Here the beloved Son, with whom the Father is well-pleased, who is one with the Father in both substance and purpose, agonistically strives with the Father. Hours later, he will cry out, asking why God has forsaken him, before he dies unanswered, still trusting. Maximus the Confessor clarifies that it is due to his humanity that Christ's will can vary with the Father's, for as divine,

---

22 See, e.g., Karl Rahner, "Christology within an Evolutionary View of the World," in *Theological Investigations*, Electronic Centenary Edition, vol. 5 (Limerick: Centre for Theology, Culture and Values, 2005), 157–92; Martin A. Nowak and Sarah Coakley, eds., *Evolution, Games, and God: The Principle of Cooperation* (Cambridge, MA: Harvard University Press, 2013); Sarah Coakley, "Sacrifice Regained: Evolution, Cooperation and God" (Gifford Lectures, University of Aberdeen, 2012).

there is no difference between his and the Father's will.[23] Nevertheless, the human Christ does indeed strive with God, and this striving is by no means a disruption of his relationship with the Father, in no way incompatible with his filial identity or the divine unity.[24]

None of this contestation should be construed as enmity, though there is, of course, striving that is also hostile. It is this latter sort of strife that God has overcome in the redemptive missions of the Word and the Holy Spirit, which are yet another divine embrace of diversity.[25] By the incarnation, the eternal Word has embraced creaturely difference so fully as to, in a manner of speaking, *be* a creature—"the Word became flesh and lived among us" (John 1:14). Of course, the person of the Word is eternally God, not a creature at all. But the humanity of the incarnate Word is a creature, and in this assumed humanity, the Word lives a fully human life.[26] He does so accompanied and empowered by the Holy Spirit. St. Irenaeus wrote of this in terms of the Spirit becoming accustomed to humanity through familiarity with Christ, who

---

23 Maximus the Confessor, *Opusculum 6* in *On the Cosmic Mystery of Jesus Christ*, trans. Paul M. Blowers and Robert Louis Wilken (Crestwood, NY: St. Vladimir's Seminary Press, 2003), 173–76.

24 E.g., Hans Urs von Balthasar, *Theo-Drama: Theological Dramatic Theory*, vol. 4, *The Action*, trans. Graham Harrison (San Francisco: Ignatius Press, 1994), 349. While Tonstad warns against the sorts of projections Balthasar makes, and particularly against the importing of suffering, death, or even obedience into God—all well taken points!—(*God and Difference*, 27–57) my claim is once again more modest. The strife of the passion is not a disruption of the relationship between the first and second persons of the Trinity. See also Christopher M. Hadley, *A Symphony of Distances: Patristic, Modern, and Gendered Dimensions of Balthasar's Trinitarian Theology* (Washington, DC: CUA Press, 2022).

25 The most classic statements on the divine missions are found in Augustine, *trin.*, 4 [WSA, 1/5:152–85]; Aquinas, *Summa Theologiæ* 1.43.1–8. The basic Western position on the divine missions is that they are identical to the eternal processions, only with the addition of an external, created term, rather than remaining internal to God. On most points, I follow the further developed articulations of Bernard J. F. Lonergan, *The Triune God: Systematics*, ed. Robert M. Doran and H. Daniel Monsour, trans. Michael G. Shields, CWBL 12 (Toronto: University of Toronto Press, 2007); Robert M. Doran, *The Trinity in History: A Theology of the Divine Missions*, vol. 1, *Missions and Processions* (Toronto: University of Toronto Press, 2013); Robert M. Doran, *The Trinity in History: A Theology of the Divine Missions*, vol. 2, *Missions and Relations* (Toronto: University of Toronto Press, 2019).

26 Bernard J. F. Lonergan, *The Incarnate Word*, ed. Robert M. Doran and Jeremy D. Wilkins, trans. Charles Hefling, CWBL 8 (Toronto: University of Toronto Press, 2016); *The Ontological and Psychological Constitution of Christ*, ed. Michael Shields, Frederick Crowe, and Robert M. Doran, CWBL 7 (Toronto: University of Toronto Press, 2002); Aquinas, *Summa Theologiæ* 3.2–19.

was now also human, in order to now embrace Christ's human siblings in the same manner that she has eternally embraced him.[27]

From Enmity to Friendship

In this way, humans are brought into friendship with God, for with the incarnate Christ, a human being is embraced with the same love that God has for the eternal Son, so that this love may be shared with other human beings (see John 14:21–24; 17:23).[28] We shall return to this with greater focus in chapter 2. For now, the point to grasp is that by the divine missions we are embraced precisely in our variance from God so that we might, even as still different than God, be brought into unity with God. The Definition of Chalcedon holds that in the single person of the Word, the divine and human natures are united without confusion, change, division or separation. They are truly united, and they remain integrally themselves. Diversity is upheld in this unity.

These missions of the Word and Spirit allow for the elevation of humanity to share in the life of God. Though there is nothing *bad* about the fact that humans are infinitely distinct from God, nevertheless, there is an infinite disproportion between them, which must be bridged for us to share in the divine life.[29] There is nothing automatic about deification. It is a supernatural reality. Hence, even apart from an account of sin, humanity is radically dependent upon divine grace if we are to be "saved"—that is, elevated into union with God. While the divine missions *are* redemptive, insofar as they overcome human sinfulness, they would still be "needed" even apart from sin in the sense that they respond to this more fundamental exigence.

The sin overcome by Christ, the hostility that he transforms into charity, the alienation that he transforms into friendship, the division that he

---

27 Irenaeus, *Against Heresies* 3.17.1. See also the elaboration of this basic position in Eugene F. Rogers, *After the Spirit: A Constructive Pneumatology from Resources outside the Modern West* (Grand Rapids: Eerdmans, 2005).

28 See Bernard J. F. Lonergan, "Supplementary Notes on Sanctifying Grace," in *Early Latin Theology*, ed. Robert M. Doran and H. Daniel Monsour, trans. Michael G. Shields, CWBL 19 (Toronto: University of Toronto Press, 2011), 562–665; Doran, *Trinity in History*, 1:19–32.

29 Bernard J. F. Lonergan, "The Supernatural Order," in *Early Latin Theology*, 52–255; *Triune God: Systematics*, 467–521; Henri de Lubac, *Augustinianism and Modern Theology*, trans. Lancelot Sheppard (New York: Herder & Herder, 2000); *The Mystery of the Supernatural*, trans. Rosemary Sheed (New York: Herder & Herder, 2012); *Surnaturel : Études Historiques*, ed. Michel Sales (Paris: Desclée de Brouwer, 1991).

transforms into communion is, in this sense, a detour within the intelligibility of the divine plan for humanity. And yet while we do not "need" to be sinful in order to be "saved," we in actuality are so. We need not detain ourselves with details of atonement theory beyond affirming that by his embrace of the cross, Christ has loved, borne with, and embraced human creatures in all our hostility, to the very end, and that by his resurrection, he has demonstrated that the divine love is stronger and more resilient than the whole of human sinfulness. Chapter 2 will develop this further with an account of charity, but this rather schematic account will suffice for now.

UNITY, DIVERSITY, AND THE ONE BODY OF CHRIST

Against this backdrop of unity, diversity, and hostility, we are in a position to interrogate what sort of unity actually obtained in the earliest Christian churches, and how diversity relates to that unity. We must first recognize that in this account of redemption, we have also articulated a nascent ecclesiology. In gathering hostile humanity back to God, Christ and the Holy Spirit constitute the church, for the redemption is directed not toward isolated individuals, but toward the entire human family.[30] There is a fundamental unity to the human race, which provides the backdrop assumption for the Christian belief in redemption by Jesus Christ.[31] Only if humanity is a unity in this way can the act of one man provide redemption for all.

It is here, then, that I would posit an original unity to the church, should we be inclined to insist upon it, not in the community itself, but in its one foundation, Jesus Christ. Rowan Williams has argued that all the famous Nicene marks of the church—unity, sanctity, catholicity, apostolicity—are in the end attributes of Christ before they are those of the church.[32] As Henri de Lubac famously argued in his *Catholicism*,

---

30 *LG*, no 9 [Tanner, 2:855]

31 Henri de Lubac, *Catholicism: Christ and the Common Destiny of Man*, trans. Lancelot C. Sheppard and Elizabeth Englund (San Francisco: Ignatius Press, 1998), 25–33; *GS*, no. 22 [Tanner, 2:1081–83]

32 Rowan Williams, "One Holy Catholic and Apostolic Church: Archbishop's Address to the 3rd Global South to South Encounter Ain al Sukhna, Egypt," Archbishop of Canterbury website, October 28, 2005. Williams's address was first brought to my attention by Ephraim Radner, *A Brutal Unity: The Spiritual Politics of the Christian Church* (Waco: Baylor University Press, 2012), 443.

For a change of metaphor there is that in which Christ is likened to a needle the eye in which, pierced most painfully at his passion, now draws all after him, so repairing the tunic rent by Adam, stitching together the two peoples of Jew and Gentile, making them one for always. . . . Such from the very beginning is the effect of the Incarnation. Christ from the very first moment of his existence virtually bears all [humanity] within himself. . . . For the Word did not merely take a human body. . . . He incorporated himself in our humanity, and incorporated it in himself. . . . In making a human nature, it is *human nature* that he united to himself, that he enclosed in himself, and it is the later, whole and entire, that in some sort he uses as a body. . . . Whole and entire he will bear it then to Calvary, whole and entire he will raise it from the dead, whole and entire he will save it. Christ the Redeemer does not offer salvation merely to each one; he effects it, he is himself the salvation of the whole, and for each one salvation consists in a personal ratification of his original "belonging" to Christ, so that he be not cast out, cut off from this Whole.[33]

In his singular act of redemption, Christ represents the people of God reduced to one, which seems to be the function of the deutero-Isaian servant songs, in which at times the servant appears to be the community, at other times an individual. And it is in this singularity that any original unity of the church is found.[34] "For by his incarnation the Son of God united himself in some sense with every human being."[35] The church, in other words, results from the unity of the human nature with Christ, rather than forging or even discovering this unity itself.

Among other things, this means that the various divisions we enact among ourselves (by race, sex, gender, nationality, politics, etc.) are, in some measure, fictive. A Jewish man has redeemed not only Jewish men, but also women and nonbinary people from every race and ethnic configuration. In recognizing the fictive character of our divisions, we gain an important insight for understanding the unity of the church. For here fictive doesn't necessarily mean "not real." Such realities are social constructions—who gets racialized into what group shifts around historically; gender is performed differently from culture to culture; political ideology exists strictly in the

---

33 de Lubac, *Catholicism*, 37–39.

34 So also Ramsey, *Gospel and Catholic Church*, 10–27. "Jesus Christ, in His solitary obedience, *is* the Church. Its existence does not begin with the addition of Jesus to men or of men to Jesus. The Israel of God is Jesus on the Cross; and those who will be united with Him will enter an Israel which exists already" (21). In appealing to Israel, we must be ever vigilant against any sort of supersessionism, though appeal to Israel we must, for Jesus lived as a faithful Jew and the God who sent him is the one God, the God of Israel.

35 *GS*, no. 22 [Tanner, 2:1082]

way we envision social arrangements—but they also profoundly affect us.[36] Those who are racialized as BIPOC in the United States face systemic and structural obstacles. The patriarchy limits the outcomes available to women. Folks who transgress the gender norms of their culture face tremendous hardship and opposition, including legislation that approaches genocidal intent in the contemporary United States. Nor is it all negative: the assertion of Black power, women's dignity, and LGBTQ pride, even in the face of social opposition, are profound witnesses to life's resilience. Socially constructed realities are among the most real things we encounter! And yet, the Christian confession of redemption by and in Jesus Christ demonstrates that they lack ontological purchase or theological basis. Within the fundamental unity of humanity, there exists tremendous diversity.

The unity of the human family in all its diversity is not merely the backdrop of redemption but also its concrete form.[37] The fourth evangelist writes that Caiaphas the high priest predicted that Jesus would die for the nation, and indeed "not for the nation only, but to gather into one the dispersed children of God" (John 11:52). And the author of the Letter to the Ephesians explains,

> But now in Christ Jesus you who once were far off have been brought near by the blood of Christ. For he is our peace; in his flesh he has made both groups into one and has broken down the dividing wall, that is, the hostility between us. He has abolished the law with its commandments and ordinances, that he might create in himself one new humanity in place of the two, thus making peace, and might reconcile both groups to God in one body through the cross, thus putting to death that hostility through it. (Eph 2:13–16)

The effect of redemption, then, is the formation of a new community, in which the hostility between human beings and God, and between different human factions, has been overcome. This occurs precisely in a single body, in the flesh of Jesus, by his blood, and through the cross, which kills the enmity itself.

---

36 See especially Barbara J. Fields and Karen E. Fields, *Racecraft: The Soul of Inequality in American Life* (New York: Verso, 2022); Willie James Jennings, *The Christian Imagination: Theology and the Origins of Race* (New Haven, CT: Yale University Press, 2011); J. Kameron Carter, *Race: A Theological Account* (Oxford: Oxford University Press, 2008); M. Shawn Copeland, *Enfleshing Freedom: Body, Race, and Being* (Minneapolis: Fortress Press, 2009); Ibram X. Kendi, *Stamped from the Beginning: The Definitive History of Racist Ideas in America* (New York: Nation Books, 2016).

37 Bernard J. F. Lonergan, *The Redemption*, ed. Robert M. Doran, Jeremy Wilkins, and H. Daniel Monsour, trans. Michael Shields, CWBL 9 (Toronto: University of Toronto Press, 2018), 237; Copeland, *Enfleshing Freedom*, 101–28; de Lubac, *Catholicism*, 33–81.

And yet, even as we consider the nature of this single body, we must recognize that its singularity is more a theological judgment than something already out there now. Here's what I mean. The New Testament speaks of both *the* church (singular) and the *churches* (plural). This recognition lies at the heart of what has been called the ecclesiology of communion, which seems to have characterized the first several Christian centuries, before its eventual occlusion, and recent recovery. Complex factors are at play in this occlusion and recovery, and we need not detain ourselves with them here. Others have ably done this work.[38] Instead, we can focus on the basic affirmation. The church (singular) exists in and through the churches (plural) and their communion with each other. In subsequent chapters, we'll note that this communion is largely a matter of mutual recognition. The bishops of the churches recognize each other's churches as authentically church, as expressions of the one church. I follow Michael Ramsey in regarding the emergence of the episcopate as a necessary implication of this ecclesiology. It is a structure that allows the life and communion of the churches to be expressed.[39] While matters of church order and polity are subject of intense ecumenical deliberation, and while they must be resolved for the churches to be united, precisely because of the practicalities of recognition, they are secondary to the matter at hand. Different church orders are a barrier to reunion, but they are not a cause of division. Instead, they have emerged in order to allow for the continued existence of churches after the fact of division.[40] We shall return to this question in chapter 5.

The point is this, when we speak of *the church* we are in fact speaking of multiple communities with their own histories, cultures, and practices. For instance, even the Catholic Church is in fact twenty-four autonomous particular churches, with their own distinctive liturgical rites, in communion with each other and the bishop of Rome (hence, throughout, I'll avoid

---

38 Jean-Marie R. Tillard, *Church of Churches: The Ecclesiology of Communion*, trans. R. C. de Peaux (Collegeville, MN: Liturgical Press, 1992); *Flesh of the Church, Flesh of Christ: At the Source of the Ecclesiology of Communion*, trans. Madeleine Beaumont (Collegeville, MN: Liturgical Press, 2001); *L'Église locale: Ecclésiologie de communion et catholicité* (Paris: Les Éditions du Cerf, 1995); Henri de Lubac, *The Motherhood of the Church Followed by Particular Churches in the Universal Church and an Interview Conducted by Gwendoline Jarczyk*, trans. Sergia Englund (San Francisco: Ignatius, 1982).

39 Ramsey, *Gospel and Catholic Church*, 55–119.

40 Ephraim Radner, *The End of the Church: A Pneumatology of Christian Division in the West* (Grand Rapids: Eerdmans, 1998), 136–70.

the misnomer "Roman Catholic," which, properly speaking, applies only to the Latin Rite). "The church" is not one single monolith, but rather a unity forged out of and amid plurality. There is no unity of the church apart from the diversity of the churches.

Corinthian Fracture

In his Letters to the Romans and the Corinthians, Paul adverts to the metaphor of a body in his exhortations to the communities to whom he writes. This ecclesiological image, which the subsequent theological tradition has developed at great length, and which was a mainstay of twentieth-century ecclesiological reflection, is a lodestone for considering the church's unity.[41] This status is augmented and modified when we consider it against the backdrop of the purpose to which Paul put it. As we shall see, the image of the church as a body is especially well-suited for expressing the twin affirmations of unity and diversity within the Christian community, emphases that both the Romans and Corinthians needed underscored in their common lives. In fact, often enough, the failure to uphold the church's unity is, equally, a failure to embrace the church's diversity and to recognize its place within and compatibility with ecclesial unity.[42]

Paul knows the situation in Corinth—having established that church—far more intimately than he knows the situation in Rome, which he had never visited at the time he was composing his letter to them (appropriately, probably during a stay in Corinth). For this reason, the Corinthian correspondence provides far more detail about the community's dynamics. The bulk of Romans is spent articulating the gospel that Paul proclaims and hopes to

---

41 E.g., Henri de Lubac, *Corpus Mysticum: The Eucharist and the Church in the Middle Ages*, ed. Laurence Paul Hemming and Susan Frank Parsons, trans. Gemma Simmonds, Richard Price, and Christopher Stephens (Notre Dame, IN: University of Notre Dame Press, 2007); *Catholicism*, 93–101, 314–19; Pope Pius XII, *Mystici Corporis Christi*, Vatican website, June 29, 1943.

42 This perspective then, both aligns with and differs from the one proposed by Yung Suk Kim, *Christ's Body in Corinth: The Politics of a Metaphor* (Minneapolis: Fortress Press, 2014). Kim plays unity and diversity against each other, with "unity" standing in for forced uniformity and hegemony. Against this reading, he posits a Pauline affirmation of diversity, which envisions the Christian community as embracing those at the margins of society in imitation and participation of the life and especially the crucifixion of Jesus. His reading of 1 Corinthians is persuasive, but I argue that instead of opposing unity and diversity, we must allow diversity to inform our understanding of unity.

bring to Spain with some assistance from the Romans, though he also provides concrete instructions to them regarding the ordering of their community. Hence, our focus will be on the Corinthian letters.

From the outset, the First Letter to the Corinthians evinces a preoccupation with maintaining unity. Paul exhorts them "that all of you be in agreement [τὸ αὐτὸ λέγητε πάντες/to auto legete pantes – all say the same thing] and that there be no divisions [σχίσματα/schismata] among you, but that you be united in the same mind and the same purpose" (1 Cor 1:10). The conditions to which he exhorts them, though, do not obtain. Instead, it he has received reports of "quarrels" among them. These quarrels seem to be rooted in factions, such that some claim loyalty to Paul, others to Apollos, or Peter/Cephas, or even to Christ, reducing him to one factional identity among others.[43] Paul finds this state of affairs risible. Christ is not divided; he and no other has been crucified for the Corinthians; into Christ, not Paul or Cephas, have they been baptized.

Importantly, the problem is the factionalism, not the diversity of leaders who were respected by the Corinthians. Paul, Apollos, and Peter were all faithful ministers, whose teachings and examples the Corinthians would do well to follow. However, they were not simply interchangeable, nor were their views. Paul records his conflict with Peter over gentile inclusion in Galatians 2:11–14. And, whomever their author may have been, the outlook of the Petrine epistles is not the same as those written by Paul. The author of 2 Peter even notes that Paul's letters can be difficult to understand and are prone to destructive twisting (2 Pet. 3:15–16). This is written in a basic affirmation of Paul, but not without a subtle dig. While on some issues (e.g., gentile inclusion) someone is right and someone else wrong, this does not preclude a unified diversity. One could hold Pauline or Petrine or Apollan views and preferences and still function healthily within Corinth. An analogy would be the existence of theological schools within the Catholic Church. Dominicans and Franciscans, for instance, held different, mutually incompatible views, but one could be either a Dominican or a Franciscan and still be a faithful Catholic in full communion with the Church. The problem was that these figures became figureheads and rallying points, with an implicit judgment upon and exclusion of those who looked to a different apostolic leader.

---

43 This is how the NRSV translates it. It is also possible that Paul asserts loyalty to Christ as a contrast to any factional loyalty. Either interpretation coheres with the basic thrust of my argument.

Since Christ is one, so should the community be. It is for this reason that they should agree (literally "say the same thing") and be of one mind and purpose. The later Pauline letter to the Ephesians operates with a similar logic in its exhortation to unity: "There is one body and one Spirit, just as you were called to the one hope of your calling, one Lord, one faith, one baptism, one God and Father of all," and for this reason the community must endeavor "to maintain the unity of the Spirit in the bond of peace" (Eph 4:4–6, 4:3).[44] And from this logic, Paul moves naturally into his famous exposition of the folly of proclaiming a crucified Christ (1 Cor 1:18–2:16). This in itself is telling: the letter's rather famous exposition of the gospel is given for the purpose of counteracting intrachurch divisions. The Corinthians' factions are evidence of their immaturity, of not having fully appropriated the gospel message or learned the way of Christ (1 Cor 3:1–9), who remains the one foundation of the church or the Christian life (1 Cor 3:10–15).

Beyond their factionalism, the Corinthians seem to have also been infected by an egoism that threatened the community. Confident about their perceived rights, community members were insistent on exercising those rights at the expense of other community members. In Corinth, the presenting issue was the eating of meat that had been offered in sacrifice to idols before being made available to the markets. While those of us who obtain meat from the grocery store find this to be a rather strange set of concerns, it was fairly ubiquitous in antiquity. Lacking refrigeration, meat tended to be eaten in a more occasional manner, and in both Jewish and pagan contexts, sacrifices were often the occasion for meat procurement. Again lost to our contemporary imagination, meal and sacrifice were tightly bound in Graeco-Roman antiquity.[45] Any public meal was likely sacrificial in nature, a fact that ought to inform

---

44 I view Ephesians as in enough continuity with the undisputed letters that it should be considered "Pauline," whether or not it was written by Paul himself, a question on which I am agnostic, and so do not wish to stake out a definitive claim. Hence, my designation "later Pauline."

45 See, e.g., Andrew B. McGowan, *Ancient Christian Worship: Early Church Practices in Social, Historical, and Theological Perspective* (Grand Rapids: Baker, 2014); *Ascetic Eucharists: Food and Drink in Early Christian Ritual Meals* (Oxford: Clarendon, 1999); Matthias Klinghardt and Hal Taussig, eds., *Mahl Und Religiöse Identität Im Frühen Christentum = Meals and Religious Identity in Early Christianity* (Tübingen: Francke, 2012); Jonathan Schwiebert, *Knowledge and the Coming Kingdom: The Didache's Meal Ritual and Its Place in Early Christianity* (New York: Bloomsbury, 2008); Matthias Klinghardt, *Gemeinschaftsmahl und Mahlgemeinschaft: Soziologie und Liturgie früchristlicher Mahlfeiern* (Tübingen: Francke, 1996); Panayotis Coutsoumpos, *Paul and the Lord's Supper: A Socio-historical Investigation* (New York: Peter Lang, 2005).

our understanding of the Christian eucharistic meal, both in its origins and in our contemporary setting where the optics of meal and sacrifice are often opposed in a zero-sum manner.

In either case, certain members of the community regarded meat offered to idols as inconsequential, and, therefore, fit for consumption by Christians. After all, the idols are not actually deities, so it's not as if such meat had somehow become religiously contaminated. Other members of the community regarded the eating of such meat as, at least implicitly, an act of idolatry, often due to their former practices. Like a recovering addict, certain settings and behaviors are just too evocative of past patterns, and simply needed to be avoided, lest the temptation to relapse become too strong (1 Cor 8:7–10). Similar dynamics also seem to have occurred in Rome, though the concern over idolatry is not explicit, with discussion centering on eating meat or vegetables only (Rom 14:1–23).

Paul agrees with the meat eaters in both cases. Idols are fictive and no food is, of itself, unclean (1 Cor 8:4–6). Those who demur from the meat are "weak" in their faith. If they understood the matter rightly, they would recognize that such food carries no actual risk of religious compromise. Though he is also resolute that to participate in the sacrificial act itself would be utterly incongruous with Christian identity, outside the sacrificial context, Paul regards such meat as simply meat, morally neutral. However, the "strong," who eat such meat at the cost of scandalizing the "weak" misunderstand the faith even more profoundly. They risk being an instrument in the destruction of their siblings for whom Christ has died. Despite being "right" on the principle involved, the strong, in their unwillingness to bear with, support, and uphold the weak, were wrong in a far more grievous and destructive way (1 Cor 8:11–13; 10:14).

In Acts 15 the so-called Council of Jerusalem determined that gentiles need not observe the Jewish law, but that they should abstain from food offered to idols, from sexual immorality, from blood consumption, and from food that had been strangled, in order to avoid scandalizing Jewish believers (Acts 15:19–21). The same basic principle seems to be in play here. The prescriptions of the Mosaic law are not binding on the conscience of any gentile Christian, but one's rights should not be exercised in a way that proves harmful to a fellow Christian or the community. We shall need to return to this from a different angle in chapter 3, and consider how it has been weaponized and deployed in manners opposite to what seems to have been its original intent. But for now, we can observe that these communities seem to have been characterized by an antigospel willfulness that refused to recognize the rights of one's fellows to a place within the community.

By contrast, Paul offers his own example. Though bound by nothing other than the gospel of Christ, he accommodated himself to the conflicting, even contradictory needs, desires, and convictions of those among whom he ministered so that they could receive his gospel (1 Cor 9:19–23). Because one has died for all, all have died, and now live not for themselves, but for him who died and rose for them (2 Cor 5:14).[46] The claims of Christ are all-encompassing, and so, the Pauline position is not at all one of moral indifference. There are some bright lines. Idolatry is not to be countenanced (1 Cor 10:14), though to eat sacrificed meat is not necessarily idolatrous. There are standards of moral behavior that brook no compromise. Paul calls for a member of the community engaged in an inappropriate sexual relationship (with his stepmother) to be removed from the community, because such sin contradicts one's union with Christ (1 Cor 5:1–13). But throughout, the controlling principle is fidelity to Christ. Whatever serves union with him is to be held fast and promoted, that which hampers or undermines this union should be repudiated.

All of this leads into Paul's discussion of the church as the body of Christ, which begins, appropriately, in a discussion of sacrificial meals.

> The cup of blessing that we bless, is it not a sharing in the blood of Christ? The bread that we break, is it not a sharing in the body of Christ? Because there is one bread, we who are many are one body, for we all partake of the one bread. (1 Cor 10:16–17)

The church is somehow a unified plurality because of its sacramental Eucharist. With this statement, the trajectory that leads Henri de Lubac to famously write, "Literally speaking, therefore, the Eucharist makes the Church," is inaugurated.[47] In context, the instruction opposes eucharistic participation with idolatry. True to the antique logic that meals are sacrificial, Paul notes that those who share in the table of the Lord are formed into a cohesive community with one another and with that Lord—the body of Christ—and that those who share in the table of demons are bound together in demonic communion. One may share in the Lord's table or the demons' table, but not both (1 Cor 10:18–22).

---

46 This text is central to the argument of Ramsey, *Gospel and Catholic Church*.
47 de Lubac, *Corpus Mysticum*, 88.

Shortly thereafter, this body imagery will reappear, once more in a eucharistic context. As noted in the Introduction, social divisions in the Corinthian community made mockery of the Eucharist. At what was ostensibly a communal meal, the haves and have nots were separated [*schismatai*], enacting their division through their participation in a meal no longer recognizable as the "Lord's supper." In doing so, the rich failed to "discern the body," and so courted judgment and damnation, sickness and death (1 Cor 11:20–34). Their exclusion of some from the community, even just performatively, was a grave matter. It is a failure of the church's unity, but is so precisely by being a failure to embrace the community's diversity.

The logic of this corporal metaphor for the church becomes clearer when Paul turns to the matter of spiritual gifts. From the letter's outset, he has made mention of the community's various charisms, which were apparently a point of pride for the Corinthians, and so another occasion for fragmentation (1 Cor 1:7). Within the community, certain gifts were regarded as especially worthwhile, and others as lackluster, leading community members to regard others, and, at times, themselves, as lesser members of the community on the basis of which spiritual gifts they had, or lacked (1 Cor 12:4–11, 28–31).

In the face of this dynamic, Paul insists that all of the diversity in charism, ministry, and activity within the community flows from and serves a fundamental unity. The gifts, ministries, and activities are given by and according to the will of the one Holy Spirit and for the common good of the whole community. The community's unity is, then, pneumatological, and for precisely this reason, it is also sacramental and Christological, "For just as the body is one and has many members, and all the members of the body, though many, are one body, so it is with Christ. For in the one Spirit we were all baptized into one body—Jews or Greeks, slaves or free—and we were all made to drink of one Spirit" (1 Cor 12:12–13).

Several features of Paul's argument are remarkable, beyond the already noted confluence of pneumatological, sacramental, and christological bases for church unity. Paul appeals to the metaphor of the body before making the statement, "So it is with Christ," not, crucially, with the church, but with *Christ*.[48] While in the letter to the Romans, Paul will use the same imagery for essentially the same purpose, that use of the body is rather more generic:

---

48 I owe this observation to Tarcisius van Bavel, "The 'Christus Totus' Idea: A Forgotten Aspect of Augustine's Spirituality," in *Studies in Patristic Christology*, ed. Thomas Finan and Vincent Twomey (Portland, OR: Four Courts Press, 1998), 84–94.

21

the community is like a body. Here, though, he specifies that it is Christ's body. With this affirmation, which essentially proposes an identity between Christ and the church, we have the basis for the subsequent development of the notion of the mystical body of Christ or the whole Christ (*totus Christus*), which shall occupy us in the next chapter. Later, in Ephesians, the Christ's body imagery will be further refined, with Jesus himself as the body's head, such that there is both identity and distinction between Christ and the church; they are not simply collapsed into each other.

Beyond this, Paul's deployment of the body metaphor is precisely in the service of highlighting the church's diversity. A body is a unity, but it is a differentiated unity, a point upon which Paul will elaborate, as he notes that each member of the body serves an important function, none of which may simply be dispensed with. This diverse unity encompasses ethnic backgrounds (Jew and Greek) and social and economic positions (slave or free). A similar statement in the letter to the Galatians includes gender within the Pauline affirmation of diversity. In chapter 3, we shall need to interrogate the somewhat glib, status-quo-maintaining acquiescence to the reality of slavery. For now, though, let it suffice to note that the various socially constructed distinctions that human beings deploy to make sense of ourselves and our differences are all embraced within the diverse unity of the church.

A RECONCILED COMMUNITY?

Various New Testament authors conceive of the Christian community as the concrete effect and form of redemption. Christ reconciles us at once to God and to one another by his redemptive act upon the cross, gathering into one body those who had been enemies. Given what we have surveyed in the First Letter to the Corinthians, it could seem that this statement of crucified peace making, of the church as the community of reconciled humanity, of hostility having been put to death has been empirically falsified. The empirical reality in Corinth would seem to reflect just about anything but the theological ideal articulated here. (And let us remember that the Ephesian community, to whom the statement about reconciliation in one body through the cross was made, was hardly pristine; it is because of intraecclesial hostilities that these assertions of reconciliation and peace are made.)

Two considerations help us to make sense of this disjuncture in such a way as to both affirm the ideal statement and acknowledge the empirical reality.

The first is to recognize that in enacting a supernatural solution to the problem of human hostility and enmity, God has done so in a manner that respects the integrity of the nature God has created and is now redeeming.[49] Difference and even agonism can become division and hostility because we choose for them to be. The will is and remains free. And God's solution to the problem of evil, a problem whose locus is our will, must also uphold that will's freedom, for to do otherwise would be an act of violence, and so not a salvation at all.

Hence, grace does not abolish but preserves, perfects, and elevates nature. By grace, we are enabled to engage in acts disproportionate to our nature, namely faith, hope, and love.[50] Old school scholastic theology was insistent that this occurred by way of habit, which is to say as a new disposition. Habits enable us to perform acts more readily, but are not themselves those acts.[51] Bernard Lonergan attempted to explain this by recourse to our experience of being in love.[52] To be in love is to exist in a certain state, which informs all of one's life. But within this state of being in love, not every act is necessarily an act of love. At every moment, including now, as I type this paragraph, I am in love with my wife. But most of my life is taken up with acts other than loving her. Much of the time, she is not explicitly in my thoughts, as I focus on other matters, such as the writing of books. But my love for her still informs all of my acts, including writing. Similarly, my state of being in love with her does not preclude my acting in ways that are not loving to her, alas.

By grace God has called us into friendship with Godself and each other, enacting this act on the cross and in the new community of the church, enabling us to hold one another fast by the same Holy Spirit who is the Father's and the Son's mutual love.[53] But this habit does not replace our wills, nor mean that at any given moment we act lovingly. In one sense, intrachurch enmity is incompatible with this love, because it fails to live in accordance with it. Just as truly, though, there is nothing incompatible with being in a state of love and acting unlovingly, because it happens all the time. It must be possible because it is actual.

The ideal ecclesiology sketched in Ephesians and elsewhere is presented so as to be recognizable and unmistakable. Lonergan writes that the indwelling of the divine persons in the faithful "exists more in acts and is better known

---

49 Lonergan, *Insight*, 718–25, 740–50.
50 Lonergan, *Insight*, 719–20; Lonergan, "The Supernatural Order," 97–122.
51 Aquinas, *Summa Theologiæ* 2-1.49.1–55.4.
52 Lonergan, *Method in Theology*, 99–104.
53 Augustine, *trin.* 15.17, 27–31 [WSA, 1/5:421–24]; Aquinas, *Summa Theologiæ* 1.37.2

in acts," but "is constituted by the state of grace."[54] To return to my example about being in love with my wife: while my being in love with her is not any particular loving act, nor even their sum total, but rather a state that informs such acts, nevertheless, that state is recognizable through those acts, which can be empirically grasped in a way that the state of being in love cannot. My showing that I love my wife is not being in love with her, but my being in love with her is known through my showing it. In a similar way, what God intends in the church is more readily grasped through the ideal statement, even though in its actuality, it exists more as a habit or a state than as this enacted ideal. Thus, the overcoming of hostility is not a punctiliar matter or fait accompli, but a process, which proceeds according to the free actions of those to whom grace has come.

The second consideration is our effort to disaggregate agonism and enmity. Vociferous disagreement and contestation are not at odds with the sort of unity that God enacts. Often enough, we assume that church unity is a matter of agreement. Of course, agreement is wonderful. And while Paul would even seem to endorse this in part, urging the Corinthians to "say the same thing" (1 Cor 1:10), the remainder of the epistle demonstrates that it is not necessary for Christian unity. The Corinthians' failure was to insufficiently embrace the diversity of their community. This failure was a blight upon their unity. The proper forum for the agonistic contestation of Christian disagreement is the church. Indeed, Paul affirms this in his prohibition of lawsuits among believers. It would be better for them to defer to one another and not have these disagreements, but barring that, they should hash them out within the community, not beyond it (1 Cor 6:1–11).

A UNITY EMBRACING ENMITY?

The unity of the Corinthian community was rather capacious indeed. Within this unity were competing factions, mutually incompatible moral convictions, egoists who insisted on following their ostensible rights at the expense of more vulnerable members of the community, even those who doubted such corner-stones of orthodoxy as the resurrection of the body. Meanwhile, the existence of Second Corinthians, with Paul's further intimations of a disciplinary visit

---

54 Lonergan, *Triune God: Systematics*, 513-21 [513].

to the community, indicates that this was not simply a confused or disordered community, but one resistant to apostolic instruction, prone even to preferring false apostles to their genuinely apostolic founder (2 Cor 11:1–15). This fact suggests a fairly radical expansion of the bounds of what is considered to be acceptable diversity.

Generally, leeway is granted for adiaphora, things indifferent, while insisting upon agreement on some set of essentials. And yet the failures of the Corinthians would seem to extend beyond adiaphora. The resurrection is not an indifferent matter, but of first importance (1 Cor 15:1–10)! Beyond this, appeal to *adiaphora* is arbitrary. One community's *adiaphoron* is another's essential. How are we to adjudicate between the two? The fact of the matter is, the only thing two parties need to agree upon in order to be in communion is that they are in communion. A union based in agreement can only be precarious, for as Radner notes, all it takes to sunder this union is the emergence of some new disagreement.[55] Robert Jenson demonstrates that consensus-based union has turned out to be an asymptotic goal, no matter what new agreements are achieved, they prove insufficient to reunite the church once its unity has been sundered. Differences that were not previously church dividing turn out to be barriers to reunion, even after the originally church-dividing issues have been satisfactorily resolved.[56]

This is, once more, not to suggest an indifferentism, precisely the opposite. Instead, I suggest that the church's unity can and should encompass dissensus even on matters that are *not* indifferent, and the conflictual processes whereby these matters are adjudicated. Even when all is going well, Christian unity is far from uniformity, but instead a celebration and embrace of rather wide diversity (in background, status, moral conviction, theological position, etc.). But it often goes far beyond this, to include a diversity that is not just variety, but also deformity, a diversity that is lived in hostility.

In his controversial work *A Brutal Unity*, Ephraim Radner wrote a line that has stuck with me ever since: "But what if they are, division and unity, in a sense the same thing, only lived in different ways?"[57] Radner's work in that book has, understandably, come under fire, particularly his engagement

---

55 Radner, *End of the Church*, 170.

56 Robert W. Jenson, *Unbaptized God: The Basic Flaw in Ecumenical Theology* (Minneapolis: Fortress Press, 1992), 1–8.

57 Radner, *Brutal Unity*, 427.

with William Cavanaugh's work *The Myth of Religious Violence*.[58] Whatever we make of the rest of the work, though, this question is almost certainly right, for it best accounts for the data of reality, while locating the problem precisely in our wills. We are divided because we reject each other in our disagreements, rather than holding each other fast amid them.

What the Corinthians did performatively in their factionalism, in their elitism, in their divided Eucharists and disordered gatherings, subsequent Christian generations have done jurisdictionally. The Corinthian contestation, as toxic as it may have been, occurred within a single community. In our divisions, we regard ourselves as severed from one another. This is the kernel of truth that can be found in the primitivist thesis that I mentioned above. Not that the earlier Christians were any more "unified" than we are, but that they lived their divisions in communion with one another. It is this that we have lost. Our contemporary denominational landscape reads like 1 Corinthians 1's account of factionalism, only no longer encompassed within the single community of Corinth.[59]

Seen in this light, Christian unity can be variously expressed. Indeed, the high-minded ideals we often have in mind when we think of the church's unity are a possible expression of it. But such unity has likely never been actual. It can also be the union of diverse folks holding diverse, perhaps mutually incompatible, views and convictions, who nevertheless recognize one another as siblings for whom Christ died, and, so themselves as bound together. It can be the agonistic unity of intense contestation, as opposed parties struggle within the community, recognizing that nowhere else but this community could be the home of their struggle, because, in the end, they belong together, because God in Christ has brought them together. It can be the factionalized unity of the Corinthians, who for all their fractiousness, were one church. It can be, finally, as Ephraim Radner suggested nearly a decade ago, the union of enemies.[60] In the end, the first expression of Christian unity was such a

---

58 William T. Cavanaugh, *The Myth of Religious Violence: Secular Ideology and the Roots of Modern Conflict* (Oxford: Oxford University Press, 2009). See Radner, *Brutal Unity*, 22–53.

59 For an incisive critique of denominationalism, see Avis, *Reconciling Theology*, 21–48. See also Ephraim Radner, *Hope among the Fragments: The Broken Church and Its Engagement with Scripture* (Grand Rapids: Brazos, 2004), 23–38.

60 Radner, *Brutal Unity*, 443–47. See also my own development of this notion in *Sacrificing the Church: Mass, Mission, and Ecumenism* (Lanham, MD: Lexington Books/ Fortress Academic, 2019), 147–50.

unity: "While we were still sinners Christ died for us" (Rom 5:8). Ideally, enmity gives way to friendship. But when it does not, "Love your enemies and pray for those who persecute you" (Matt 5:44), for this is what Christ has done. *Father, forgive them* . . . (Luke 23:34).

In the end, failures of unity are failures of diversity, failures to believe that the gospel could be true, and that the love of Christ could or should embrace us in all our differences, all our hostilities. The "New Testament church" is hardly what we have in mind when we think of ecclesial unity, but it sets forth the only sort of unity we are likely to ever find, that of enemies, reconciled by the cross, yet resisting that reconciliation.

CHAPTER TWO

The Heart of Unity

Having loved his own who were in the world, he loved them to the end.

John 13:1b

As the Father has loved me, so I love you; abide in my love.

John 15:9

I give you a new commandment, that you love one another. Just as I have loved you, you also should love one another.

John 13:34

God's love has been poured into our hearts through the Holy Spirit that has been given to us.

Romans 5:5

This work is an ecclesiology of love and of love's refusal.

The church, like all things, exists because of the love of God. In an ecclesiology of love, we begin with God, for God is love. Eternally and infinitely God loves God, for God is infinite goodness, and love is the proper response to the good. This eternal divine self-love is not the self-love of the narcissist, for God is the Trinity. Eternally God speaks God's Word, loving and affirming that Second Person of the Trinity with a love analogous to that of a parent for their child. Eternally the Speaker and the Word breathe forth the Holy Spirit, who is the bond of love between them.[1] God's love, then, is love of an-other.

This infinite and eternal communion of loving affirmation of the good could have been the whole of existence without existence being any the poorer for it. But, fittingly, this love-of-another has determined to love an-other that is not God, and so there has been a creation. All reality exists by the love of God, whether because it is identical to that love (i.e., is God), or because God has lovingly caused it to be. The creation, then, is infinitely loved by God. And because a mutual, reciprocated love is better than unilateral, unrequited love, God has also created free rational creatures, capable of loving God in turn. This is where human beings (in company with the angels) fit into the picture. The intradivine love is reciprocal, and so it is, once more, fitting—though, again, by no means necessary—that there be a finite expression of reciprocal love.

God, though, has done this love one better. Rather than merely loving the nondivine other with the divine love, God has become the nondivine other, and so has loved God as a human being, in both senses of that phrase. The eternal Word has become human, and lived out the Word's eternal love for the Speaker over the course of a genuinely human life. As human he has loved God. And throughout his human life, he was not bereft of God's love for him. The eternal love of the Speaker for the Word was given to this human being, Jesus of Nazareth, because the human nature was assumed into union with the second person of the Trinity, meaning that the *person* he was is the Word eternally spoken by God. In loving the human being Jesus in this way, God still loves God, and so loves God as a human being.

With this trinitarian sketch, we have the nucleus of an ecclesiology, for Christ did not become human for his own benefit. The second person of the Trinity did not stand to gain anything by loving God as a human being, nor by being the God loved as a human being. The same divine love would have been his regardless. Instead, the Word became flesh so that other human beings could come to love and be loved with the divine love itself.[2] This belovedness

---

1 Lonergan, *Verbum*; *The Triune God: Systematics*, 181–207; "Christology Today: Methodological Considerations," in *A Third Collection*, ed. Robert M. Doran and John D. Dadosky, CWBL 16 (Toronto: University of Toronto Press, 2017), 91–93; Doran, *The Trinity in History*, 31–11, 145–48.

2 See Maximus the Confessor, "*Ambiguum 42*: On Jesus Christ and the 'Three Births,'" in *On the Cosmic Mystery*, 79–95; Rogers, *After the Spirit*, 136–48.

is what older scholastic theology meant by sanctifying grace, which is itself a synthetic concept, derived from several strands of biblical testimony, which Bernard Lonergan summarizes thus:

> To those whom God the Father loves [1] as he loves Jesus, his only begotten Son, (2) he gives the uncreated gift of the Holy Spirit, so that (3) into a new life they may be (4) born again and (5) become living members of Christ; there for as (6) just, (7) friends of God, (8) adopted children of God, and (9) heirs in hope of eternal life, (10) they enter into a sharing of the divine nature.[3]

By this grace we come to share in the life of the God who is love. Recognizing our own belovedness for the sake of and in Christ, we love God in return.[4] "God's love has been poured into our hearts through the Holy Spirit that has been given to us" (Rom 5:5), which is roughly what scholastic theologians meant by the habit of charity.[5] While the scholastics' abstruse reflections on the metaphysics of grace and charity may strike us as hopelessly antiquated and arcane, the reality they sought to describe is earth-shattering in its implications and far less removed from our lives and experiences than their rarified presentation might imply: our recognition that God loves us for the sake of and in Jesus and our loving God in return are not extrinsically related to God, but rather share in God such that by them we are enfolded in the God who is love.[6]

And our enfolding in the love of God is no individual affair, because the love of God is diffusive. If we are bound to God in love, we will also be bound to each other, for to love God is to love all those whom God loves. While there is more to say about the church than this, in these affirmations we have articulated the basic theological substance of the church: the binding together of humanity to Christ (and, so, to one another) in love, a love by which we share in the love that is God and God's own.

---

3 See Lonergan, "Supplementary Notes on Sanctifying Grace,", 581.

4 This notion is a refinement and transposition of Lonergan's basic position by Robert Doran, *Trinity in History*, 1:19–34.

5 Doran, *Trinity in History*, 1:22–23, 32, 34–39.

6 This is the basic thesis of Bernard J. F. Lonergan, "The Supernatural Order," in *Early Latin Theology*, 52–255, which affirms that creatures share in a created communication of the divine nature in a manner analogous to and which participates in the uncreated way that the divine nature is communicated within the life of the Trinity.

LOVE AND SACRIFICE: EUCHARIST AND CROSS

The gesture of love that is the incarnate Christ reaches its apex in the events of his crucifixion and resurrection, where due to his love for us and for the one who sent him, Jesus suffered death, and where, due to that same love, he was restored to life, never to die again. We must acknowledge this, especially because in much of the foregoing, I have more or less sidestepped such theologically significant matters as sin. This may strike readers as a rather glaring omission, but I contend it is not. While the actual accomplishment of redemption—and, so, of the church—has involved the overcoming of sin, sin is fundamentally irrational, and, so adds nothing to the meaning of redemption or of the church. All that has positive meaning/intelligibility can be expressed without recourse to sin, which lacks meaning or intelligibility. The meaning of the formation of a new humanity bound together by supernatural charity would be the same without the surd of sin, though some of its material trappings would probably vary. For instance, while I believe that Christ would have become incarnate and united us to himself and, through himself, to the first person of the Trinity, and thus into the loving communion that God is even if we had not fallen into sin, I doubt that this mission would have involved his suffering, and perhaps not even his death. While counterfactuals cannot, by definition, be proven, fellowship with God is nevertheless the positive meaning of the reconciliation that has occurred. In what follows, sin shall factor far more prominently.

In the world order that actually exists, human beings have fallen into sin and need to be not just elevated to share in the divine life, but be reconciled from their sins, in what Henri de Lubac describes as "a darksome . . . bloody drama,"[7] and which Black theologians have shockingly, though fittingly, compared to the horror of lynching.[8] This latter comparison is important, for it moves us to deromanticize the cross. This shall be especially important in chapter 3, when we note the ways that the word of the cross has been used to justify the ongoing crucifixions of oppressed communities. To recognize that we have to do not just with a generic "Christ

---

7 Henri de Lubac, *A Brief Catechesis on Nature and Grace*, trans. Richard Arnandez (San Francisco: Ignatius, 1984), 135.

8 James H. Cone, *The Cross and the Lynching Tree* (Maryknoll, NY: Orbis, 2013); Copeland, *Enfleshing Freedom*, 121–28.

crucified," but rather with the "lynched Jesus," calls us away from any and all such applications.

Within the Christian tradition there is no side-stepping the cross. The confession that it is the instrument of our redemption is primordial and endemic. And, while feminist theologians in particular have leveled searing criticisms of the crucicentric character of the tradition—critiques to which we shall attend and more fully incorporate in the next chapter—there is no avoiding the cross, for this is precisely what Jesus did not do, even when given the opportunity (Matt 26:52–54; John 18:4–11). Instead, the theological task is to ensure that our understanding and articulation of the cross is authentically life-giving, offering no quarter to systems of abuse or oppression, but rather leading to their dismantling.

"Having loved his own who were in the world, he loved them to the end," writes the fourth evangelist (John 13:1). In this statement we find the essential meaning of the crucifixion. While Jesus suffered upon the cross, the redemptive meaning and effect of the cross is not found in that *suffering*, but in the *love* that informed his suffering: he loved his own to the very end. For a free creature, the outcome of our life is in suspense until its final moment. Repentance and apostasy remain possibilities —however remote—until the foreclosure of death. In his crucifixion, Jesus maintains his loving solidarity with the human race up to the bitterest of ends, showing that there are no lengths to which the divine love will not go in order to enact and maintain communion with human beings, even in our hostility to divine love.

This meaning is not immediately discernible in the phenomenology of the crucifixion—wherein all that appears to the eye is a man being tortured to death (though the Lucan and Johannine passion narratives provide theologically motivated commentary that leads more to this view—Jesus praying for his killers and offering paradise to the penitent thief in Luke; completing the mission given by the Father in John). It is, though, far more clearly displayed in the Last Supper narratives, by which Jesus interprets his death, and which stand at the heart of the church's common life.

As Jesus approaches his final hours, he does what he has so often done, he shares a meal with his friends. This meal, though, is unique, for in it he offers himself as food to the gathered disciples: *Take, eat. This is my body. Drink this, all of you, for it is my blood of the new covenant.* In this way, Jesus asserts his agency in the face of his impending arrest and crucifixion. It is not merely something that happens to him, whether as an accident of history or as the result of immanent political forces.[9] Instead, as the Johannine Jesus says, "No one takes my life from me; I lay it down of my own accord" (John 10:17–18). He has agency not only over his impending death, but also over its meaning, providing this meal as an interpretation of this death.[10] Crucially, though not uncontroversially, the meaning he indicates both for the meal and the death is sacrificial.

Immediately, we must disabuse ourselves of whatever notions we may have had in mind regarding sacrifice. A conceptualism that derives its knowledge from ideas rather than an intellectualism that derives its concepts from acts of understanding will do us no favors here, and has, in fact, caused untold harm in the history of the church's reckoning with sacrifice.[11] In the face of this, some have, understandably, opted to abandon the notion altogether. However, given its ubiquitous presence in Scripture, in the theological tradition, in the churches' liturgies—and the fact that the Catholic Church has dogmatically defined that the Mass is a sacrifice—this strikes me as dead end. Better to insist that sacrifice does not mean what it has been taken to mean within the churches' legacies of harm, better to insist that it bears that meaning given to it by Jesus himself, than to attempt its jettison.

While in the popular imagination, sacrifice refers more or less to the slaughter of an animal, often interpreted as the substitution of an innocent

---

9 However, liberation, Black, and womanist theologians have rightly pointed our attention to the way that the crucifixion stands in continuity with the social and political stances enacted by Jesus. See, e.g., Gustavo Gutiérrez, *A Theology of Liberation: History, Politics, Salvation*, trans. Caridad Inda and John Eagleson (Maryknoll, NY: Orbis, 1988), 130–35; James H. Cone, *Black Theology and Black Power* (Maryknoll, NY: Orbis, 2019), 39–48; M. Shawn Copeland, *Knowing Christ Crucified: The Witness of African American Religious Experience* (Maryknoll, NY: Orbis, 2018), 110–26, 136–47; *Enfleshing Freedom*, 58–65, 121–28. Especially helpful is Jon Sobrino's distinction between two questions: Why did Jesus die? (a theological question that terminates in the mystery of God), and Why was Jesus killed? (a question that must attend to the political realities of the clash between the kingdom of God and the antikingdom of death-dealing idols). *Jesus the Liberator: A Historical Theological Reading of Jesus of Nazareth*, trans. Paul Burns and Francis McDonagh (Maryknoll, NY: Orbis, 1994), 195–211. We shall return to this in chapter 3.

10 See the rather lovely image of the Eucharist as a "deathbed wedding" in Eugene F. Rogers, *Sexuality and the Christian Body: Their Way into the Triune God* (Oxford: Blackwell, 1999), 249–68.

11 On the distinction between intellectualism and conceptualism see Lonergan, *Insight*, 717–18; *Verbum*, 194–96, 218–24.

victim's death in place of the guilty party's,[12] and, in especially abhorrent forms, with this death construed as a punishment: *God is furious and wants to kill you because of your sins, but he'll let you kill this animal instead, and, later, he'll punish Jesus with the death penalty and get all that wrath out of his system, so that he doesn't have to take it out on you.* Such a framework is far removed from biblical or ancient Christian understandings of sacrifice, which, rather than being a matter of punishment or even violence, were construed as an exchange of gifts.

I've written about this more directly elsewhere, and there's no need to reproduce that work here, but a few summary statements can help to solidify the point.[13] First, note that the Old Testament prescribed not just animal sacrifices, but also grain and wine sacrifices, which ought to put to paid any notion that the point of sacrifice is killing or violence (Lev 2:1–14; 6:14–23; 23:9–21). Second, while animals were indeed killed in Old Testament sacrifices (as Jesus was in his own), (1) this death was not construed as a punishment, and (2) the operative theology was of the offering of the victim's *life*, not its death (Lev 17:11, 14).[14] Finally, given the close association between meal and sacrifice that we observed in chapter 1, our notion of sacrifice should be far more convivial than punitive. Indeed, it is in a meal that Jesus bestows theological meaning and sacrificial significance to his death upon the cross. To put a finer point on it: animals must be slaughtered before they can be eaten, and, while the ethics of meat eating are worth discussing—and all the more so when we consider the ecological impact of the meat-production industry—to assume that when meat is on the table that those seated are there because they desire to inflict death upon the animal, rather than to eat, is rather to miss the point.

---

12 This degradation of meaning is symbolized in the way that "victim," originally a sacrificial term merely denoting what was offered in the sacrifice, has come to mean someone who suffers some sort of (usually violent) wrong.

13 Schlesinger, *Sacrificing the Church*, 33–37; "Eucharistic Sacrifice as Anti-violent Pedagogy," *TS* 80, no. 3 (2019): 653–72.

14 Robert J. Daly, *Christian Sacrifice: The Judaeo-Christian Background before Origen* (Washington, DC: CUA Press, 1978); *Sacrifice Unveiled: The True Meaning of Christian Sacrifice* (London: T&T Clark, 2009); David M. Moffitt, *Atonement and the Logic of Resurrection in the Epistle to the Hebrews* (London: Brill, 2011); "Blood, Life, and Atonement: Reassessing Hebrews' Christological Appropriation of Yom Kippur," in *The Day of Atonement: Its Interpretation in Early Jewish and Christian Traditions*, ed. Thomas Hieke and Tobias Nicklas (Leiden: Brill, 2012), 211–24.

What, then, does sacrifice mean, in the Christian tradition? Its origin is, obviously, Jesus's own action and words. In his offer of the bread and wine, Jesus gives his body and blood, first to the disciples, and then, upon the cross, to his Father. Thus, he gives himself. This is the fundamental meaning of sacrifice. From at least Augustine onward, outward acts of sacrifice have been construed as symbolizing interior states, namely the disposition of charity.[15] This is crucial, for it is the charity that informed Jesus's act upon the cross that made it sacrificial and redemptive, not his suffering. On this Thomas Aquinas is clear. Jesus, by loving, offers a sacrifice upon the cross. His crucifiers, who caused his suffering and his death, do not offer a sacrifice, but instead commit a grave evil.[16] To state the matter emphatically once more: Love, not suffering, not death, constitutes the Christian meaning of sacrifice.

All these notions are gathered together in what Robert Doran, drawing upon and expanding the thought of Bernard Lonergan, calls the "just and mysterious law of the cross," which is the fundamental meaning of redemption, and which is "where the long history of 'sacrifice' as a theological category comes to fulfilment, transcending all other notions of sacrifice and even definitively negating some of them."[17] Lonergan summarized the principle thus:

> This is why the Son of God became [human], suffered, died, and was raised again: because divine wisdom has ordained and divine goodness has willed, not to do away with the evils of the human race through power, but to convert those evils into a supreme good according to the just and mysterious law of the cross.[18]

The law of the cross is that according to which one would rather suffer evils than to bring them about, and according to which one is willing to bear evils in order to reverse them.[19] This law "is the intrinsic intelligibility of

---

15 Augustine, *civ.* 10.5 [WSA, 1/6:309–10]; Aquinas, *Summa Theologiæ* 2-2.81, 85.1–2; Bernard J. F. Lonergan, "The Notion of Sacrifice," in *Early Latin Theology*, 2–51.

16 Aquinas, *Summa Theologiæ* 3.48.1–3; 3.22.2

17 Robert M. Doran, *The Trinity in History: A Theology of the Divine Missions*, vol. 3, *Redeeming History*, ed. Joseph Ogbannaya (Milwaukee: Marquette University Press, 2022), 96; Doran wrote extensively about the law of the cross elsewhere. *Theology and the Dialectics of History* (Toronto: University of Toronto Press, 2001), 108–35; *Trinity in History*, 1:231–40; *Trinity in History*, 2:37–50.

18 Lonergan, *The Redemption*, 197. The bracketed substitution is my own, drawn from the original Latin *homo* (196).

19 Lonergan, *The Redemption*, 97–205, 223–51.

the redemption."[20] This is how we have been redeemed and what it means to have been redeemed.

As the crucifixion gives way to the resurrection, as the way of Jesus's love is vindicated by the God of love, the law of the cross is given expression. Definitively enacted and openly revealed in the events of the life death and resurrection of the incarnate Word, the law of the cross is the secret energy operative in those contexts where the grace of God is at work to overcome human sin.[21] It is this law that comes to constitute the lives of Christ's members, as the Christian community devotes itself to reversing evil and promoting good, not by power or coercion, but by a supernaturally empowered forbearance.[22] In this way the mystical body of Christ, bound together by charity, "is the supreme good into which human evils are converted."[23]

Love, then, is the meaning of sacrifice, of the cross, of the Eucharist, and of the church understood as the body of Christ. This detour into the notion of sacrifice is needed because it serves as the connective tissue between the church's founding event upon the cross and its ongoing liturgical life in the Eucharist. By participating in the Eucharist, Christians are brought into the same reality that informed the cross: Christ's loving gift of self to the Father and to the world. It is for this reason that the Catholic Church has defined the Eucharist as a sacrifice. As we shall see shortly, the divisions of the church turn upon a stultification of this movement of love, and are concretely expressed in eucharistic terms. Before we take that turn, though, one further dimension of the Eucharist-church connection needs to be established.

The Sacrifice of the Church

Returning to the discussion of 1 Corinthians 10:15–17, the church is one body because it partakes of the one eucharistic loaf. Or, as Henri de Lubac has said, "Literally speaking, the Eucharist makes the church."[24] As influential as this statement has become in the decades since the publication of *Corpus Mysticum*,

---

20 Lonergan, *The Redemption*, 237.

21 These statements are drawn from Theses 91, 92, 97, and 98 of Doran, *Trinity in History*, 3:97, 169, 172. See also Cone, *Cross and the Lynching Tree*, 155–66.

22 Lonergan, *The Redemption*, 203, 219–23, 227–31; Doran, *Theology and the Dialectics of History*, 108–35; *Trinity in History*, 3:162–86; Copeland, *Enfleshing Freedom*, 101–5, 124–28.

23 Lonergan, *The Redemption*, 199.

24 de Lubac, *Corpus Mysticum*, 88.

little attention has been paid either to the question of what it actually means or how it might work or to the role that sacrifice plays in de Lubac's argument. These two lacunae are related.[25]

The Eucharist makes the church precisely because it is the sacrifice of Christ, his loving self-gift, brought into our lives and received by us here and now. Eating his body and drinking his blood, we are incorporated into him, a sort of metabolic reversal whereby rather than us assimilating the food into our bodies, this food assimilates us into his body.[26] And, just as eternally, the love of the Speaker and the Word breathes forth the notional love that is the Holy Spirit; just as in the economy of salvation, the gift of the love of God (sanctifying grace) calls forth our own loving response (habitual charity), so in the Eucharist, our reception of Christ's gift-of-self brings forth our response. In the words of Paul, "I appeal to you therefore, [siblings], by the mercies of God, to present your bodies as a living sacrifice, holy and acceptable to God, which is your spiritual worship" (Rom 12:1). Or, in the words of *Lumen Gentium*, "When they take part in the eucharistic sacrifice, the source and the culmination of all Christian life, they [the faithful] offer to God the divine victim and themselves along with him."[27] Or, in the words of Jesus himself, "This is my body, which is given for you. *Do this* in remembrance of me" (Luke 22:19, emphasis added).

So then, in the Eucharist, we receive Christ's gift of himself, and are led by that gift to make a gift of ourselves. This gift is directed ultimately toward God, but also proximately to our fellow human beings, for to love God is to love what God loves. In this way, the eucharistic sacrifice calls forth and constitutes the charity that binds together the church as Christ's mystical body, and in this way, Christ's members share in the life of God as beloved children of adoption, interior to the Son, loving with the same love that is the Holy Spirit.[28]

---

25 On the former question see my *Salvation in Henri de Lubac*, chapter 6. On the latter, see "Opus Dei, Opus Hominum: The Trinity, the Four-Point Hypothesis, and the Eucharist," *Irish Theological Quarterly* 88, no. 1 (2022): 56–75.

26 Cf. *conf.* 7.10.16 [WSA: 1/1:173].

27 *LG*, no. 11 [Tanner, 2:857]

28 This is beautifully, and poignantly expressed in Shawn Copeland's account of "eucharistic solidarity," wherein the gift of receiving and becoming the body of Christ calls the Christian community to a stance and praxis of radical solidarity with those whom the world despises, because Jesus was so despised, putting himself in their position and at their service. *Enfleshing Freedom*, 124–28.

By his gift of himself, Christ has gathered a new humanity in one body, within which and as which we are presented by him to the Father in an act of perfect worship. This is the essential meaning of both the eucharistic sacrifice and of the mystical body of Christ, which, according to Augustine is constituted by the sacrifice of Christ and bound together by the same charity that provides the interior meaning of that sacrifice.[29] To be the body of Christ is to be bound together by love.

This vision coheres with and is operative within the ecclesiology of communion articulated in chapter 1. The church exists in and through the churches in their mutual communion with each other. The ecclesiology of the Second Vatican Council defines the particular church as a "community of the altar, under the sacred ministry of the bishop," foregrounding the eucharistic character of the church.[30] Two dimensions of this are worth particular note. First, the church, as the community constituted by the Eucharist, is a community that coalesces around the cross and the redemptive love that informed Christ's act there. Second, a eucharistic ecclesiology must necessarily foreground the local church, for the Eucharist can only be celebrated locally, only in a particular time and place by a particular community. In its celebration, that community joins with the whole church of all times and places in the one body of Christ, offering the one sacrifice of Christ, but nevertheless, there is no universal celebration of the Eucharist, only local ones. Because of the meaning of the church and the Eucharist, these local churches recognize their connection to one another, and celebrate in openness toward one another, or so the logic should go.

Division in the church occurs primarily between these particular churches rather than within them per se. Yes, sometimes local assemblies can be split, whether because of interpersonal conflict, doctrinal disagreement, or what have you, but by and large, this is not the sort of division with which we are concerned. Instead, we are dealing with nonrecognition on the part of the churches, whereby one (or more) churches refuse to acknowledge another as church, and determine to live not just an existence that is distinct from the other, but independent of or separate from them. The classic sign of this division has been the establishment of separate eucharistic celebrations. The separateness of the celebration is not the same as a numerical increase of

---

29 Eugene R. Schlesinger, "The Sacrificial Ecclesiology of *City of God* 10," *Augustinian Studies* 47, no. 2 (2016): 137–55.

30 *LG*, no. 26 [Tanner, 2:870].

celebrations. Within a single parish, there might be several Masses over the course of a weekend. Within a diocese, the various parishes will carry out their own liturgical lives. There is not necessarily any division involved here. Instead, the division occurs when, to borrow Augustine's phrase, one raises "altar against altar," when there is a eucharistic celebration carried out in isolation from or rivalry with the other churches in question.

At issue is not that there are multiple churches. Even in an undivided church, there would be multiple churches, for *the* church is none other than the communion of the particular churches. The problem is that these multiple churches live their lives out of communion with each other, either failing or refusing to recognize in each other the church, or able or willing to extend only partial recognition. In a united church, these churches in all their diversity and difference would not cease distinct existence. Rather, they would acknowledge and embrace one another as particular churches within the wider communion of churches. Precisely what the shape of that recognition would be is not the issue here. The point is that the problem is not multiplicity. The problem is exclusion.

The theological meaning of the church is redemptive charity. In love, God has become human, suffered and died—an act whose meaning is not suffering or death, but rather the love that informed that suffering and the death—and risen again. In so doing the Word has gathered a new humanity, which shares in his identity, as his body, itself bound together by charity, the same charity that informed Christ's redemptive act, the same charity that constitutes the divine life, the same charity by which human beings come to share in that divine life. We share it, not isolated from each other, nor as an aggregate, but as a unity, as the mystical body of Christ. The redemption overcomes hostility, transforming it into charity.

CHARITY LOST, THE BODY RENT

The foregoing is a nice enough story, and I am persuaded that it is true, indeed, persuaded that if it were not true, there would be no purpose in engaging in Christian theology. Nevertheless, we must ask, "What's gone wrong?" As early as the second century, our first witness to the monarchical episcopate, the letters of Ignatius of Antioch, even as they articulate the time-honored (though, honored by time, not by actual practice) principle of one altar one bishop, urging their recipients to "do nothing without the bishop," must do so precisely because of those who would carry on with the life of the church in isolation from the bishop.[31] Writing in the fourth and fifth centuries, Augustine must combat the Donatists. Since the mid-eleventh century, the Eastern and Western Churches have been formally divided from one another. And, though the mutual anathemas have been lifted, communion has not been restored. The sixteenth-century reformation led to further splintering of Catholic from Protestant, Lutheran from Reformed from Anglican from Anabaptist from Baptist. In the last couple of centuries Protestants of the same tradition have divided from one another, leaving rival Baptist, Presbyterian, Methodist, and Anglican denominations. Even the church at Corinth no longer celebrated the Lord's Supper in their fractious gatherings.

The mystical body of Christ is ruptured indeed.

For all the divisions just listed, the parties involved would list different causes. And the particulars of each case matter to an extent. In the end, though, it is my contention that they have one particular feature in common, which relativizes all the rest, and which is the true cause of division. They all represent a failure or refusal of charity, a turning away from the law of the cross, which would have us cleave to one another despite any cost involved, and, so a severance from the fundamental meaning of the church.

Tellingly, these schisms all involve, at least at some point, the refusal of eucharistic communion to the divided parties. This is rather central to our considerations, because communion is a sacramental reality, not a matter of opinions. Christians are not divided from each other because they disagree. You can disagree with someone and kneel down beside them to receive the Lord's body and blood.

Instead, they are divided from each other because they refuse to kneel down beside one another and receive the Lord's body and blood. This is a rather damning realization, for this refusal undercuts the very source of the church's identity and its principle of life. It refuses the prospect of being reconciled, at least not if that reconciliation involves being reconciled to *these people*.

Here I do not advocate for a glib or hasty intercommunion that overlooks our real divisions. The Catholic Church is right to insist against this, arguing in their Decree on Ecumenism, *Unitatis Redintegratio*, "Worship in common [*communicationem in sacris*] is not to be considered as a means to be used

---

31 E.g., Ephesians 3–6; Magnesians 2–4, 6–7; Trallians 2–3; Philadelphians 3–4; Smyrneans 8 (in Michael W. Holmes, ed., *The Apostolic Fathers: Greek Texts and English Translations*, 3d ed. [Grand Rapids: Baker, 2007]).

indiscriminately for the restoration of christian unity.... Witness to the unity of the church generally forbids common worship [*communicationem*]."[32] The Eucharist is an ecclesial act, and if we are not yet willing to wholeheartedly throw in our lots with one another, we ought not engage in intercommunion. Doing so simply trivializes the reality of division and of the Eucharist.[33]

This is not to suggest that those churches that invite members of other churches to communicate at their altars (as does my own) are wrong to do so, but rather to affirm that sacramental intercommunion without restored ecclesial communion does not resolve the problem, and risks making matters worse by softening the pain of division. Pain serves a medically important function, calling our attention to the fact that something is not right. The problem is not the pain caused by division but the division itself. We ought to be pained by our divisions, and seeking to alleviate the pain without ending the division could prove medically disastrous, akin to a premature transition to palliative hospice care.

We ought to be celebrating and receiving the Eucharist together, but our common celebrations should be the expression and enactment of a common life. If they are not, then the celebration risks devolving into a mockery, despite all the best intentions that lead to it. It is striking that no one seems to take to heart Jesus's warning in the Sermon on the Mount, to leave our gift at the altar and first be reconciled with our siblings before offering our sacrifice, despite the frequent application of those words to eucharistic contexts.

Augustine against the Donatists

These themes of charity, unity, and the Eucharist are distilled with a particular clarity in Augustine's anti-Donatist writings. Throughout his ministry, Augustine was embroiled in controversy with the Donatists, who were the predominant expression of Christianity within Northern Africa at the time.[34]

---

32 *UR*, no. 8 [Tanner, 2:914].

33 Contra Geoffrey Wainwright, *Eucharist and Eschatology* (New York: Oxford University Press, 1981), 141–46. So also Radner, *End of the Church*, 235.

34 So Maureen Tilley, "General Introduction" in WSA, 1/21:13. For historical treatments of the Donatist movement, see, e.g., Maureen A. Tilley, *The Bible in Christian North Africa: The Donatist World* (Minneapolis: Fortress Press, 1997); W. H. C. Frend, *The Donatist Church: A Movement of Protest in Roman North Africa* (Oxford: Clarendon Press, 1952); James P. Keleher, *Saint Augustine's Notion of Schism in the Donatist Controversy* (Mundelein: Saint Mary of the Lake Seminary, 1961).

Insisting upon purity for the church's ministers, the Donatists had broken away from the Catholic Church in the aftermath of the Diocletian persecution, when certain clergy who had caved to pressure during the persecution, handing over (*tradere*) the Scriptures, were elected to the episcopate. Such *traditores* contaminated the church and were incapable of bestowing authentic sacraments, thereby setting off a chain reaction of apostasy, for those baptized or ordained by *traditores* were likewise incapable of bestowing authentic sacraments, for one cannot give what one does not have. The only hope of salvaging a faithful church, and saving the souls who cleave to it was to divide from the morally compromised church of the *traditores*, or so the logic went.

Against the Donatists, Augustine advanced several arguments, most famously the insistence that the true minister of every sacrament is Christ,[35] which means that even heretics and schismatics can validly administer the sacrament, even if this administration is unlawful. For this reason, those who were baptized among the Donatists, but who wished to enter the communion of the Catholic Church did not have to be and, indeed, should not be rebaptized.[36] But the most relevant dimension of Donatism is not its heresy, but its schismatic character. And it is schism, more than anything else, that concerned Augustine.[37] This fact is borne out by his view of Cyprian, to whom the Donatists appealed as a patron of sorts. Earlier, in the third century, Cyprian was embroiled in a similarly motivated controversy surrounding the Novatian schism. After the Decian persecution, Christians disagreed over how, or if, the *lapsi* could be restored to the communion of the church. The Novatians insisted that they could not. In the context of this dispute, Cyprian held a line not all that dissimilar to the later Donatists: salvation could not be found outside of the church, so those who would be saved must adhere to the communion. Moreover, as one cannot give what one does not have, those who were baptized by heretics or schismatics needed to be rebaptized in order to enter the communion of the church, because any sacrament they had received outside this saving communion was null and void.[38] Augustine,

---

35 This statement is made explicit in *c. Litt. Pet.* 49,59 [WSA, 1/21:250], but is implied throughout *bapt.* Particularly in the continuous use of the "baptism of Christ" to refer to the sacrament. See also *bapt.* 3.4.6 [WSA, 1/21:446]; 5.9.11 [WSA, 1/21:508–9]. Cf. *In Io eu.* 6.1,7 [WSA, 3/12:127].

36 E.g., *bapt.* 1.1,2–3,4 [WSA, 1/21:391–95].

37 See Keleher, *Augustine's Notion of Schism*, 7–8, who notes that only relatively late, and out of desperation, did Augustine regard the Donatists as heretical.

38 Keleher, *Augustine's Notion of Schism*, 13–18.

we should not be surprised to learn, thought that Cyprian was wrong about this. And yet, he was also insistent that Cyprian offered no support to the Donatist position, for Cyprian's entire motivation was to maintain the bond of unity with the Catholic Church.[39] Those who left this communion left the community of salvation. In the case of the Donatist controversy, this position was occupied by the Donatists. So, despite their appeal to Cyprian, they found themselves opposite him on the issues. Moreover, Cyprian deferred to the principle of unity, holding to his view about baptism, but "not judging anyone or depriving him of the right to communion if he should hold a different opinion."[40]

In other words, while Augustine thought that Cyprian's position on the sacraments' efficacy (a position that, at least superficially, agreed with the Donatists') was wrong, Cyprian was no heretic, because he was no schismatic. He remained within the communion of the Catholic Church. The Donatists, though, were both wrong and heretical because they had left that communion, setting up "altar against altar."[41] The difference is not in the material positions they held, but in their formal position vis-à-vis the communion of the church. The body of Christ is bound together by charity, and to break this bond is to turn away from charity. But to turn away from charity is also to turn away from salvation, for it is in charity that our salvation consists.[42] This is the heart of Augustine's anti-Donatist position.

It is crucial to understand that Augustine's disagreement with the Donatists revolves entirely around the issue of maintaining or breaking communion. In terms of the moral principle, he thought they were correct. The *traditores* should not have handed over the Scriptures. But his doctrine of sin granted him a certain realism that recognized that all fall short of the glory of God, and, so will depend entirely upon grace if they are to be saved (Rom 3:23). It was, in the words of R. A. Markus, a Christianity for the mediocre.[43] We

<hr>

39 Much of books 2–5 of *bapt.* are taken up with Cyprian and his legacy. See especially 2.4,5–5,6 [WSA 423–26]; 2.7,12 [WSA, 1/21:431-33]; 2.13,18 [WSA, 1/21:437–38]; 3.1,1–4,6 [WSA, 1/21:441–47];

40 Quoted in Augustine, *bapt.* 6.6,9 [WSA, 1/21:539]

41 E.g., *ps. c. Don.* [WSA, 1/21: 34, 36, 38, 41, 46].

42 See, e.g., *c. litt. Pet.* I. 77,172 [WSA, 1/21:150]; 81,180 [WSA, 1/21:154]; *bapt.* 1.9,12 [WSA, 1/21:403–4]; 18,27 [WSA, 1/21:415–18]. See also discussion in Keleher, *Augustine's Notion of Schism,* 49–55.

43 R. A. Markus, ed., "Augustine: A Defence of Christian Mediocrity," in *The End of Ancient Christianity* (Cambridge: Cambridge University Press, 1991), 45–62.

shall return to this with greater force in chapter 3, but for now, we can note that, while Augustine would not endorse errant theological views nor moral failings (in other words, mediocrity is an accurate description, but not an adequate goal), he also insists that the church's communion can and does embrace them, and that the presence of the mistaken or the morally lacking cannot contaminate the rest of the church, whose entire hope lies in Christ and not in any ostensible moral purity.[44] We do not risk our salvation by remaining in communion with them. Instead, it is in our withdrawal from community that the risk lies, for such withdrawal is a repudiation of charity, and, so, salvation.[45]

In *De doctrina christiana*, Augustine notes that there are right and wrong ways to interpret Scripture, but that, depending on the nature of the error, different evaluations are in order. The purpose of Scripture is to facilitate our journey to our true homeland, the triune God, through the incarnate Word, so that we can be truly happy.[46] This is accomplished by setting our loves in their proper order. Scripture, then, is intended to promote the twofold love of God and neighbor. Mistaken interpretations that promote this love are still wrong; they should be corrected, because it is better to be correct than mistaken, but they are not dangerous or harmful, for we still reach the same destination. On the other hand, interpretations that lead away from the love of God or neighbor are not only wrong, but dangerous, for they lead away from the goal of happiness in God.[47] As 1 Peter 4:8 notes, "Love covers a multitude of sins."

Error should not be allowed to go uncorrected, but those who are in error can also be embraced in the bonds of charity. And, as noted in the introduction, as the church journeys through history, as our understandings of ourselves and our world shift, as we recognize further the ambiguity of texts and their interpretation, particularly those that reflect rather different cultural and historical contexts than our own, the question of error and truth becomes a matter of discernment, even contestation. It is only together that we will be led into all truth by the Holy Spirit sent by the Father and the

---

44 *c. litt. Pet.* I. 4,5 [WSA, 1/21:57–58]; *bapt.* 2.6,8 [WSA, 1/21:427]; *cath. fr.* 2,3 [WSA, 1/21:607–9]; *c. ep. Parm.* III 20,39–22,42 [WSA, 1/21:338–40].

45 Hence, Aquinas's judgment that schism is more dangerous than heresy. *Summa Theologiæ* 2-2.39.1.

46 *doctr. chr.* 1.11.11–14.13, 34.38 [WSA, 1/11:110–12, 122–23].

47 *doctr. chr.* 1.36.40–37.41 [WSA, 1/11:124–25]

Word, and this Holy Spirit is the bond of love. When we refuse love, we stop our ears to the voice of the Spirit, not unlike those who stoned St. Stephen the protomartyr (Acts 7:57).

Here I do not suggest either endless deferral of decisions, nor the impossibility of definitive decisions, nor do I suggest that we should assume that those with whom we disagree are right after all, nor even that we should forgo polemics. Decisions must be reached; someone *is* wrong; and rather vociferous argumentation is in order. What I suggest instead, is that this contestation properly belongs within the church's communion. If we would be faithful to the God revealed in Jesus Christ, the God to whom we are reconciled by the cross and resurrection, the God who bestows upon us the Holy Spirit, then we must hold fast to one another in love, even when we are convinced that our interlocutors are sorely wrong. The law of the cross constitutes the supernatural aid we need for this bracing stance.

Jesus himself models sharp opposition and rebuke within the context of love. To Peter he declaims, "Get behind me, Satan." Yet, clearly, he loves this rock upon whom the church is to be built. Overlooking Jerusalem, on his way to meet his fate, he laments, expressing his desire to gather those who stone prophets and kill those sent to them under his wings like a mother hen, despite their unwillingness (Matt 23:37; Luke 13:34). Nailed to the cross, he prays for his killers' forgiveness, demonstrating his insistence upon holding fast to sinful humanity in love, even at the height of their opposition to God (Luke 23:34). The point here is twofold: (1) holding fast to one another in love is not a call for laissez-faire approaches to doctrinal or moral matters, and (2) doing so replicates the very shape of our redemption. We are reconciled to God because in Christ, God has held fast to the morally and theologically bankrupt, loving his enemies to the utmost extremity. To refuse to do the same is its own implicit rejection of redemption (cf. Matt 18:23–35).

The Donatist schism is now long behind us, but the prevailing problem that informed it has reasserted itself time and again. There have been a variety of other schisms over the centuries, some larger and others less so. Two have been especially prominent and deserve mention, the division of the Eastern and Western Churches from 1054 onward, and the fracture of the Western church beginning in the sixteenth century. There is no need to linger over the details nor to relitigate the controversies, so we can be somewhat brief. The main point we need to grasp is that these two instances of division run afoul of the basic anti-Donatist logic we have surveyed so far.

The Great Schism

The presenting issue of the Great Schism of 1054 was the addition of the phrase *filioque* into the Latin version of the Nicene-Constantinopolitan Creed, initially at the Third Council of Toledo (589), but eventually throughout the West. With this addition, a relatively standard Western trinitarian theologoumenon, namely, that the Holy Spirit proceeds from both the Father and the Son, was elevated to credal status,[48] provoking no small consternation among Eastern Christians. Neither the filioque nor disagreement about it caused the schism, though. These causes were far more complex, revolving especially around questions of authority, jurisdiction, and primacy, with a significant overlay of political rivalry between Rome and "New Rome" (i.e., Constantinople).[49] Eventually the conflict reached such a fevered pitch that the churches of Rome and Constantinople mutually excommunicated one another, leading to a division between East and West that perdures to this day.

The refusal of charity is relatively easy to recognize when we consider the political and jurisdictional dimensions of the schism. Rival factions vying for power are more or less a textbook example of failing to love. Unable to get their way or impose it on others, the two sides sought to exclude each other from the community of salvation. At issue isn't even whether one side was right regarding the questions of authority and jurisdiction, and, if so, which one was right. Such rivalries and disagreements were nothing new. And even if with the controversy over the filioque, they'd reached a new stage or intensity, the fact remains that there was a time when all the parties disagreed over these matters and were still in communion. That this had ever been the case means that maintaining communion even amid these same disagreements was possible. What changed was the willingness to remain in communion. We shall return to this consideration in chapter five.

Similarly, regarding the filioque itself, there is nothing necessarily church dividing about it. Augustine affirmed it in the fifth century and Gregory of Nazianzus, writing in the fourth, did not (though I'd not say he rejected it; he doesn't seem to have considered the matter). But the churches remained

---

48 That the Spirit proceeds from both the Father and the Son is attested by, e.g., Tertullian (*Ad Praxeas* 13), Hilary (*De Trin.* 2.29), Ambrose (*On the Holy Spirit* 1.11.20), Augustine, *Trin.* 4.5.29 [WSA, 1/5:182]; 15.17,29 [WSA, 1/5:422–23]

49 See, e.g., Aidan Nichols, *Rome and the Eastern Churches: A Study in Schism* (Collegeville, MN: Liturgical Press, 1992); Philip Sherrard, *Church, Papacy, and Schism: A Theological Enquiry* (London: SPCK, 1978).

united. If the filioque is wrong, and one still affirms it, the orthodox faith is not challenged, for the equality and full divinity of the trinitarian persons is still upheld. Similarly, if it is correct, but one denies it, nothing essential to the faith is lost, for the same reason. And, in the present day, prominent Orthodox theologians have suggested that it is an acceptable theological position, though it should not be imposed doctrinally.[50] More importantly, the Catholic and Orthodox Churches have both rescinded the anathemas by which they had formerly condemned one another. What this demonstrates is that there is nothing inherent in the theological disagreement that would require the churches to divide. This being the case, the division was purely the result of a decision. The parties were no longer willing to bear with one another in love amid their real and serious disagreements.

The Reformation's Schisms

The divisions of the Protestant reformation were similarly so complex as to defy easy summary, but many if not all of the disputed issues flowed from disagreement over the doctrine of justification. This doctrine, which was elevated by these controversies into a status that it had never before held (previously it was one metaphor for salvation among many; Martin Luther shifted it to a fulcral position). The Lutherans considered it the article upon which the church stands or falls, and it is generally regarded as the material principle of the reformation. Disputes about theological authority were motivated by questions of the criteria whereby the proper doctrine could be established. Protestant opposition to ministerial priesthood, to the idea of the Mass as a sacrifice, and various other principles of Catholic sacramental doctrine, and so on and so forth, was based on a conviction that the Catholic Church's teaching and practice on these matters obscured or denied the notion of justification by grace alone through faith alone.[51]

---

50 David Bentley Hart, "The Myth of Schism," in *Ecumenism Today: The Universal Church in the 21st Century*, ed. Francesca Aran Murphy and Christopher Asprey (Aldershot, UK: Ashgate, 2008), 99–100; Sergius Bulgakov, *The Comforter*, trans. Boris Jakim (Grand Rapids: Eerdmans, 2004), 75–151; Timothy Ware, *The Orthodox Church: An Introduction to Eastern Christianity*, 3d ed. (London: Penguin, 2015), 204–12.

51 This is noted in the *JDDJ* (Vatican website, October 31, 1999), no. 1. Jakob Karl Rinderknecht provides further analysis of this ample documentation from historical sources in *Mapping the Differentiated Consensus of the Joint Declaration* (New York: Palgrave Macmillan, 2016), 4.

Once more, we need not detail all of the developments that led from Luther's initial desire to bring about reform within the Catholic Church to the mutual condemnations of Lutherans and Catholics, nor the emergence of other types of Protestantism and their inability to maintain or establish full communion with each other. These are well known and thoroughly documented elsewhere. What matters for our purposes is to note that the Catholic Church and the Lutheran World Federation have achieved sufficient consensus on the doctrine of justification that they consider their former mutual condemnations not to apply to each other, and have done so in such a way that neither party has had to repudiate their distinctive historical teaching.[52] The two communions no longer regard their differences surrounding justification to be church dividing. This consensus shows that the differences never had to be church dividing. A differentiated consensus, one that does not erase the differences, while also not condemning them, is possible.[53] It was found near the end of the twentieth century because the parties involved were willing to work toward it. It was not found in the sixteenth century because neither party was willing to do so. They mutually refused to bear with one another while they strove to resolve the issue. This is, once more, a failure of charity.

While at the sixteenth century, the dividing churches viewed the very gospel message at stake, requiring a separation for the sake of the salvation of souls, the *JDDJ* shows that this was not the case. They could have stayed together and worked through matters. Hence, in both the East-West schism and the Western schism of the Protestant reformation, the cause was, in the end, not disagreement, but failures of charity. This, of course, begs the question: What if there were to emerge a sufficient reason for division, whether on moral or doctrinal grounds? Neither affirming or denying the filioque, nor holding to a Catholic or Protestant understanding of justification puts one outside the bounds of Christian recognition, but might there be *some* aberration that would?

---

52 *JDDJ*, nos. 5–7.

53 See the thorough analysis of Rinderknecht, who demonstrates that the two churches maintain their own distinctive, mutually-incompatible modes of talking about justification within the context of this consensus. *Mapping the Differentiated Consensus*, especially 147–244.

O Love That Will Not Let Me Go? The Limits of Communion

The entire assumption of this book is that Christian division is never excusable or justifiable. This leaves unaddressed the question of divisions from those who are not recognizably Christian. In such cases, Christian communion is, by definition, impossible. We have just considered two examples of this, as Catholic and Orthodox, Catholic and Protestant mutually condemned one another for subverting the very heart of the faith. And yet, we have also seen that after centuries of division, the divided parties have come to see that the issues at hand have not, in fact, placed either party beyond the pale. Other divisions operate on a similar logic: the divisions of the Anglican Communion over the place of LGBTQ people and relationships in the life of the church, for instance, has seen accusations that the churches that affirm queer folks have placed themselves beyond the bounds of Christian orthodoxy. We shall return to this with greater focus in the next chapter.

While I have argued that neither the East-West schism nor the Reformation-era divisions actually involved either party moving beyond the bounds of Christian recognition, we must note that accusations of doing so are not in all cases unacceptable, having some basis in the New Testament, where in the Johannine epistles, we read about "antichrists," those who deny that Christ has come in the flesh (2 John 7). Such antichrists have, apparently, departed from the Johannine community, prompting this assessment: "They went out from us, but they did not belong to us, for if they had belonged to us they would have remained with us. But by going out they made it plain that none of them belongs to us" (1 John 2:19). If those who depart are antichrists, then, clearly, they have no claim to belonging to the community.

While the movement is reversed—expulsion, rather than departure—a similar logic would govern the excommunication of heretics by conciliar decrees. Those who deny that Christ has come in the flesh are outside the bounds of what can be recognized as Christian confession. While God's love for them remains, and while the grace of God may yet embrace them (this is for God to know), they are not *recognizably* Christian, and so their not being included in the Christian community is not a matter of church division.

In his classic study *Arius: Heresy and Tradition*, Rowan Williams persuasively locates the Arian controversy not as an instance of "the church" reacting against and expelling a heresy from its midst, but rather as a matter of the forging of orthodoxy in the face of newly emergent questions. Anti-Nicene and Nicene Christians both appealed to the same Scriptures, to the same structures of authority, to the same sense of a Catholic tradition. The Arian crisis instead represented an inflection point beyond which mere repetition of formulae and slogans from before the crisis would no longer suffice. Some discontinuity with the past was needed. The question was *which* discontinuity would be most adequate to maintaining the integrity of the faith. It is, in a sense, the invention of theology.[54] The point here is to, once more, locate contestation and disagreement within the communion of the church. Even if certain positions are eventually excluded as incompatible with the faith, this outcome is never a foregone conclusion. Indeed, as Williams demonstrates, Arius was deeply conservative and in profound continuity with much of the received common tradition. So it is not merely a matter of maintaining some sort of pristine doctrinal status quo.[55] Conservative positions can and have become heretical.

What, then, are the boundaries? While I will not mount a defense of this position—such a defense would belong to fundamental theology, not systematics—I follow my own Anglican tradition's identification of the Nicene-Constantinopolitan Creed as "the sufficient statement of Christian faith."[56] Those who affirm the Nicene faith, which outlines the basic parameters of the doctrine of the Trinity, by asserting the full equality, but also the distinction on the basis of their eternal relations of origin, of the Father, the Son, and the Holy Spirit, as well as a confession that the eternal Word of God has become truly human (viz., that he has "come in the flesh," per 1 John 2:19), are properly recognized as Christian. They may be grievously wrong about any number of things, but their errors are the errors of Christians, and any disagreement among those who hold to this faith should be regarded as an intrachurch disagreement.

---

54 Rowan Williams, *Arius: Heresy and Tradition* (Grand Rapids: Eerdmans, 2002). Bernard Lonergan attributes a similar axial significance to Nicaea, see, e.g., *The Triune God: Doctrines*, ed. Robert M. Doran and H. Daniel Monsour, trans. Michael G. Shields, CWBL 11 (Toronto: University of Toronto Press, 2009); "The Origins of Christian Realism," in *A Second Collection*, 202–20.

55 Williams, *Arius*, 233–45.

56 The "Chicago-Lambeth Quadrilateral" was first passed by the House of Bishops (though not the House of Deputies) at the Episcopal Church's General Convention in 1886, and subsequently adopted in modified form by the Bishops of the Anglican Communion, gathered at the 1888 Lambeth Conference. *BCP* (New York: Church Hymnal Corporation, 1979), 876–78. For a similar identification of the Nicene Creed as the sole doctrinal criterion for ecclesial communion from a Catholic perspective, see Heinrich Fries and Karl Rahner, *Unity of the Churches—an Actual Possibility* (Philadelphia: Fortress Press, 1985).

Even as I say this, though, I am haunted by the words of James Cone, who, in *The Cross and the Lynching Tree*, issues a challenge to Christians complicit in white supremacy:

> Black people did not need to go to seminary and study theology to know that white Christianity was fraudulent. As a teenager in the South where whites treated blacks with contempt, I and other blacks knew that the Christian identity of whites was not a true expression of what it meant to follow Jesus. Nothing their theologians and preachers could say would convince us otherwise. We wondered how whites could live with their hypocrisy—such a blatant contradiction of the man from Nazareth. (I am still wondering about that!) White conservative Christianity's blatant endorsement of lynching as a part of its religion and white liberal Christians' silence about lynching placed both of them outside Christian identity. . . . There was no way a community could support or ignore lynching in America while still representing in word and deed the one who was lynched by Rome.[57]

And I recognize the judgment of Kelly Brown Douglas that the credal tradition is not so much *wrong*, according to the womanist theological tradition, as irrelevant.[58] If one can affirm the Nicene faith and either participate in or turn indifferently away from chattel slavery, lynching, the war on drugs, and mass incarceration, what good does that faith do for Black folks? (Or, for that matter, white folks, whose own souls are distended by such abominations?)

Returning to Williams, we may indeed be now at another inflection point, one where the boundaries of Christian recognition are being interrogated. "Arianism" was not ruled out of bounds until Nicaea, and the judgment was not solidified until after Constantinople. I am confident that the judgment of history will be to similarly rule out white supremacy, along with patriarchy, homophobia, and all other structures of oppression. Until such time, white supremacist Christians can still be recognized as Christian, even as they should be called to repentance and amendment of life.[59]

---

57 Cone, *Cross and the Lynching Tree*, 133.

58 Kelly Brown Douglas, *What's Faith Got to Do with It? Black Bodies/Christian Souls* (Maryknoll, NY: Orbis, 2005), 74–84; *The Black Christ* (Maryknoll, NY: Orbis, 1993), 111–13.

59 Here again the development of dogma is a useful analogue. Justin Martyr, Origen, and others displayed subordinationist tendencies in their Christologies, but they lived and worked before Nicaea, and so are not formally heretical. Similarly, when the Christian churches definitively exclude racism, sexism, homophobia, et cetera, as incompatible with the faith, there will not be a retrospective exclusion of racists, et alia, from the communion of saints, though there can and should be a retrospective judgment that they were wrong. Meanwhile, their individual eschatological destinies are God's to know and determine.

Churches, then, do need standards and practices of accountability and discipline. About this, the Donatists were right. The New Testament contains frequent admonitions for discipline within the church, and calls for excommunication under certain circumstances (e.g., Matt 18:15–20; 1 Cor 5:1–13; 1 Tim 1:20). We are presently witnessing a reaping of the whirlwind as the Catholic Church reckons with the lack of accountability and discipline that not only allowed clergy sexual abuse to run rampant, but also protected abusers, favoring institutional reputation over the well-being of the flock. While the Catholic Church has been the most visible instance of this, probably because it's just so much larger than any other Christian communion, they are hardly alone in it. We Anglicans have our own cultures and legacies of abuse. As I write this paragraph, the Southern Baptist Convention is under investigation by the United States Department of Justice for fostering a culture of abuse.

To take another example, in February 2022, Russia launched an invasion of Ukraine. In this act of aggression, the Russian government was enthusiastically supported by Kirill, the Orthodox Patriarch of Moscow, who deployed religiously couched rhetoric, casting the invasion as a nearly Manichaean struggle of good against evil. In response, an array of clergy and theologians, including some whose canonical residence was in the Moscow Patriarchate, called for the Russian Orthodox Church to be expelled from the World Council of Churches.[60] Importantly, such an act would not be a break of communion, per se. The WCC is not a church, and most of its member churches are not in full communion with Moscow anyway. Andrew Louth, who spearheaded this call, as a priest of the Moscow Patriarchate, would remain in communion with that church, and with Patriarch Kirill. Hence, the struggle for accountability and discipline is properly located within the communion of the church. About this the Donatists were wrong, as are their contemporary heirs.

Paul makes it clear, and the subsequent theological tradition maintains this principle, that excommunication is always for the purpose of restoration and that the excommunicate is still embraced by bonds of charity, even if they are not eligible to receive the Eucharist until the cause of their excommunication is removed (1 Cor 5:5b; 2 Cor 2:5–11; 1 Tim 1:20).[61] Further, and especially pertinent to our concerns, the Pauline instruction is to excommunicate

---

60 Andrew Louth, "Should the WCC Expel Patriarch Kirill?," *Public Orthodoxy* (blog), August 26, 2022.

61 See, e.g., David P. Long, "Eucharistic Ecclesiology and Excommunication: A Critical Investigation of the Meaning and Praxis of Exclusion from the Sacrament of the Eucharist," *Ecclesiology* 10, no. 2 (2014): 205–28.

individuals, not churches. He regards the division of the church with horror and as an impossibility. One may ask about the prudence of disciplinary exclusion of individuals from the church, but there is no basis whatsoever in the New Testament for division at the level of the church.

The most prominent divisions of the church are marked out as inexcusable by the very progress made by divided Christians toward overcoming the divisions. In regaining something of our lost love for another, in coming to recognize that the issues over which we had divided from one another and condemned one another are not sufficient to warrant such condemnation and division, we clarify that they were never sufficient to do so. Our divisions are instead rooted in a refusal to bear with one another in love, a bearing with that, had we done it, would have allowed us to come to such realizations earlier and without the division. This is not to condemn those efforts that have led to the realization. They are their own sign that God has not abandoned us to our lovelessness, a matter that we shall consider in chapter 5. Rather, the progress shows how inexcusable the divisions were, shows that the real issue has been the refusal of charity.

Free Love: Charity Clarified

This conclusion calls for its own clarification, for charity by its nature must be free. Apart from our free consent to the grace of God, there could be no redemption, there could be no charity, there could be no Christian unity. For the infinite freedom of God, it is impossible to fail to do the good, for God is simply identical to goodness, and so it is impossible to fall short of love, for God is love. Our created freedom, though, by virtue of its finitude, is capable both of defection and of failure to love. This capacity is not a flaw, but rather just an entailment of being both finite and free. There is no necessity that requires that finite freedom should fall from the good or refuse love, just as there is no necessity that would require that we should attain it or always be loving, facts that I must consistently underscore with my students, who tend to feel that God has set us up for failure by making us in such a way that we are capable of sin. And, while I tell them that the Grand Inquisitor's objection in *The Brothers Karamazov* that the freedom with which God has bestowed us is not worth the cost is always a viable option,[62] indeed, the only viable

---

62 Fyodor Dostoyevsky, *The Brothers Karamazov*, trans. David Magarshack (New York: Penguin, 1958), 288–311.

intellectual argument left regarding the problem of evil, we all intuitively recognize that it is better for us to be free than not.[63] In any case, it has pleased the divine wisdom to make us free, and, so here we are, whether we think it's worthwhile or not.

In other words, that which makes us capable of redemption, capable of being joined to one another in love in the mystical body of Christ is also that which has allowed ourselves to stand in need of redemption, and which allows us to sunder the church's unity by refusing that charity which would bind us together. God has saved us not by violence, but by bringing forth in us a free response of love beyond what we would be able to do on our own, a love by which we are brought to share in God's life, a love by which we are enabled to bear with one another in all our joys and griefs, in all our concord and disagreement, if only we would.[64]

CONCLUSION: A EUCHARISTIC PARABLE

Love is the meaning of all existence, whether that necessary existence that is the Trinity or the contingent existence of creatures that the Trinity has loved into being. It is love that led God to make creatures capable of freely given reciprocal love, and love that led God not to abandon us when we turned away from God's love, but rather to consistently and persistently call us back into the way of love, to overcome our resistance not by power, nor any violence, but by a further, supernatural gift. It is love that led the second person of the Trinity to become one of us, to share our existence to the full, to love God as a human being, and to receive the love of God as a human being, so that the love God has for God could be granted to humanity. It is love that led him to the cross, where he bore with our resistance to love to the very

---

63 See Lonergan, "God's Knowledge and Will," in *Early Latin Theology*, 257–411 for an articulation of how the classic Augustinian-Thomistic commitment to the intelligibility of being and its attendant notion of evil as privation, and so fundamentally irrational, resolves the logical and theological aporia. That this solution leaves us wanting something more is a sign that the problem of evil is not an intellectual problem, but rather a practical one. The issue is not "Why does God allow evil?" but rather, "What has God done to overcome evil?" See Lonergan, *Insight*, 708–51; *The Redemption*, 455–65; Doran, *Theology and the Dialectics of History*, 108–38; *Trinity in History*, 1:231–45; Copeland, *Enfleshing Freedom*, 92–95, 99–105.

64 Lonergan, *The Redemption*, 455–65.

end, never giving up on us, no matter the cost—love for us and love for the Father who sent him to redeem us in this manner. It is love that raised him from the dead, and love that led him to give the Gift of the Notional Love that is the Holy Spirit, so that we could not only receive the love of God, but love with that same love. It is love that constitutes the Christian church as the community called and bound together by the love of God, as we learn to love all those whom God loves as God loves them. Love is the meaning of the eucharistic meal, which sets forth Christ's redemptive sacrifice to be received and entered into here and now through the gift of Christ's very self, his body and blood, his soul and divinity, and which calls forth our own return of love as members of his body.

And it is in the Eucharist that our refusals of love are crystalized, for in the end communion is not a matter of our agreement with each other, but of our acknowledging one another as members of the same body and so sharing in the same sacrificial meal. Schism is enacted when rival altars are erected, providing alternative Eucharists to those of other Christians. And the relaxation of the churches' eucharistic disciplines does not change this basic fact, but rather obscures it by ignoring the reality of our divisions, for our ministries and sacraments are not fully interchangeable. It is a well-intended gesture, no doubt, but amounts to saying "'peace, peace,' when there is no peace" (Jer 6:14). Whatever our pretensions, we are not united with one another.

Week by week, we come to this table in isolation from each other. Week by week, we come to the table in *willful* isolation from each other, for we do so not in full unity, but knowing that we are divided. On the one hand, how could we do otherwise? Our only hope lies in the Lord who was crucified for us, whose body and blood are offered for our redemption. On the other hand, how dare we? For our gathering at the table in isolation from each other, essentially enacts a desire to have access to the Lord for ourselves, but not for others. We would be reconciled to God, but not to these other Christians for whom the Son of God died.

Week by week we come to the table, and observe as the host is fractured. Originally, this gesture was utilitarian, breaking the one loaf so that all may share in it.[65] Over time, rather naturally, it accrued a sacrificial valence: the body of Christ is broken for us. Crucially, these two dimensions of meaning are not opposed to one another. For sacrifice is just that gift of love whereby

---

65 See Louis-Marie Chauvet, "Le pain rompu comme figure théologique de la présence eucharistique," *Questions Liturgiques* 82, no. 1 (2001): 9–33.

Jesus invites us to share in him as members of his body. As Eugene Rogers beautifully puts it,

> The broken bread is the broken body of Christ, which is the broken body of the Triune God, the body by the breaking of which on the cross the Son was forsaken by the Father and the Trinity risked its unity, the persons threatening to come apart. Better: for humanity's sake the persons *promise* to come apart, their unity restored in the same way that human unity with them begins, in the Holy Spirit. . . . The body's grace is first of all what identifies the Trinity by the crucifixion and reunites it in the resurrection. At the Eucharist, secondarily, the fraction breaks open the Trinity to let the body in. The Trinity is entered by the body of a believer through the broken body of the Lord, and the body of the Lord is also broken to enter into the bodies of believers.[66]

And yet, under the conditions of division, this originally generous gesture, intended to invite us to the table of love, the body broken so that more can share, becomes a parable of our divisions. The body is broken not so that more can share, but in order to exclude. Our divisions do what the fraction cannot: divide the body of Christ. What we do to the host does not happen to Christ, this is at least part of the point of the doctrine of transubstantiation, which developed to overcome crude realisms in conceiving eucharistic presence.[67] It is Christ's body, but we aren't chewing Jesus, nor breaking him.[68] Schism, though, does rupture the body, and it does so by refusing the love that placed that body here on the earth, upon the cross, and upon our altars, the love that ought to bind us to one another and to the one who loved us and gave himself for us. "Love so amazing, so divine, demands my soul, my life, my all."

When we refuse each other, we refuse that love.

Christ, have mercy.

---

66 Rogers, *Sexuality and the Christian Body*, 241.

67 See the overview of the history in Edward J. Kilmartin, *The Eucharist in the West: History and Theology*, ed. Robert J. Daly (Collegeville, MN: Liturgical Press, 1998), 97–102, 143–45.

68 See Aquinas, *Summa Theologiæ* 3.76.1–6. And anyone worried about transubstantiation probably has a less realistic view of the sacrament, so the point would hold just as, if not more strongly. For an excellent restatement of the classic doctrine, see Joseph C. Mudd, *Eucharist as Meaning: Critical Metaphysics and Contemporary Sacramental Theology* (Collegeville, MN: Liturgical Press, 2014).

CHAPTER THREE

Crucifying Unity

Woe to those who call evil good and good evil, who put darkness for light and light for darkness, who put bitter for sweet and sweet for bitter!

Isaiah 5:20

Jesus prays for the unity of his people. By that unity, the church expresses the charity in which salvation consists. We are bound to one another in love because Christ has bound himself to us in love, to the point of death, even death on the cross. And, because love is stronger than death, he has borne us in himself through death into the new life of the resurrection. The unity of the church is premised on the same charity by which we are saved, the same charity by which we come to share in the life of God.

The churches' divisions, whatever other factors are involved, stem from a failure of charity, and, with it, a departure from the way of salvation. A divided church is a performative contradiction of the gospel, of salvation. Whatever other factors may be involved in church division, the "cause" is a lack of charity, and so not a cause at all. It is deficient, rather than efficient. Like trying to hear silence or see the shadow.[1]

But we must broaden and nuance this basic and unremitting Augustinian position, with the recognition that "unity" is not always an unqualified good, but can, in fact, become a cudgel, a tool of oppression by which the status quo is maintained at the expense of vulnerable, marginalized populations.

---

1 See Augustine, *ciu.* 12.7 [WSA, 1/7:43–44]; Lonergan, "God's Knowledge and Will" in *Early Latin Theology*, 257–411.

A discourse of church unity that trades upon the subjection of others is a crucifying unity, for as we shall see, it reproduces the domineering logic of violence that crucified Jesus.

Lodged within the heart of this Augustinian tradition itself is a grim legacy. As the Donatist controversy wore on and persuasion failed to attain the desired results, Augustine advocated for a policy of violent coercion whereby the power of the state would "compel them to come in," a return to Catholic unity at sword point. Perversely, this compulsion was cast as itself an act of charity: better to enact violence against the bodies of schismatic dissenters for the sake of their souls' salvation than to allow them to go their own way into everlasting perdition.[2]

Much as I esteem Augustine, I deem such arguments unworthy even of refutation. On this point, the Doctor of Grace was categorically and unequivocally wrong and we honor him more by dismissing his position here out of hand as utterly out of step with the heart of his theological vision than by regarding it as worthy of counterargument. His advocacy of violence against the Donatists was a repudiation of the caritative ecclesiology he constructed in his arguments against them. Momentarily, this shall be our starting point. In the meantime, it affords us an important insight, one that further refines an Augustinian antischismatic ecclesiology. Division's wounds are not limited to the departing party.

While the argument of *On Baptism* warns that departures from the Catholic Church are departures from the body bound together by charity, thereby imperiling the schismatics' salvation, Augustine's advocacy for violence against the Donatists represents his own repudiation of charity. Division's wounds cut both ways. It is not that the Catholic Church remains unaffected in pristine unity, while the schismatics cut themselves off from that nourishing root. Rather, all of us wither in our divisions to varying extents. Division is deformity, and the deformed church does not just suffer its divisions, it inflicts harm. It is to this harm that we now turn.

Not all divisions are equivalent, and therefore different responses and analyses are needed when we consider dominant groups' coercive appeals to unity than those used for other disruptions of unity. In such cases, a heuristic structure obtains: the dominant group excludes, denies, suppresses, or otherwise seeks to eliminate the perspectives, experience, questions, or witness of those who are defined as "other," leaving them the choice, departure or

---

2 See, e.g., Augustine, Letter 93 [WSA, 2/1:377–408].

assimilation. In response, some notable examples of church division have occurred in order to allow for a flourishing of oppressed persons and groups within communities that affirm their fundamental dignity and their share in Christ. Examples could be multiplied, alas, but we shall fill this structure out principally with reference to divisions surrounding race and sexuality, each of which remains pressing in its own right. I hasten to note that, while I engage with Black, womanist, and queer theologies in this chapter, I do not endeavor to contribute to any of these discourses (such contributions are not mine to make), but rather to learn from them and apply their insights to my own theological vision. I can occupy no position other than my own, that of a cisgender heterosexual white man, but I endeavor to be the self that I am, in the network of relations in which I am embedded, in solidarity with all others, most especially those rendered marginal by cisheteronormative patriarchal white supremacy.

As we traverse this troubled and troubling terrain, we shall supplement and even correct our earlier engagements with the role of the cross in the Christian tradition. The cross casts a long shadow with a dual aspect. Symbol of the redeeming love of God, it offers hope to a world bound by its own tragic histories. Symbol of imperial terror and subjugation, it menaces those deemed marginal by the powerful. At their intersection is the Word made flesh: Christ crucified, Jesus lynched.

THE LAW OF THE CROSS AND LEGACIES OF CRUCIFIXION

As I've already intimated, there are (at least) two valences to the crucifixion. For clarity, I shall refer to them as the law of the cross (or just the cross), and crucifixion, respectively. We have explored the law of the cross in this book's earlier chapters. The cross is Christ's great act of love, whereby he gathers us to himself (and, so, to one another), binding us together with one another and with the God. Charity is the heart of the church, as well as of the cross. And yet, this does not tell the full story of what transpired on Calvary. We have mentioned in passing feminist and womanist critiques of the cross and of cross traditions (or, in my more restricted use in this chapter, "crucifixion"). We must more squarely face these critiques, for they tell a terrible truth.

In some ways, the matter is encapsulated by Jon Sobrino, who posits a twofold question regarding Calvary. We can ask, "Why did Jesus die?" which invites a theological answer, one ultimately terminating in the mystery of

God. The law of the cross is the answer to this question. We must also ask, though, "Why was Jesus killed?" and as we do, we find a historical answer. The Romans crucified not out of love, but to maintain political control. Crucifixion was the price paid for the fabled Pax Romana, as dissidents were kept in their place through the threat of meeting a similar fate. Jesus was killed because of the sort of life he led, a life that put him consistently in solidarity with those at the margins of society, a life that exercised a preferential option for the poor and excluded, a life that apparently threatened the stability of the political order.[3] Crucifixion, then, was also a practice of subjugation. It has, unfortunately, continued to function in this way, even within the Christian tradition, both theoretically and practically.

The critiques of atonement theory, particularly in its post-Anselmian forms, and particularly by feminist and womanist theologians are well-established. The notion of a divine retribution—especially one that must be meted out upon an innocent in order to forgive the guilty—results in an image of God unworthy of worship or devotion.[4] Of course, one can protest and clarify: the simplicity of God and the inseparable operations of the Trinity mean that there is no divine imposition of punishment upon Jesus; the notion of punishment is foreign to Anselm's "satisfaction model" anyway, because he explicitly distinguishes satisfaction from punishment, such that to make

---

3 Jon Sobrino, *Jesus the Liberator: A Historical Theological Reading of Jesus of Nazareth*, trans. Paul Burns and Francis McDonagh (Maryknoll, NY: Orbis, 1994), 195–211, 219–32. Ignacio Ellacuría, *Freedom Made Flesh: The Mission of Christ and His Church*, trans. John Drury (Maryknoll, NY: Orbis, 1976), 24–78; James H. Cone, *A Black Theology of Liberation* (Maryknoll, NY: Orbis Books, 2020), 116–36; *Cross and the Lynching Tree*, 1–29; *God of the Oppressed* (Maryknoll, NY: Orbis, 1997), 99–126; Copeland, *Enfleshing Freedom*, 55–84; *Knowing Christ Crucified*, 1–47.

4 Joanne Carlson Brown and Carole R. Bohn, eds., *Christianity, Patriarchy, and Abuse: A Feminist Critique* (New York: Pilgrim, 1989); Delores S. Williams, *Sisters in the Wilderness: The Challenge of Womanist God-Talk* (Maryknoll, NY: Orbis Books, 1993); Rita Nakashima Brock and Rebecca Ann Parker, *Proverbs of Ashes: Violence, Redemptive Suffering, and the Search for What Saves Us* (Boston: Beacon, 2001). Especially noteworthy is Elizabeth Johnson's treatment of the question, which is able to read Anselm within his historical context, appreciate the partial truths in multiple metaphors for the cross (some of which have fallen into disrepute), while also insisting that the language of faith can and should purge itself of metaphors that no longer resonate, or that, due to changes in cultural meanings, now communicate a message at variance with their original intent. *Creation and the Cross: The Mercy of God for a Planet in Peril* (Maryknoll, NY: Orbis, 2019).

satisfaction is precisely not to undergo punishment;[5] and so on. As helpful as those correctives are—for it is always better to operate with an adequate doctrine of God, always better to properly understand one's interlocutors— they can only take us so far. "The Symbol of God functions," and the fact of the matter is that notions of the cross have generated grim crucifying histories of subjugation, particularly of women, people of color, and sexual minorities.

Our primary guide shall be Delores Williams, who has uncovered the ways that so much atonement theory has lodged surrogacy into the Christian imagination, with deleterious effects for Black women especially. Beginning with Hagar's experience recorded in Genesis 16 and 21, Williams traces a lineage whereby enslaved women are forced into surrogate roles, serving the sexual whims of their enslavers, bearing the resulting children, and finding God apparently unconcerned with their liberation, but rather arrayed on the side of the masters. Hagar and other enslaved women have found not liberation, but rather survival in the wilderness.[6]

Within this legacy of surrogacy, the crucifixion of Jesus has served to establish Christ as the ultimate surrogate, who serves as the exemplar that justifies the surrogacy asked of and imposed upon others. Here it is important to note that voluntary surrogacy is just as, if not more, pernicious than coerced surrogacy. Through religious formation and devotion to the cross, women, and especially Black women, have internalized a surrogate role that leads them to suffer for others in imitation of Christ.[7] For this reason, Williams deems surrogacy as just too harmful to allow for any positive role for the cross in Christian teaching, devotion, or spirituality:

> Humankind is, then, redeemed through Jesus' *ministerial* vision of life and not through his death. There is nothing divine in the blood of the cross. God does not intend black women's surrogacy experience. Neither can Christian faith affirm such an idea. Jesus did not come to be a surrogate. Jesus came for life, to show humans a perfect vision of ministerial relation that humans had very little knowledge of. As Christians black women cannot forget the cross, but neither

---

5 A generally sympathetic, and, by my lights, accurate, albeit transposed statement of Anselm's basic view can be found in Lonergan, *The Redemption*, 79–195. As we shall see, Robert Doran found even Lonergan's transposed elaboration of Anselm unacceptable. *The Trinity in History*, 3:95–112, 121–27. See also David Bentley Hart, "A Gift Exceeding Every Debt: An Eastern Orthodox Appreciation of Anselm's Cur Deus Homo," *Pro Ecclesia* 7, no. 3 (1998): 333–49.

6 Williams, *Sisters in the Wilderness*, 1–83.

7 Williams, *Sisters in the Wilderness*, 161–67.

can they glorify it. To do so is to glorify suffering and to render their exploitation sacred. To do so is to glorify the sin of defilement.[8]

While I cannot ultimately follow Williams in her complete rejection of the cross as salvific (a point to which I shall return), I find myself compelled to affirm her critique, to join her in rejecting all forms of surrogacy (whether voluntary or involuntary) and to commend her strategy of opting for what promotes the survival of oppressed communities.

Through this engagement with the ways that crucifixion has functioned as a practice of subjugation theoretically, we have already ventured into the practical, for, as we've noted, the symbol of God functions. Beyond explicit reflection on the cross and atonement, crucifixion's legacy continues to echo throughout the church's history. Augustine's endorsement of force against the Donatists is one clear example of it. With apparently no irony, Augustine advocates for the same sort of state-sponsored violence that killed his Lord to be wielded against his opponents, all in the service of maintaining proper order and promoting salvation. In a perversely appropriate flourish, Augustine even appeals to the violence enacted against Hagar:

> Did not Sarah rather punish the rebellious serving girl when she was given the power? And she, of course, did not cruelly hate her since she had previously made her a mother by her own generosity; rather, she was subduing pride in her in a way conducive to her salvation.[9]

In the end, the Donatists who are compelled to come in will be grateful to have been forced to conform to the church's unity for the sake of their salvation.[10] Such statements demonstrate the accuracy and urgency of Williams's critique and merit any excoriation with which they meet.

In similar fashion, the history of lynching in the United States continued this crucifying drama, allowing the dominant social group to exert control through terrorism by way of violence made spectacle. While much of the white imagination surrounding lynching is formed by the mythology present in, say, Harper Lee's *To Kill a Mockingbird* (a crime of passion, done under cover of night, and ideally thwarted by a white savior!), the reality of lynching was rather different. It was a social event, often planned in advance with

---

8 Williams, *Sisters in the Wilderness*, 167.

9 Augustine, Letter 93, 6 [WSA, 2/1:380].

10 Augustine, Letter 93, 15–16 [WSA, 2/1:387–88].

advertisements in the newspaper. Food might be provided, and souvenirs were often taken.

The entire point of the lynching was its social function: cohesion for the white community and a warning to the Black community, a dimension powerfully, if disturbingly depicted in James Baldwin's short story "Going to Meet the Man."[11] The story unfolds from the point of view of a bigoted white police officer, Jesse, who reminisces in the night, after a failure to perform sexually. Something of a rogue's gallery of racist tropes flit across the page:[12] the hypersexualization of Black folks, especially Black women (229–30, 239); that Black inferiority is essential, cultural, and somehow God-ordained, and that the "good ones" would be grateful for the brutality enacted against their less docile Black siblings, who "had taken it into their heads to fight against God and go against the rules laid down in the Bible for everyone to read" (235–36 [235]).

The story culminates in a graphic depiction of a lynching, the first Jesse has witnessed. His parents explain the function of social control when he wonders why his Black friend Otis is hiding away since he had done nothing: "'Otis *can't* do nothing,' said his father, 'he's too little . . . We just want to make sure Otis *don't* do nothing'" (240). The lynching itself is organized around a picnic, to which all resort after the brutal, sexualized torture and death of the man who is lynched (243–49). "At that moment [just after the man's death] Jesse loved his father more than he had ever loved him. He felt that his father had carried him through a mighty test, had revealed to him a great secret which would be the key to his life forever" (248). Here bonds of love are forged and conviviality enacted through the killing of the victim— a perverse inversion of eucharistic logic. Fittingly, the story ends with the cock's crow as day dawns, perhaps an echo of Peter's denial of Christ before his crucifixion (249).

Here it is vital to recognize that lynching was, by and large, carried out by Christians (and visited upon Christians). The Klansman's burning cross, at once an instrument of terror and also intended to symbolize the spreading of Christ's light, is a betrayal of that cross, an outworking of the impulse toward crucifixion that so often animates the tradition.

---

11 James Baldwin, "Going to Meet the Man," in *Going to Meet the Man* (New York: Dial Press, 1965), 227–49. Subsequent references will be parenthetical in the text.

12 On these tropes see Ibram X. Kendi, *Stamped from the Beginning: The Definitive History of Racist Ideas in America* (New York: Nation Books, 2016).

While it has been especially the Black community that has been terrorized by lynching, we must also recognize the violence done to the LGBTQ community as sharing this logic as well. Matthew Shepard's 1998 murder by lynching is a notable example of this, but it is hardly solitary. Patrick Cheng gathers historical testimonies of the violence done to LGBTQ folks, and especially to "queers of color" in his *Rainbow Theology*.[13] In several countries, LGBTQ behavior and even identities are criminalized, with punishments ranging from imprisonment to death. While they are presently unenforced, fourteen states in the US still retain antisodomy laws on the books, and as I write, several of them are proposing legislation that will further ostracize and limit the care and accommodations available to LGBTQ folks, with a particular focus on trans people. Meanwhile, LGBTQ youth are about four times more likely to attempt suicide than their peers, and nearly half of LGBTQ youth report suicidal ideation.[14] These figures are only related to their sexual identity insofar as they face bullying, hostile home environments, and messages that lead them toward existential self-contradiction and away from integration and self-acceptance. In other words, they are not suicidal because they are queer. They are suicidal because of the ways that queer youth are crucified in our society.

HISTORY, PREMOTION, AND TRADITIONS OF DEFORMITY

Faced with such deplorable legacies, we should be outraged, saddened, moved to compassionate solidarity and action on behalf of those who've been crucified.[15] Following Ignacio Ellacuría, we should, in the spirit of the Ignatian Exercises, ask, "What have I done to crucify these people? What am I doing to end their crucifixion? What am I doing so that they might rise from the dead?" We shall return to this below. Theologians, engaged in the enterprise of faith seeking understanding, have a further task, though. We must account

---

13 Patrick S. Cheng, *Rainbow Theology: Bridging Race, Sexuality, and Spirit* (New York: Seabury, 2013).

14 "Facts about LGBTQ Youth Suicide," *The Trevor Project* (blog), accessed May 26, 2023.

15 The "we" here refers to all people, regardless of the relationship they bear to these realities. In other words, it is not just a call to solidarity for relatively privileged people (though it is that), but for all. This is important to note, because, as we shall see, there is a tendency to construct the church as a white and heterosexual space. But this chapter insists that the ecclesial "we" includes all the baptized, and any uses of such the first person should be understood in this sense unless I explicitly differentiate.

for *how* such horrors have come to characterize the Christian tradition. While a full answer to this quandary is beyond the scope of this present work, traversing a few segments of the path to such an answer will prove useful, for it intersects with our own and can shed light on our task.

At the outset, we must locate the church within the dynamics of history. It is, after all, a historical process, a pilgrim community journeying along the way to the perfected reign of God. As we saw in chapters 1 and 2, its foundation is historical—the missions of the Word and the Holy Spirit, and its life plays out over time as the gift of God's love given in those missions is more deeply appropriated. The law of the cross serves as the common meaning around which the life of the Christian community coalesces, as, through a transformed human cooperation, God works out the divine purpose of reversing evil, overcoming it with good. This is the meaning and the mission of the church, to collaborate with God in this project.

Central to the life of the Christian community has been tradition, a handing on (*tradere*) of what has been received. Of this the letters of Paul are an important early witness. He writes of how he has passed on what he first received (1 Cor 11:23; 15:3). Importantly, the earliest of Paul's writings date from nearly two decades after Christ's resurrection. Until these writings, the faith had been transmitted solely as *traditio*.

That there are any Christians in the contemporary world is the result of tradition. From our forebears we receive; to our successors we pass on. Tradition is an action (*tradere*) that passes along its objects (*tradita*). The most fundamental *traditum* is the life-giving message of the divine love given in the incarnate Word and poured into our hearts by the indwelling Spirit. This gift, though, can only be given and received to and by historical subjects, within their own cultural horizons (which are themselves passed on and received). As a result, it is passed along not "purely," but from within those horizons and outlooks. This lack of "purity" is not necessarily a contamination, just a recognition of the conditioning effect of culture. It occurs by necessity, and no traditioning process could unfold without it. Even under the most ideal of circumstances, cultural goods would be passed along this way, along with the gospel message, and indeed, as that with which the gospel message is clothed.[16] There is no naked gospel.

---

16 See the painstaking analysis in Anne M. Carpenter, *Nothing Gained Is Eternal: A Theology of Tradition* (Minneapolis: Fortress Press, 2022). We shall return to these matters in chapter five.

In one of his last writings, the late Robert Doran appealed to the early Bernard Lonergan's notion of premotion to explain these dynamics. Premotion itself is a fairly opaque category deployed by scholastic theologians as they tried to account for the interplay of divine grace and human freedom, but the point Doran drew from it is easily enough grasped. Premotion names the anterior conditions or prerequisites for any given motion or activity.[17] For a campfire to "move" upon marshmallows by toasting them, those marshmallows must first be positioned close enough for the fire's heat to affect them (this is not a far cry from the first of Aquinas's five ways, all finite motion depends upon some prior motion).[18] Similarly, our acting upon the world's stage as Christians is dependent upon the premotion of having received the Christian message from those who preceded us, who depended on their predecessors. And our activity is the premotion for those who will come after us.

This premotion also provides constraints for our activity. Materially, parents' socioeconomic status colors the opportunities available to their children. Intellectually, we inherit cultural notions and values, which we can either assent to or repudiate. Of course, in neither of these cases are the constraints absolute. Such absolutes can indeed occur: the evolutionary pathway by which we've arrived at *Homo sapiens sapiens* means that I cannot fly, nor breathe underwater (at least not without mechanical assistance). In general, though, these relative constraints are quite enough to have significant effects. To anticipate our subsequent discussion of race, the centuries-long financial head start whereby white Americans gained wealth through the uncompensated labor of enslaved Black Americans and the subsequent legacies of redlining and other legally encoded suppressions of Black success mean that in general Black Americans inherit less generational wealth and its attendant opportunities than do their white counterparts. Yes, a Black man can be elected president of the United States; the constraints are not absolute. But taken as a whole, the effects are telling. Examples could multiply, not least the legacy of stolen lands whereby Americans of European descent have come to own any real estate on this continent, but by now the general picture should be clear.

Premotion, then sets the condition for historical agency. Under ideal circumstances, we inherit horizons (and material circumstances) that enable us to act authentically and justly, leading to a closer approximation between our

---

17 Doran, *Trinity in History*, 3:59–94.
18 Aquinas, *Summa theologiæ* 1.2.3.

world and the coming reign of God. But ideal conditions do not obtain. The frameworks we inherit are often distorted, and such distortion tends to have a compounding effect, due to what Lonergan calls the "social surd." Inattentive, unintelligent, unreasonable, irresponsible, unloving actions give rise to states of affairs where the intelligible is alloyed with the irrational. This partially irrational state of affairs further conditions the horizons within which people act, variously constraining the possibility of their action, which in turn tends to add to the irrational component, expanding the social surd,[19] further constraining our ability to act authentically. Both the law of the cross and the expanding social surd—or to recast the matter in the terms we developed above, the law of the cross and the impulse to crucifixion—provide something of the premotion that informs our actions, including within the church.

An example can illustrate. M. Shawn Copeland reflects upon how the legacy of slavery has conditioned the American, and especially the Black American, Catholic experience. But the roots go deeper:

> Chattel slavery led Christianity to a crossroad: discipleship or duplicity. That choice was made centuries before the American form of chattel slavery came into existence, but the option for duplicity has made all the difference. Slavery was part of the social and cultural fabric of the ancient world . . . it was part of the fabric of the early Christian community. Jennifer Glancy offers a thought-provoking experiment. She asks us to "ponder how differently Christianity might have developed if early Christian communities had made freeing one's slaves a precondition of baptism."[20] It appears that early on, we followers of Jesus compromised the gospel.[21]

As a result, we have inherited an entire complex of ideas that have constrained Christian fidelity: the image of a master-slave relationship as a metaphor for Christian discipleship, the Pauline injunctions that slaves obey their masters and his failure to challenge the institution (any affirmations of freeing slaves were individually directed), and so on. These served to reinforce and ally the church with practices of slavery, with the abolitionist witness of Gregory of Nyssa serving as an all-too-rare exception. Even Bartolomé de las Casas's resistance to indigenous enslavement was offset by his suggestion that Africans be enslaved instead, though eventually he came to oppose this too. And though

---

19 Lonergan, *Insight*, 254–57, 651–52, 711–15.

20 Jennifer A. Glancy, *Slavery as a Moral Problem in the Early Church and Today* (Minneapolis: Fortress Press, 2011), 25. Copeland's citation.

21 Copeland, *Knowing Christ Crucified*, 9.

slavery has been repudiated, a process that wasn't complete until the papacy of John Paul II,[22] its legacy of harm still dogs us, and the slavery metaphor still influences our imaginative horizons.

Closely allied with these dynamics is the construction of race which unfolded in tandem with the colonial project. As Europeans expanded their ambitions to new geographic areas, claiming territory and resources for their own, supplanting indigenous populations in the Americas, transplanting Africans, conscripting indigenous and African alike into forced labor, and so on, the notion of race was constructed, largely to justify these divisions and deformations within the *humanum*.[23] Whiteness came to bear all that was good, noble, beautiful, civilized, ordered to God and salvation. Other racial groups were constructed as the foil to whiteness, with blackness at the opposite end of the scale, representing the contraries of all that was white.[24] Within such a construction, it was only proper that those now considered white dominate all other races, and especially those now considered Black.

Three points are particularly salient for our considerations here. First, we must reckon with the fact that colonialism and racialization were explicitly Christian theological constructions.[25] Especially pertinent is Willie James Jennings's argument that underlying colonial imagination was the long-standing

---

22 Thoroughly documented in John T. Noonan, *A Church That Can and Cannot Change: The Development of Catholic Moral Teaching* (Notre Dame, IN: University of Notre Dame Press, 2005).

23 E.g., Achille Mbembe, *Critique of Black Reason*, trans. Laurent Dubois (Durham, NC: Duke University Press, 2017), 10–37; Walter D. Mignolo, *The Darker Side of Western Modernity: Global Futures, Decolonial Options* (Durham, NC: Duke University Press, 2011), 8–18; Kendi, *Stamped from the Beginning*, 1–46; J. Kameron Carter, *Race: A Theological Account* (Oxford: Oxford University Press, 2008).

24 Frantz Fanon, *Black Skin, White Masks*, trans. Charles Lam Markmann (New York: Grove Press, 1991); Mbembe, *Critique of Black Reason*, 38–76; Mignolo, *Darker Side of Western Modernity*, 82–90, 121–27; Barbara J. Fields and Karen E. Fields, *Racecraft: The Soul of Inequality in American Life* (New York: Verso, 2022), 111–31; Copeland, *Enfleshing Freedom*, 9–22.

25 See especially Jennings's account of Gomes Eanes de Zurara's christological and crucificatory construal of the arrival of a shipment of African slaves in Portugal: *The Christian Imagination*, 15–64. See further, e.g., Carter, *Race*; Mignolo, *Darker Side of Western Modernity*, 8–9; Achille Mbembe, *On the Postcolony* (Berkeley: University of California Press, 2001), 219–31. We might note also Ephraim Radner's observation that Colombus's voyage of "discovery" was motivated by a Joachimite theological horizon. *A Profound Ignorance: Modern Pneumatology and Its Anti-modern Redemption* (Waco, TX: Baylor University Press, 2019).

legacy of supersessionism within the Christian community.[26] The theological imaginary that animated colonialism's displacements was funded by the prior displacement of Israel. Colonialism and its twin progeny, race and racialized slavery, were carried out by Christians who had forgotten that they are gentiles, those with no claim upon God or God's grace. As with the failure to repudiate slavery, perhaps even related to it, the deplorable reality of supersessionism and its bitter anti-Semitic fruit does not nullify the subsequent tradition, as if divine grace could be put to flight by human sinfulness.[27] However, it does install a surd within the tradition, which conveys its own irrationality alongside the life of grace. At its inception the Christian movement failed properly to repudiate slavery, bequeathing a distorting, deformative tradition. Now, with the colonial project, slavery came to be racialized, particularly imposed on those who are now considered Black.

Second, we should note that racism is more the byproduct than the aim of colonialism. As Barbara Fields and Karen Fields argue, the product of the plantation system was not white supremacy but cotton or tobacco. Racism was used to justify the colonial and plantation systems, but their aims were power and profit.[28] Ibram X. Kendi argues persuasively that racist ideas exist downstream from racist policies. They provide the pretext that justifies Euro-American rapacity, not its motivation.[29] The primary definition of racism is not bigotry or prejudice based on "race" (which we must remember is a fiction), but rather those structures and systems that produce unequal outcomes for racial groups and the complexes of ideas that support and flow from those structures and systems, including those that blame those unequal outcomes on any ostensible inferiority of a racial group (whether biological, behavioral, or cultural).[30]

---

26 Jennings, *The Christian Imagination*, 250–88. See also Ephraim Radner's contention that anti-Judaism and supersession provide the original matrix for much church division. *Brutal Unity*.

27 Anne Carpenter puts this forward as an important corrective to the position of Katie Walker Grimes that certain distortions can indicate divine absence (*Fugitive Saints: Catholicism and the Politics of Slavery* [Minneapolis: Fortress Press, 2017], 107). *Nothing Gained Is Eternal*, 113.

28 Fields and Fields, *Racecraft*, 138–39.

29 This thesis is developed over the course of Kendi's *Stamped from the Beginning*, and distilled in the epilogue (497–515). See also Ibram X. Kendi, *How to Be an Antiracist* (New York: One World, 2019), 17–23, 27–28, 41–43, 201–17, 230–35. Or, as Fields and Fields explain, the perceived inferiority of racial groups follows from their oppression, rather than the other way around. *Racecraft*, 128–31.

30 Kendi, *How to Be an Antiracist*, passim.

This brings us to the third salient point: colonialism exemplifies what Lonergan calls a classicist understanding of culture, which stands in opposition to an empirical view of culture.[31] For the classicist, "culture" is one ideal thing, which a person or group either has or lacks. An empirical view of culture recognizes that there are multiple ways in which human beings order their lives around shared meanings and values. Such structures as white supremacy, patriarchy, heterosexism, and ableism all reproduce this basic impulse, by rendering "normal" the experience of whatever group is privileged, and viewing other experiences, not just as different, but as aberrant, departures from a norm.

Colonialism defined "culture" in terms of the shared meanings and values of European men, who were in the process of becoming "white." Because people living in Africa or in the Americas lived according to different shared values, they were deemed to be lacking culture, and so in need of civilization. Ironically, the precolonial world had been polycentric; Europeans were aware of other cultures before the colonial period, having engaged in extensive trade with Asia (recall the hope of finding a more direct route to India), but the advent of colonialism brought a shift to a monocentrism,[32] and in so doing crafted Eurocentrism and white supremacy.

To bring this section to a close, positive historical change does indeed occur, but it is a slow, halting process. Each generation inherits the horizons within which they're able to operate, through their living and activity, they transform these horizons, for better or worse, often a mixture of the two, providing the horizons that will be inherited by those who come after. Yet, as Fields and Fields note,

> If race lives on today, it does not live on because we have inherited it from our forebears of the seventeenth century or the eighteenth or nineteenth, but because we continue to create it today ... in our social life, continue to verify it, and thus continue to need a social vocabulary that will allow us to make sense, not of what our ancestors did then, but of what we ourselves choose to do now.[33]

---

31 Bernard J. F. Lonergan, "Dimensions of Meaning," in *Collection*, ed. Frederick E. Crowe and Robert M. Doran, CWBL 4 (Toronto: University of Toronto Press, 1988), 232–45; see the developments of this idea by Copeland, *Enfleshing Freedom*, 9–22; Bryan N. Massingale, *Racial Justice and the Catholic Church* (Maryknoll, NY: Orbis, 2010).

32 Mignolo, *Darker Side of Western Modernity*, 27–31.

33 Fields and Fields, *Racecraft*, 146, 148.

Thus, we must acknowledge, as we've already noted, the constraints on the operations of free intellectual creatures are not absolute (the intellect can become all things), there is no reason, in principle, why any element of the social surd cannot be transcended by any particular individual at any given time. We are responsible for our own doings. This is the case, even as the constraints of premotion make it unlikely that any one person would over-come all elements of the social surd, and even less likely that a critical mass necessary for the changing of cultural values would overcome any given one at the same time. But our premotion is also provided by the law of the cross, which continues to operate, informing our operations, so that little by little progress does occur.

UNITY AND DIVISION IN THE BLACK CHURCHES

It is within this fraught history that the legacy of historically Black churches unfolds. At once a testament to the vibrancy of African American faith and the faithfulness of God and God's grace to the Black community, and an indictment of white Christians, these churches are the outcome of premotion affected by both the crucifying surd and the law of the cross.

From the earliest days of the United States, even predating American independence, (at least) two different expressions of Christianity have been operative, the religion of the slaveholders and their allies, and the religion of the enslaved.[34] Copeland provides stirring accounts of the enslaved peoples' encounter with Jesus and his love,[35] juxtaposed with damning expositions of the distortions slave-holding Christianity underwent in order to justify that "peculiar institution." Faced with the message of liberty in Christ, British colonists first resisted attempts to evangelize enslaved people, but then opted to simply change their baptismal theology, such that becoming a Christian would not eo ipso manumit the enslaved.[36] This change allowed Christianity to become a tool for promoting docility among the enslaved, for who could be a more dependable slave than a faithful disciple, obedient to the Pauline

---

34 See, e.g., Kelly Brown Douglas, *The Black Christ* (Maryknoll, NY: Orbis, 1993), 9–29; Cone, *Cross and the Lynching Tree*, passim.

35 E.g., Copeland, *Knowing Christ Crucified*, 3–58.

36 Copeland, *Enfleshing Freedom*, 27.

injunction, "Slaves, obey your masters"?[37] Christian theological anthropology similarly underwent loathsome distortions, as persons created in the image of God were reduced to objects of production, of reproduction, and of sexual violence.[38]

Under this heavy, uneasy yoke enslaved people encountered Christianity in two forms, that mediated to them by the slaveholding class, and that mediated from within their experience. From the slavers, they received messages enjoining docility and rendering due service to the master. Yet in their own gatherings with their aural transmissions of the gospel message and the tradition of the spirituals, they found a companion and ally in Jesus, who joined them in their enslaved condition, whose cross was like unto their own experience, and who led them on to hope.[39] In their own gatherings, the enslaved were granted some measure of self-determination, even flourishing. Yet even here, the legacy is uneven. The enslavers' willingness to allow the people they'd enslaved to worship varied, with some imposing punishments for gathering or singing. And Jennings explains how even when the enslaved were gathered for worship, it occurred under the auspices of plantation logic, under the gaze of the master, sometimes even literally.[40]

Such denominations as the African Methodist Episcopal Church, the AME Zion Church, and the Church of God in Christ (among many others) were all formed so that Black Christians could worship in dignity and peace. In many cases the impetus was an unwillingness of white Christians to worship alongside their Black siblings. As with the other cases of division we have surveyed, these churches' separate existences were also borne from a failure of charity, but with a crucial difference. The Donatists separated from the Catholics because they could not countenance communion with the *traditores* or those who would tolerate them; East and West mutually condemned one another, as did Catholics and Protestants. Here the failure is not on the part of those who departed, but on those who forced their departure: white Christians, who preferred to be impoverished in their experience of God, rather than either recognize the dignity of Black folks, or have the hegemony of their cultural

---

37 Copeland, *Enfleshing Freedom*, 27–28; *Knowing Christ Crucified*, 10–13.

38 Copeland, *Enfleshing Freedom*, 29–38.

39 Copeland, *Knowing Christ Crucified*, 19–36, 41–47, 55–58. See also Cone, *Cross and the Lynching Tree*, 1–29.

40 Willie James Jennings, *After Whiteness: An Education in Belonging* (Grand Rapids: Eerdmans, 2020), 58–76.

supremacy displaced. On the part of the Black Christians who formed these congregations, it was charity that led them on, as the love of God in Christ, given through the Holy Spirit burned in their hearts, empowering them to affirm themselves and their communities. Had a call been issued for Black Christians to remain in white congregations where their basic humanity was denied, this unity would have been its own ongoing crucifixion.[41]

Racism upsets the typical ecclesiological categories for assessing division and unity, as an account from Celia A. Moore illustrates. She recounts the history of the racial reintegration of the Catholic Diocese of Raleigh, North Carolina in the 1950s. Two decades earlier, the diocese had formed St. Benedict the Moor parish in order to provide a home to Black Catholics, who had formerly worshiped at Holy Redeemer parish. Before the formation of St. Benedict the Moor, Black parishioners at Holy Redeemer were kept in a second-class position.[42]

The logic of segregation was twofold. It would allow Black parishioners to truly be at home in their own parish. This is laudable enough, though we must note that it apparently hadn't occurred to anyone that Holy Redeemer could be changed in such a way as to make its Black members truly at home. Second, it was believed that the parishes' missions could be better pursued if segregated, so that prospective white converts wouldn't have the added burden of proximity to Black folks added to the summons to take up Christ's cross.[43] This, then was a mission of expediency, one unwilling to challenge the prevailing mores of those called to conversion. We can (and should), of course deplore its failure to grasp the reconciling mission of Christ, the call

---

41 The dynamic of a marginalized group cultivating a community within which they can flourish is heuristic, given concrete specificity here by the Black churches, but by no means exclusive to them. One could undertake a parallel analysis from the perspective of, e.g., disability theology. The formation of deaf churches, for instance, provides a context where deaf Christians are able to flourish, without having to accommodate themselves to the hegemony of hearing culture. Nancy L. Eiesland, *The Disabled God: Toward a Liberatory Theology of Disability* (Nashville: Abingdon, 1994); Courtney Wilder, *Disability, Faith, and the Church: Inclusion and Accommodation in Contemporary Congregations* (Santa Barbara, CA: Praeger, 2016). NB that it is a disputed question whether deaf experience should be understood in terms of disability or as a minority group.

42 Celia A. Moore, "Dealing with Desegregation: Black and White Responses to the Desegregation of the Diocese of Raleigh, North Carolina, 1953," in *Uncommon Faithfulness: The Black Catholic Experience*, ed. M. Shawn Copeland (Maryknoll, NY: Orbis, 2009), 63–77.

43 Moore, "Dealing with Desegregation," 63–64.

for all of humanity to be united in one body through the cross. But we must also recognize that it is truly the heir to much of the theological tradition, having been premoved by the original failure to repudiate slavery, and by the overlays this failure received from colonialism and racializing. It is deplorable, but it comes by this honestly.

For all this, though, the segregated parishes were not, formally speaking, ecclesial division. Both were under the oversight of the same bishop, and so part of the same particular church, in communion with each other de jure, if not de facto. As with any division, the obstacle is lodged solely in the will. Catholics in ostensibly full communion with each other, nevertheless were de facto out of communion for two decades, with that enacted communion restored only by episcopal decree.

In 1953, Bishop Vincent Waters determined that this de facto breach in communion was unacceptable, and moved to reintegrate the parishes. While met with resistance, mainly from white Catholics, he held fast, insisting that all Catholics in Newton Grove, North Carolina would attend one Mass at Holy Redeemer.[44] On the one hand, this was a prophetic move, a corrective to the inherited social surd, a gesture intended to give expression to what had become a truncated catholicity of the church. Separate but equal is inherently unequal, and Black Catholics had and have every right to participate in the liturgy anywhere. Siloing them into a racially defined alternative parish was a denigration. Nevertheless, in reintegrating the church, *they* were asked to bear the burden of joining with those who held them in opprobrium. Their willingness to do so is its own participation in the redemptive charity of Christ. (While white Catholics also had to learn to worship alongside their Black siblings, this is not a parallel or equivalent case.)

And yet, even in a postintegration context, the National Black Catholic Clergy Caucus could issue the challenge that "the Catholic Church in the United States, primarily a White racist institution, has addressed itself primarily to White society and is definitely a part of that society."[45] And as Bryan Massingale and Joseph Flipper have recognized, even in those documents where the United States College of Catholic Bishops challenges racism, it does so in a way that presumes a white normativity and constructs the Catholic Church as a white space, with Black people and Black culture

---

44 Moore, "Dealing with Desegregation," 66–67.
45 Cited in Joseph J. Flipper, "White Ecclesiology: The Identity of the Church in the Statements on Racism by United States Catholic Bishops," *TS* 82, no. 3 (2021): 429.

external to it.[46] Hence, the cost of admission for Black Christians into white-imagined churches is assimilation to white cultural supremacy.[47]

Within white supremacy, the distinctiveness of white cultural forms is lost. They are simply "normal." Theology done by nonwhites, by women, or by queer people is "contextual," while the theology done by cishetero white men is simply "theology." Thus, just as it hadn't occurred to white parishioners at Holy Redeemer, Newton Grove (or their bishop at the time of the formation of St. Benedict the Moor) to treat their Black siblings in Christ with equal dignity, it does not occur to "not-racist" white Christians, who would have no problem with an integrated church that reflects white cultural norms, that their Black siblings might draw value from their own distinctive identity and culture. It's normal for white folks to have their culture, divisive for nonwhites to have theirs.

On the one hand, this presents an obstacle to ecclesial unity. No one should have to suppress their cultural heritage and expression for the sake of some ostensible unity. On the other hand, it is no obstacle at all, for as we've seen unity is not neither monolithic nor uniform. The inculturation of the gospel message within Black (or Latinx, or Asian, or indigenous or white, and so on) experience is unproblematic. Ethnically specific church traditions, parishes, and liturgies are a genuine good. So long as these cultural expressions are allowed to develop and flourish, not being relegated to a subalternate status, so long as the people gathered in these different parishes or liturgies are not gathered *against* or to the exclusion of or in isolation from each other, they serve to express the church's catholicity. Such churches can maintain their own distinct identity, expression, and heritage while also being in communion with each other. The obstacle is solely in the will.

Thus, we have seen a tendency for white Christians (and here they are followed by the wider white culture) to erase the reality of nonwhite Christianity. This erasure is of a piece with a Christianity that constructs itself as white, and that concomitantly expects that Black Christians suppress their blackness in order to belong, reinscribing the logic of surrogacy. Delores Williams identifies the strategy of moral suasion favored by some within the civil rights movement as doing much the same. The basic idea is that through

---

46 Flipper, "White Ecclesiology"; Massingale, *Racial Justice and the Catholic Church*.

47 See also Albert J. Raboteau, "Relating Race and Religion: Four Historical Models," in Copeland, *Uncommon Faithfulness*, 14–17, who traces the sidelining of Black cultural expression by white Christians, often in the name of avoiding racial division.

patiently living exemplary lives, the oppressed could bring their oppressors to recognize their basic humanity, leading eventually to their being granted social equality.

Kendi has offered a definitive refutation of this strategy, demonstrating that from a practical standpoint, the historical record stands against it.[48] The entire project of uplift suasion is a capitulation to white supremacy, as the Black community is invited to assimilate themselves to white cultural values in order to secure their future, rather than recognizing the equal value of Black cultural expression.[49] Instead, meaningful change has only ever reliably occurred at the level of policy. These changes lead to changes in ideas and not the other way around.

Williams's concern extends beyond this practical dimension to the moral bankruptcy of the idea. She cites the important earlier work of Joanne Carlson Brown and Rebecca Parker, who contend that "it asks people to suffer for the sake of helping evildoers see their evil ways. It puts concern for the evildoers ahead of concern for the victim of evil. It makes victims the servants of the evildoers' salvation."[50]

In answer to such erasure, or to such assimilationist demands, whether thematized or not, the historically Black churches have nourished and sustained Black faith in the face of oppression. Yet, while the historically Black churches have been a source of affirmation, liberation, and flourishing within and for the Black community, they have not been unambiguously so. Williams has noted how surrogacy (voluntary and involuntary) asserts itself within the Black church tradition as well, particularly in calling women to docility under male supremacy. Important studies by Kelly Brown Douglas have followed her lead, noting also the prevailing heterosexism in many Black church traditions.[51] Even as we oppose oppression, we must not lose sight of the "oppressed's oppressed."[52] And, while women in particular have been

---

48 Kendi, *Stamped from the Beginning*, passim, especially chapters 10, 26, 37, and the epilogue.

49 Kendi, *How to Be an Antiracist*, 81–91; Copeland, *Enfleshing Freedom*, 9–22, 66–73.

50 Brown and Bohn, *Christianity, Patriarchy, and Abuse*, 20 (cited in Williams, *Sisters in the Wilderness*, 200).

51 Williams, *Sisters in the Wilderness*; Kelly Brown Douglas, *Sexuality and the Black Church: A Womanist Perspective* (Maryknoll, NY: Orbis Books, 1999); *What's Faith Got to Do with It? Black Bodies/Christian Souls* (Maryknoll, NY: Orbis, 2005).

52 Williams, *Sisters in the Wilderness*, 144–53.

funneled into surrogate roles, placing their own wellbeing in a subservient place to that of others, the expectation of conformity to white culture as the price of admission cuts across the gender line. These dynamics are also discernible in the churches' treatment of the LGBTQ community.

A PLACE IN THE BODY? LGBTQ CHRISTIANS

As I mentioned in this book's introduction, the churches are in a period of reckoning with the massive shifts that have taken place in our understandings of gender and sexuality. While, generally speaking, the heteronormativity of the theological tradition has made the churches inhospitable places for LGBTQ folks, the last decades have seen the beginnings of a shift, as growing numbers of Christians have experienced themselves both as LGBTQ and as beloved by Jesus, beloved precisely as their queer selves, and sought to discern what faithful discipleship looks like in light of these two unmistakable facts of their existence. In response to this shift, some churches have tentatively begun exploring the viability of marriages or marriage-like relationships between Christians of the same gender. Others have insisted on the sole validity of heterosexual sexual relationships, while also committing themselves to pastoral care for and accompaniment of LGBTQ Christians. Still others have failed to come even this far, contesting the possibility of being both gay and Christian, even supporting laws that would criminalize and kill LGBTQ people. And along the way and across this spectrum, churches have found themselves increasingly divided over how to respond to this newly recognized reality.

It is not my intention to advance here an argument for LGBTQ inclusion in the church, and this for three reasons. First, others have already done yeoman's work on this front.[53] I don't have anything to add to their efforts. Second, an argument for (or against) LGBTQ inclusion would move us away

---

53 Rowan D. Williams, "The Body's Grace," in *Theology and Sexuality: Classic and Contemporary Readings*, ed. Eugene F. Rogers (Oxford: Blackwell, 2002), 309–21; Rogers, *Sexuality and the Christian Body*; Patrick S. Cheng, *Radical Love: Introduction to Queer Theology* (New York: Seabury, 2011); Robert Song, *Covenant and Calling: Towards a Theology of Same-Sex Relationships* (London: SCM, 2014); Sarah Coakley, *The New Asceticism* (London: Bloomsbury, 2015); Karen R. Keen, *Scripture, Ethics, and the Possibility of Same-Sex Relationships* (Grand Rapids: Eerdmans, 2018).

from our focus on ecclesial unity and division. At issue are *those* dynamics, not the status of LGBTQ people in the church. Finally, inclusion is the wrong question for us to be asking. There is no need to include LGBTQ folks in the church, because many LGBTQ people already are the church. As noted above, the driving force of this new development is the twinned experience of being at once queer and beloved by Jesus precisely in that queerness. By virtue of their baptism, they are members of Christ, sharers in the new life in the Spirit, and so within the communion of the church. The call is coming from inside the house, and the task for heterosexual Christians is not inclusion but recognition and embrace of our siblings in Christ.

Linn Marie Tonstad similarly resists the discourse of inclusion, for a distinct, but perhaps related reason. Similar to Massingale's and Flipper's observation that the Catholic Church in the United States, even when it seeks to address and redress racism, constructs itself as a normatively white space, language of LGBTQ inclusion reflects a heterosexism. The logic of inclusion presumes that those "we" (cisgender heterosexual Christians) need to include are the "decent gays" (i.e., gay couples who conform themselves to "straight" culture), while no space is made for "indecent queers" (those whose sexual or gender expression subverts or threatens the heterosexual norm). The cost of inclusion is assimilation.[54] Another instance of the logic of surrogacy in the form of moral suasion.

Lost in all of the furor over inclusion is Eugene F. Rogers's injunction that the most important fact for most of us to remember is that we are gentiles.[55] When heterosexual Christians construct the church as a heterosexual space and ask whether LGBTQ folks should (or can) be included within it, we do so from a position that presumes that we heterosexual gentiles have any right to be here ourselves. It is into Israel's vine that we have been grafted, and this itself "contrary to nature" (Rom 11:24; cf. 1:26–27). In other words, anyone's inclusion in Christ is a matter of sheer grace. Any time we question the limits of inclusion, we begin to saw out from under us the branch upon which we are perched. And here we can note a reprise of a motif from above,

54 Tonstad, *God and Difference*, 254–77. In this, Tonstad draws extensively from the challenges issued by Marcella Althaus-Reid, *Indecent Theology: Theological Perversions in Sex, Gender and Politics* (London: Routledge, 2000); *The Queer God* (London: Routledge, 2003).

55 Rogers, *Sexuality and the Christian Body*, 37–66.

for Jennings argued that colonialism, racialization, and racialized slavery were also strange supersessionist fruit.

The churches can, ought to, and will develop their teachings in light of our new understandings of gender and sexuality. This development will help transform the churches into spaces better capable of sustaining the life of all Christians, notably LGBTQ Christians. But no individual Christian, no individual church, no individual communion can effectuate this transformation. Only when all the churches fully embrace all of their members will this work of discernment have been done.[56] What I attempt here is to make sense of what unity might mean between now and that completed work.

Case Study: The Anglican Communion

Perhaps nowhere has the matter of divisions over the proper stance toward LGBTQ sexuality been more palpable than in my own Anglican Communion. In some ways, Anglicans' attempts, failures, and halting progress toward holding together while navigating differences over the place of LGBTQ people in the church is an experiment undertaken on behalf of all the churches. As we test the limits of authority and responsibility, of unity and disagreement, of interdependence and autonomy, we play out the same essential dynamics that any church or communion of churches must contend with when discerning a way forward concerning any proposed major development. Here my purpose is not to trace all of the political machinations of the Anglican Communion, but rather to highlight some of the fraught dynamics.[57]

The precursors extend earlier, but the matter irrupted onto the global stage in 2003, when a diocese of the Anglican Church of Canada authorized rites for marrying same-sex couples, and the Episcopal Church consecrated V. Gene

---

56 We shall return to this matter in chapter 5.

57 We could pursue an examination of new denominations, such as the Metropolitan Community Church, which was formed for the specific purpose of fostering LGBTQ affirmation. In such case, our analysis might roughly parallel the one undertaken for the historically Black churches above. By focusing on divisions enacted for the specific purpose of rejecting LGBTQ affirmation, as has occurred in the Anglican Communion, we provide a complement to the ground already covered.

Robinson, who is gay and was in a partnered relationship, as a bishop.[58] The denunciations of these actions were swift, with such provinces as the Church of Uganda declaring their communion with the Episcopal Church broken. Various African provinces began to provide alternative oversight for Americans who could not countenance being under the care of a gay bishop (though at this juncture, only the diocese of New Hampshire was under the oversight of a gay bishop).[59] Most of the alternative congregations were established in rather conservative dioceses, which were led by bishops who rejected same-sex sexuality, so the schism followed something of the transitive property. It was not enough for one's own bishop to be heterosexual, not even enough that this bishop hold a traditionalist view of sexuality and marriage. For that bishop to be in communion with a gay bishop was contamination enough.

Such alternative structures were a serious disruption of the well-established ecclesiological norm of canonical territory. Essentially, the basic unit of the church is the diocese, overseen by the bishop, and all ministry that occurs within that diocese should be with the consent and approval of the bishop. Readers less habituated to episcopal polity may be served by imagining someone showing up to a congregation on a Sunday morning and insisting to its pastor that they would be conducting worship and delivering the sermon, refusing to take no for an answer. To be fair, faced with this norm of church order, the schismatic groups would note that approving LGBTQ sexuality was its own departure from well-established norms, which is true enough, as we noted in the introduction.

---

58 All chronicled in Stephen Bates, *A Church at War: Anglicans and Homosexuality* (London: Hodder & Stoughton, 2005); Christopher Craig Brittain and Andrew McKinnon, *The Anglican Communion at a Crossroads: The Crises of a Global Church* (University Park: Pennsylvania State University Press, 2018). Christopher Craig Brittain also provides a helpful analysis with its scope mainly limited to the Diocese of Pittsburgh, which as the see of Robert Duncan, the first primate of the schismatic Anglican Church in North America, was a particular storm center of developments. *A Plague on Both Their Houses: Liberal vs. Conservative Christians and the Divorce of the Episcopal Church USA* (London: Bloomsbury, 2015). Miranda Katherine Hassett provides an important anthropological study of the prehistory of these developments (she reports having completed her initial research a year before the Robinson consecration), informed by fieldwork. *Anglican Communion in Crisis: How Episcopal Dissidents and Their African Allies Are Reshaping Anglicanism* (Princeton, NJ: Princeton University Press, 2007).

59 The groundwork for these schismatic congregations had been laid in the 1990s and some of the first were actually formed in 2000: three years before Gene Robinson's election.

The Archbishop of Canterbury at the time, Rowan Williams, was personally in favor of developing the church's teaching to embrace nonheterosexual relationships, and had even written a rather influential essay on the possibility of affirming LGBTQ sexuality within a more traditional Christian ethic previously.[60] Whatever his personal views, though, as archbishop, Williams felt compelled to safeguard the unity of the Communion, and these developments threatened division.[61] So he took action aimed at preserving unity. Robinson was not invited to the 2008 Lambeth Conference (a roughly decennial gathering of the Anglican Communion's bishops), and the conference format was geared toward fostering dialogue amid the tensions between provinces, opting for *indaba* (a Zulu and Xhosa word for discussion) rather than issuing resolutions.[62]

In these regards, Williams was following the directives of a working group he had called to consider the question of a way forward amid disagreement about sexuality. The result of their work was the Windsor Report, issued in 2004.[63]

The Report concluded that the previously held Anglican consensus on sexuality (the rather traditional view that sexual expression is limited to the context of monogamous heterosexual marriage, articulated at the 1998 Lambeth Conference) while still officially in force, no longer held as a consensus, per se. And so, in light of this, the churches of the Anglican Communion would need to find ways of walking together despite their disagreements on the matter. To facilitate this, they proposed a season of mutual listening and discernment, and to facilitate this discernment, called for three related moratoria: on the authorization and use of rites for blessing same-sex unions, on the consecration of bishops in same-sex partnerships, and on incursions into other churches' canonical territory. These moratoria were intended to

---

60 Williams, "The Body's Grace."

61 Note the scathing indictment of Williams's approach in Susannah Cornwall, *Controversies in Queer Theology* (London: SCM, 2011), 41–42.

62 See analysis in Peter John Lee, "Indaba as Obedience: A Post Lambeth 2008 Assessment 'If Someone Offends You, Talk to Him,'" *JAS* 7, no. 2 (2009): 147–61; Jeffrey Driver, "Beyond Lambeth 2008 and ACC14: Tuning a Polity of Persuasion to the Twenty-First Century," *JAS* 7, no. 2 (2009): 195–211; David F. Ford, "A Wisdom for Anglican Life: Lambeth 1998 to Lambeth 2008 and Beyond," *JAS* 4, no. 2 (2006): 137–56.

63 Lambeth Commission on Communion, "The Windsor Report" (Anglican Communion Office, 2004).

remove pressure and facilitate the breathing room necessary for authentic, good faith discernment to occur, until some new consensus could emerge.[64]

None of the moratoria were kept for long. Mary Glasspool, a partnered lesbian, was consecrated as a bishop for the Diocese of Los Angeles in 2010, and cross-border incursions proceeded apace, culminating in the formation of a new alternative province, the Anglican Church in North America (ACNA) in 2009. It must be noted that the formation of ACNA was at once a schismatic rupture from the Episcopal Church, the Anglican Church of Canada, and the Anglican Communion, *and* a movement of consolidation and convergence, gathering together a number of disparate bodies that had broken ties with the Episcopal Church over the years, most notably the Reformed Episcopal Church, which had broken away in 1873. Moreover, while it is not a member of the Anglican Communion, a canonically defined reality grounded in full communion with the Archbishop of Canterbury, a large number of Provinces that have broken ties with the Episcopal Church are in full communion with ACNA.

In 2015 the Episcopal Church's General Convention authorized liturgies for same-sex marriages available for use throughout the church, subject to the approval of one's diocesan bishop. In 2018, a compromise was arranged that would allow access to these rites throughout the church, even in dioceses where the bishop would not authorize same-sex marriages. In those cases, the bishop would delegate their oversight to another bishop in order to allow the rite to be used, while also not compromising their conscience or their responsibility for the liturgical activities that occur under their oversight.

The 2022 Lambeth Conference brought about yet another stage of development. Once more, significant controversy and political machination has been involved, most of which we shall skip over, to focus instead upon outcomes. Several provinces simply boycotted the meeting, refusing to be participants so long as the Episcopal Church was included. Among those who did attend, there were attempts to procure a reaffirmation of the 1998 Lambeth Conference statement as the official position of the Communion. A particularly egregious instance of this was the press release from the Global South Fellowship of Anglican Churches (GSFA), which called for "sanctions on Provinces

---

64 Varying analysis of the Windsor process may be found in Ian T. Douglas, "An American Reflects on the Windsor Report," *JAS* 3, no. 2 (2005): 155–79; Darren C. Marks, "The Windsor Report: A Theological Commentary," *JAS* 4, no. 2 (2006): 157–76. See also the Fall 2005 issue of the *ATR* 89, no. 4 (2005), which was devoted to the Windsor Report.

which ordain bishops in same-sex relations, and conduct same sex weddings," and signaled an intention to "not receive Holy Communion alongside gay-partnered bishops, and those who endorse same-sex unions."[65] Amid all of this, we can note the reproduction of the Donatist logic against which Augustine contended, and that drove the creation of alternative congregations in the US and Canada. The conference's outcome, though, was something of a different order. In the end it was recognized that a plurality of views on sexuality and marriage exist among the Communion's churches and that while we have yet to figure out how to walk together amid this disagreement, we are committed to finding that way.

Developments have continued apace, to the extent that I have had to revise my treatment several times in the course of completing this book just to keep up with the state of affairs. In February 2023, the Church of England's general synod authorized prayers of blessing for same-sex couples, while leaving unchanged the church's teaching on marriage (viz., heterosexual monogamy). This was the outcome of the Living in Love and Faith initiative, a years' long process of ecclesial discernment.[66] As might be expected, this drew denunciations from conservatives, the most notable of which are an Ash Wednesday statement from the GSFA and the Kigali Commitment, issued by the Global Anglican Future Conference (GAFCON), which announce that the churches represented by those bodies no longer recognize the Archbishop of Canterbury as an instrument of communion.[67] While neither of these bodies, nor the churches they represent, are monoliths, and the precise fallout remains unknown, given the historic understanding of what constitutes the Anglican Communion, these statements seem to amount to an exit from the Communion.

In all this, the minutiae of the history matter less than the basic dynamic: the Anglican Communion is coming apart at the seams over the question of how LGBTQ Christians fit into the life of the church. Both those who support

---

65 Global South Fellowship of Anglican Churches, "Press Release," Global South Fellowship of Anglican Churches website, July 29, 2022.

66 Much of this process is distilled in *Living in Love and Faith: Christian Teaching and Learning about Identity, Sexuality, Relationships and Marriage* (New York: Church House, 2020).

67 Global South Fellowship of Anglican Churches, "Ash Wednesday Statement of GSFA Primates on the Church of England's Decision Regarding the Blessing of Same Sex Unions" (GSFA website, February 20, 2023); GAFCON, "The Kigali Commitment" (GAFCON website, April 21, 2023).

revising the churches' teaching on sexuality to embrace LGBTQ folks and those who refuse to countenance such development have decided that the matter is important enough to allow the breaking of communion. While the communion-breaking acts have come from those who oppose LGBTQ inclusion—they are the ones who have declared communion broken, who have erected altar against altar—its proponents have gone ahead with it, knowing that the Communion as a whole was not ready to go along with them;[68] hence, all bear some responsibility.

I do not suggest that these are equivalent moves or positions, just that both sides have regarded the question of sexuality to be one that warrants ecclesial division, if need be. In this connection, and without prejudice to the question of whether or not the church's teaching should develop to embrace LGBTQ sexualities, the witness of the Communion Partners, a group of bishops in the Episcopal Church who both uphold the traditional teaching on marriage and sexuality and who remain committed to the Episcopal Church, refusing schism, is of vital importance. The Communion Partners' commitment to the Episcopal Church and the rest of the Episcopal Church's commitment to allowing for their witness and flourishing, serves as a demonstration that differences over sexuality need not lead to broken communion.

As we saw in chapter 2, Augustine's anti-Donatist writings are consistent and clear: to be in communion with the sinful does not and cannot contaminate the one who maintains communion, while breaking communion is a refusal of charity, and so a departure from the way of salvation. Hence, even if ACNA and their cohorts are right in their assessment of LGBTQ sexuality, their decision to break communion is not only unjustifiable but downright dangerous. Similarly, even if the Communion Partners are wrong in their refusal to countenance same-sex marriages, the bonds of charity can encompass them, even in a church that has made the option for LGBTQ inclusion. Their presence does not and cannot "contaminate" the rest, particularly now that rites for same-sex marriage are available throughout the Episcopal Church.

---

68 Acknowledged in Deirdre J. Good et al., "A Theology of Marriage Including Same-Sex Couples: A View from the Liberals," *ATR* 93, no. 1 (2011): 61–62. This is a particularly poignant point when one considers the reports from African Anglicans that the LGBTQ-affirming actions of the American church have led to increased persecution for Christians within predominantly Muslim contexts (see, e.g., Brittain and McKinnon, *The Anglican Communion at a Crossroads*, 54–56, 77–94.)

Colonialism, Homophobia, and Queer Crucifixion
for the Sake of Unity

In all this, intersecting legacies of colonialism and homophobia come home to roost. While we must neither ignore nor diminish the authentic evangelistic intentions of its missionaries, nor the ways that missionary and imperial/colonial goals sometimes conflicted, it is also the case that the Anglican Communion grew through the expansion of the British empire, and is in many ways a colonial project.[69] While the bishops of the 1920 Lambeth Conference recognized the need for the Communion's future to be "less Anglican and more Catholic" (i.e., less expressive of English culture and more expressive of the wide diversity of the human race),[70] nevertheless, the Communion's history involves a legacy of material plunder and cultural imposition.

And it is against this backdrop that we must recognize that the bulk of the opposition to LGBTQ inclusion has come from churches in former colonies, who tend to cast it as a matter of Western decadence and a renewed attempt to impose the cultural values of the colonizer upon them. This is not helped when African resistance to LGBTQ sexuality is dismissed as retrograde ignorance by ostensibly enlightened Americans.[71] Such dismissal merely reinscribes the discourse of the colonial "other" in need of civilization from the Northern hemisphere. Lost amid the dispute is the way that antipathy toward same-sex sexual relationships was itself a colonial export, reflecting the British mores

---

69 See, e.g., Kwok Pui-Lan, "The Legacy of Cultural Hegemony in the Anglican Church," in *Beyond Colonial Anglicanism: The Anglican Communion in the Twenty-First Century*, ed. Ian T. Douglas and Kwok Pui-Lan (New York: Church Publishing, 2001), 47–70; Michael Doe, "From Colonialism to Communion," *JAS* 7, no. 2 (2009): 213–20; Joseph F. Duggan, "The Postcolonial Paradox: Becoming Less than Whole(s) Producing Parts That Exclude Other Parts," *JAS* 7, no. 1 (2009): 67–77; "Postcolonial Anglicanism: One Global Identity or Many Contextual Identities?," *ATR* 90, no. 2 (2008): 353–67; Robert S. Heaney, "Coloniality and Theological Method in Africa," *JAS* 7, no. 1 (2009): 55–65; Ross Kane, "Tragedies of Communion: Seeking Reconciliation amid Colonial Legacies," *ATR* 97, no. 3 (2015): 391–412.

70 1920 Lambeth Conference, "Report on the Committee on Reunion" (in *The Lambeth Conferences (1867-1930): The Reports of the 1920 and 1930 Conferences, with Selected Resolutions from the Conferences of 1867, 1878, 1888, 1897, and 1908* [London: SPCK 1948]).

71 Documented in Hassett, *Anglican Communion in Crisis*, 72–73, 111–12, 167–207. It is worth noting that even some of the more ostensibly positive characterizations of African Christianity (e.g., zeal) reproduce the logic of colonialist discourse. See also Kane, "Tragedies of Communion," 403–4.

of the day.[72] As we enter a more fully postcolonial reality, we cannot expect the formerly colonized to be cajoled into acquiescence; we must also reckon with and respect the dignity of their newly reasserted agency.[73]

And yet the complexity goes deeper still, for it is not the case that LGBTQ sexuality is a Western invention.[74] LGBTQ folks exist everywhere, regardless of geography or culture. As a result, even as we respect the agency of formerly colonized peoples, we must also consider the plight of "the oppressed's oppressed," in Delores Williams's memorable phrase.[75] This became particularly apparent in 2021 when Ghana introduced legislation not only criminalizing homosexual activity (which had been illegal since the 1800s), but also advocacy for LGTBQ rights, or even identifying as LGBTQ. The bill was enthusiastically endorsed by the Anglican Church of Ghana.

Initially, the Archbishop of Canterbury, Justin Welby, expressed "grave concern" over the bill, calling upon the Ghanaian church to remember the commitments expressed by the 1998 Lambeth Conference, which while limiting sexual activity to heterosexual marriage and finding that it "cannot advise" blessings for same-sex relationships, had also declared,

> We commit ourselves to listen to the experience of homosexual persons and we wish to assure them that they are loved by God and that all baptised, believing and faithful persons, regardless of sexual orientation, are full members of the Body of Christ . . . [and call] on all our people to minister pastorally and

---

72 E.g., Pui-Lan, "The Legacy of Cultural Hegemony in the Anglican Church," 64–65. She argues this at greater length in *Postcolonial Imagination and Feminist Theology* (Louisville, KY: Westminster John Knox, 2005). See also Mignolo, *Darker Side of Western Modernity*, 18. The intertwining of heterosexism with colonialism is argued throughout Althaus-Reid, *Indecent Theology*.

73 And yet, see the insightful critique of Charlotte Dalwood, who demonstrates that much of the anti-LGBTQ rhetoric from the Global South, especially that decrying colonialism, actually reinscribes the bio-and-necro-political imaginary of colonialism. "Orthodoxy and the Politics of Christian Subjectivity: A Case Study of the Global Anglican Future Conference (GAFCON)," *JAS* 18, no. 2 (2020): 235–50; Also relevant is the question of the extent to which the globalization of the controversy over sexuality is the result of manipulation by Western conservatives. See, e.g., Esther Mombo, "The Windsor Report: A Paradigm Shift for Anglicanism," *ATR* 89, no. 1 (2007): 69–78; Brittain and McKinnon, *The Anglican Communion at a Crossroads*, 69–73; Hassett, *Anglican Communion in Crisis*, 47–101. In observing this, I have no intention of denying Global South agency in the matter! Yet, Mombo's observation from her own Kenyan context and the concerns raised by Brittain and McKinnon's African interviewees are worth notice.

74 See especially Cornwall, *Controversies in Queer Theology*, 72–113.

75 Williams, *Sisters in the Wilderness*, 150–51.

sensitively to all irrespective of sexual orientation and to condemn irrational fear of homosexuals.[76]

However, a short time later, he retracted and apologized for the statement, citing the evils of colonialism along the way.[77]

Like his predecessor, Rowan Williams, Welby has had to engage in all sorts of maneuvering to prevent the dissolution of the Anglican Communion over the issue of sexuality, including taking such steps to avoid alienating the Global South. To an extent this is laudable, but amid this solicitude for the unity of the Anglican Communion, and amid this concern to avoid reinscribing the colonialist past, the most vulnerable population in the mix, criminalized LGBTQ people, were, apparently, dispensable. Their ongoing crucifixion was the price to be paid for the preservation of unity.

Even more recently, in March of 2023, Uganda passed legislation that criminalized not just same-sex sexual activity, but even identifying as LGBTQ, even making some forms of LGBTQ expression punishable by death. As in Ghana, these laws have been endorsed by the Anglican Church of Uganda. What the larger response throughout the Anglican Communion will be to these laws is not yet clear as I write. However, Justin Welby has once more weighed in, condemning the laws and calling for protections for LGBTQ Ugandans.[78] His statement recognizes the history of colonialism, while insisting that his call to respect and protect LGBTQ people is not a Western imposition, but a matter of fidelity to the gospel. In response, GAFCON has reiterated their rejection of the Archbishop of Canterbury's legitimacy (and, by extension the legitimacy of the Anglican Communion), accusing him of "colonisation and patronizing behaviour," and of taking "the path of rebellion against God." In this exchange, Welby has held the line thus far.[79]

I will not speculate as to the archbishop's motivations, but it strikes me that a key difference is that in the case of the exchange over the Ugandan legislation, unity has already been taken off the table. By their rejection

---

76 Justin Welby, "Archbishop of Canterbury's Statement on Ghana's Anti-LGBTQ+ Bill," Archbishop of Canterbury website, October 26, 2021.

77 Justin Welby, "Archbishop of Canterbury's Statement Following a Meeting with the Archbishop, Bishops and Senior Clergy of the Anglican Church of Ghana," Archbishop of Canterbury website, November 21, 2021.

78 Justin Welby, "Archbishop of Canterbury's Statement on the Church of Uganda," Archbishop of Canterbury website, June 9, 2023.

79 GAFCON, "GAFCON Response to Archbishop of Canterbury" (GAFCON website, June 14, 2023).

of Canterbury, GAFCON has made it clear that they have no intention of remaining in the Anglican Communion. That being the case, with no unity to maintain, Welby has been freed up to more consistently advocate for vulnerable LGBTQ Ugandans. Their situation remains dire, but with the Anglican Communion's unity already ruptured, their crucifixion can no longer be demanded as the price to be paid for its maintenance.

The Windsor process was meant to create the conditions wherein authentic good faith discernment could occur for the churches of the Anglican Communion. On the surface, this is a worthy enough goal. Had all parties been willing to engage in the process, the Communion might find itself in a rather different position than it presently is, though there are enough contingencies involved in this counterfactual that it is impossible to say. It seems, though, that both sides viewed the moratoria not as an invitation to further discernment, but as a clamping down upon change, not the starting point for a conversation, but its termination.[80] I have had several conversations with conservatives that have borne this out: their commitment to the moratoria was a way to slow down gay marriage. Frankly, when this is the case, the revisionists can hardly be blamed for moving forward with and acting upon their own discernment. For how long can one be expected to wait for someone who declares they have no intention of joining you?[81]

Amid this, some autobiographic details can bear the complexities out further. My entry into the Anglican tradition was through the ACNA. I was a young conservative evangelical, enamored of the liturgical and sacramental heritage of the church, yet unable to recognize in the Episcopal Church a viable expression of Christian faith. Part of this was borne from my seminary formation, which warned me against the dangers of "liberalism" and apostasy, of which the Episcopal Church, particularly its decisions to ordain women and to embrace LGBTQ sexualities, was often Exhibit A. I was drawn to the

---

80 Oliver O'Donovan presents an important case for viewing Windsor as opening a process of discernment, and a winsome commendation of such discernment. *Church in Crisis: The Gay Controversy and the Anglican Communion* (Eugene, OR: Cascade, 2008). At times his frustration with revisionists in the Episcopal Church for moving forward instead of waiting for the rest of the Communion to catch up is palpable.

81 Shortly after the publication of Windsor, others recognized that this dynamic was in play. E.g., Timothy W Bartel, "Adiaphora: The Achilles Heel of the Windsor Report," *ATR* 89, no. 3 (2007): 401–19. Similarly, for all of the overtures towards the Global South, including Welby's walking back of his denunciation of the Ghanaian legislation, these churches remain unplacated, and seem to be ready to leave the Communion.

liturgical heritage of the *Book of Common Prayer*, but could not countenance entry into the Episcopal Church. ACNA provided a liturgically grounded expression of the faith where I could feel comfortable in my conservative convictions.

Yet, as soon as I entered ACNA and began learning about my newfound tradition, I was confronted with the troubling realization that Anglican ecclesiology is not supposed to work like this, and that the schism was indefensible. Meanwhile, relationships with Episcopalians led to the (shocking!) recognition that they were, in fact, Christians. Most of the excesses of the Episcopal Church about which I'd been warned were caricatures.[82] Not that they weren't grounded in any reality, but they were hardly representative of the preponderance of the facts on the ground. Moreover, the existence of the Communion Partners provided a witness that a conservative/traditionalist position on sexuality could still be held with integrity in the Episcopal Church. This allowed me to become an Episcopalian in good conscience.

Since then, the witness of faithful LGBTQ people and couples, in concert with learning from and listening to them, has brought me to a rather different place on the question of sexuality than I was when I entered the Episcopal Church. Were it not for the Communion Partners or the Windsor process, I'd probably not have wound up here. Patience and space for discernment allowed my positions to shift in a way that they wouldn't have been able to had the Episcopal Church decided to purge itself of the "homophobes." Returning to one of this book's basic theses, ecclesial unity is not opposed to agonism nor contestation, but rather the context where these are properly situated. Allowing for dissent is vital to authentic unity, and persuasion, rather than coercion must prevail.

Yet, I do not wish to suggest that this autobiography should be normative. I concurred with the rejection of uplift suasion in the pursuit of equality for the Black community. I do not suggest we apply that strategy for the LGBTQ community. To do so is precisely to reinscribe the logic of surrogacy, making this marginalized and suffering community responsible for my growth, asking

---

82 There's a cottage industry among schismatic Anglicans of cataloguing the most extreme examples of heterodoxy by Episcopalians and marshaling them as evidence to justify the schism. See, e.g., Foley Beach, "A North American Perspective: Neo-Pagan Anglicanism," in *The Future of Orthodox Anglicanism*, ed. Gerald R. McDermott (Wheaton, IL: Crossway, 2020), 81–102. Also documented in Brittain, *A Plague on Both Their Houses*, 19–21; Brittain and McKinnon, *The Anglican Communion at a Crossroads*, 95–120.

them to continue their suffering so that others might come around as well. No one should be expected to live a morally heroic life just so that others will recognize their humanity, nor defer the living of their lives until that coming around occurs. Moreover, I noted above that it is not uplift suasion, but policy change that brings change. My journey was no exception. It is precisely the authorization of same-sex marriage within the Episcopal Church that has made visible in new ways the witness of faithful LGBTQ Episcopalians. Had the moratoria kept them locked away in the closet, my own group bias could not have been corrected.

While to a certain extent, slow change following upon careful consideration seems the only viable path for authentic development (and, I think, more likely to lead to deep and lasting change), we must not forget the human cost of taking the "long view" in this way. In his "Letter from Birmingham Jail," Martin Luther King Jr. excoriates the "white moderates," who claim to be on the side of racial justice, but urge the Black community to wait for a more opportune time, as more destructive to the cause of justice than the Klan.[83]

While I am committed to Communion-wide ecclesial discernment, King's words haunt me, as do James Baldwin's, "I was born here almost sixty years ago. I'm not going to live another sixty years. You always told me it takes time. It has taken my father's time, my mother's time. My uncle's time. My brother's and sister's time. My niece's and my nephew's time. How much time do you want for your progress?"[84] As Rowan Williams once put it to his predecessor as Archbishop of Canterbury, George Carey, "Who bears the cost" of such protracted processes with no end in sight?[85] The aspirations of LGBTQ people cannot be endlessly deferred. Life is too precious, too brief.

The churches need to discern, yes. But two factors are vital to bear in mind. First, that discernment is already underway in the lives of LGBTQ Christians. Their pursuit of queer faithfulness is not something other than the churches' discernment, for they are the church to an equal degree with heterosexual and/or non-affirming Christians. Second, while no one individual is more important than the church community as a whole, nevertheless, the community exists for the sake of the people who compose it. It is a good of order,

---

83 Martin Luther King, "Letter from Birmingham Jail," African Studies Center—University of Pennsylvania, 1963.

84 *James Baldwin: The Price of the Ticket* (Maysles Films; PBS American Masters, 1989).

85 Bates, *A Church at War*, 203.

promoting their salvation by promoting the occurrence and recurrence of faith, hope, and love. The immolation of the individual for sake of the collective is not a valid ecclesiological principle. Therefore, LGBTQ Christians must not be expected to shoulder the burden of the rest of the churches' discernment. Their crucifixion is too high a price to pay for unity, and indeed counteracts the very purpose of unity. Christ has bound us together not for crucifixion, but by the law of the cross.

THE CROSS REPRISED

In the opening of this chapter, we noted the dual aspect of Calvary: the law of the cross that gives life and the subjugating impulse to crucifixion that deals death. The former is exemplified in Augustine's ecclesiology of love; the latter in his advocacy of violence against the Donatists. We have surveyed various forms that crucifixion has taken, most potently, the lynching tree.

The Black community has long recognized the affinity between their experience of lynching and Jesus's crucifixion,[86] and here the two dimensions of the cross meet. As James Cone explains it,

> The lynching tree frees the cross from the false pieties of well-meaning Christians. When we see the crucifixion as a first-century lynching, we are confronted by the reenactment of Christ's suffering in the blood-soaked history of African Americans. Thus the lynching tree reveals the true religious meaning of the cross for American Christians today. The cross needs the lynching tree to remind Americans of the reality of suffering—to keep the cross from becoming a symbol of abstract, sentimental piety. Before the spectacle of this cross we are called to more than contemplation and adoration. We are faced with a clear challenge: as Latin American liberation theologian Jon Sobrino has put it, "to take the crucified down from the cross."[87]

At the same time, the cross holds out the prospect of redeeming the lynching tree, because on it, in Christ, God has entered into solidarity with the crucified and lynched of history.[88]

---

86 Cone, *Cross and the Lynching Tree*, 1–29, 65–119; Copeland, *Enfleshing Freedom*, 117–24; *Knowing Christ Crucified*, 136–49.

87 Cone, *Cross and the Lynching Tree*, 161 (citing Jon Sobrino, *The Eye of the Needle: No Salvation outside the Poor: A Utopian-Prophetic Essay* [London: Darton, Longman, & Todd, 2008], 1–17).

88 Cone, *Cross and the Lynching Tree*, 161–62.

Shawn Copeland develops this further. Throughout his ministry, Jesus placed himself alongside and in solidarity with those who were marked as inferior and dispensable by the logic of empire. In exercising this preferential option for the marginalized, Jesus signals his mission's priorities and gestures toward where he can be found in here and now, as his mission continues to unfold in his resurrection life.[89] The solidarity enacted by Jesus, then, is to characterize his followers, who are instructed to take up their own crosses and follow him (Mark 8:34–37). In this sense, solidarity offers a more pointed and specific rendition of the charity we have already discerned to be at the heart of the cross, of redemption, and of the life of the body of Christ. "Through a praxis of solidarity, we not only apprehend and are moved by the suffering of the other, we confront and address its oppressive cause and shoulder the other's suffering."[90] In this way, "solidarity sets the dynamics of love against the dynamics of domination."[91]

The dual nature of the cross "exposes our pretense to historical and personal innocence, to social and personal neutrality. It uncovers the limitation of all human efforts to meet the problem of evil. Thus, the praxis of solidarity is made possible by the loving self-donation of the crucified Christ, whose cross is its origin, standard, and judge."[92] Copeland's words here are vital on a number of fronts.

The disavowal of neutrality and innocence reminds us that we have to do not just with "Christ crucified," but with the "lynched Jesus." Both dimensions of the cross are kept in view here, which disallows safe or saccharine pieties that would invite the surrogacy against which Delores Williams rightly warns us. Instead, the cross empowers self-affirmation and self-love on the part of those upon whom white supremacy, or cisheteronormative patriarchy, or any other oppressive structure would impose crosses. Christ's cross is not a call to crucify others, nor a call to acquiesce to one's own crucifixion. It is instead God's radical affirmation and embrace of those whom history crucifies.[93] It is an invitation to share God's evaluation of them: radical love and solidarity.

The recognition of our limitations in addressing the problem of evil prevents us from confusing any immanent political order with the reign of God, warns us away from the Pelagian effort to attain to salvation by social engineering, even as it refuses to allow inaction or indifference. In Christ,

---

89 Copeland, *Enfleshing Freedom*, 55–105; *Knowing Christ Crucified*, 148–73.
90 Copeland, *Enfleshing Freedom*, 93–94 [94].
91 Copeland, *Enfleshing Freedom*, 94.
92 Copeland, *Enfleshing Freedom*, 99.
93 Copeland, *Knowing Christ Crucified*, 25, 36.

God has taken a side. If we would follow this Christ, we must go where he has led. We cannot manufacture the reign of God, but we must work in light of its values, knowing that we ourselves shall be judged according to them.

Copeland, thus, offers a different rendition on the eucharistic sacrifice, one in continuity with the classic account sketched in chapter 2, but also aware of and so designed to overcome the liabilities lodged in the heritage of crucifixion. This is a eucharistic solidarity, wherein we recognize that Christ has taken the despised and lynched bodies of history and made them his own, thus inviting us to recognize that

> in Christ, there is neither brown nor black, neither red nor white; in Christ there is neither Creole nor *mestizo*, neither senator nor worker in the *maquiladoras*. In Christ, there is neither male nor female, neither gay/lesbian nor straight, neither heterosexual nor homosexual [neither cisgender nor transgender, neither sighted nor blind, neither hearing nor deaf, etc., etc., etc.,]. We are all transformed in Christ: *we are his very own flesh.*
>
> If my sister or brother is not at the table, we are not the flesh of Christ. If my sister's mark of sexuality must be obscured, if my brother's mark of race must be disguised, if my sister's mark of culture must be repressed, then we are not the flesh of Christ. . . . Unless our sisters and brothers are beside and with each of us, we are not the flesh of Christ.[94]

Through this eucharistic solidarity, we are drawn into the dangerous memory of the lynched Jesus, whose cross reminds us both of the lengths to which divine love will go to ensure that we are all included at the table, and of the deadly results of our refusal to others of their seats at that table.[95] It warns us that none of us are free until all of us are free, that so long as any are shut out from this table, we eat and drink without discerning the body of Christ, and so court our own damnation by our eating and drinking. Our only hope, then, are the bonds of solidarity by which Christ refuses to let us go. This being the case, we dare not refuse this same relentless solidarity in our own lives.

CONCLUSION: ICHABOD

The cross has been and remains an inescapable feature of the Christian tradition, and this in two senses. On the one hand, Christians are continually confronted by those upon whom they have imposed crosses (or those crosses

---

94 Copeland, *Knowing Christ Crucified*, 78.
95 Copeland, *Enfleshing Freedom*, 128.

imposed upon them), often enough in the name of unity. On the other hand, we all are confronted by the cross of Christ, by which he has embraced the despised, the forgotten, the excluded, the lynched, the crucified, making them his own, refusing any future which does not include them and their flourishing. By this same cross, all the failures of his people can be redeemed, including those legacies of harm whereby we have crucified his beloved. But this redemption occurs by way of the repudiation and dismantling of any and all structures of oppression.

Seen in this light, the traditional emphasis on the imitation of Christ, and especially participation in his cross, cries out for refinement. We have seen the ways that crucifixion validates and sacralizes suffering, either imposing surrogacy or courting its "voluntary" embrace. The danger here is real, and yet I am persuaded that we must hazard it. Jesus bids us take up our crosses and come after him. The call is to solidarity, not to subjugation, whether of ourselves or of others. Eugene Rogers provides an incipient and evocative criterion. Faced with a "pattern [that] invites women and sexual minorities to 'take up their own cross and follow Jesus.' Ask whether someone making that demand is willing to join you on the cross, as Jesus joined the thief. Ask who holds the hammer and the nails."[96] The cruciformity of Jesus will not impose the cross on others, nor ask them to bear the cross for others. It will instead, join with those who are crucified in the embrace of solidarity, working for their liberation, working for their resurrection into fulness of life.

Throughout this chapter, we have explored the ways that unity can be a crucifying unity, as oppressed communities are either kept in their marginal situation by force, or enjoined to voluntarily endure their crucifixion for the good of the whole. The way of Jesus is the outright refusal of either of these crucifixions. The God who raised him from the dead in so doing signals their intention for all who've been crucified, whether in the name of holiness, or good order, or unity. Until they are properly seated at the table, we are not the flesh of Christ. Until they are seated at the table, our keeping of the eucharistic feast occurs under a sign of contradiction, and invites our condemnation.

---

96 Eugene F. Rogers, *Blood Theology: Seeing Red in Body- and God-Talk* (Cambridge: Cambridge University Press, 2021), 124. See also Paul G. Crowley, *Unwanted Wisdom: Suffering, The Cross, and Hope* (New York: Continuum, 2005) for a reckoning with this dual aspect of the cross and an affirmation of the need for solidarity, particularly with regard to the suffering of LGBTQ people.

In the end, the resolution of the divisions enacted by the churches over race, sexuality, gender (or disability, or any other analogous mark) will be the reversal of the exclusion of marginalized identities. But it will not occur through the acquiescence of white or cisgendered heterosexual Christians deigning to include their BIPOC, or API, or queer siblings in Christ.[97] Rather, in a twofold movement we will recognize that they are the church every bit as much as we are, that our attempts to conceive of and enact the church in ways that exclude them, are self-mutilating acts, maiming that body we all together are, moving us further away from our identity as church, and, as suppliants, we will beg for their forgiveness, and implore them to enrich our impoverished precincts by their presence, so that we may finally and fully experience the presence of Christ.

---

97 In this final sentence, my use of the first-person plural is deliberate. As a white heterosexual man, who tends to operate in these white-and-straight-constructed spaces, I must take responsibility for my own part in their crucifying ways. I cannot hold myself at a distance.

CHAPTER FOUR

To Gather the Fragments:
The Nature and Possibility of Unity

I lay down my life for the sheep. I have other sheep that do not belong to this fold. I must bring them also, and they will listen to my voice. So there will be one flock, one shepherd.

John 10:15–16

The last chapter ended with a challenge. Until all who belong to Christ are united in eucharistic fellowship, we are not yet true to our identity as his body. This thesis, of course, is nothing new. From Paul's admonitions to the Corinthians to Augustine's anti-Donatist writings to the modern ecumenical movement this thread runs, indicting us in our divided state. Yet it bears repeating, and all the more so in light of the historically embedded processes by which (for the most part) white heterosexual men have constructed the church as an imaginatively white, heterosexual, and patriarchal space, thereby marginalizing and excluding the witnesses of BIPOC, API, and LGBTQ voices, especially those of women.

The imaginative excision of these voices and perspectives amounts to a performative amputation of limbs from the mystical body of Christ, leaving him in whom all things hold together disfigured and maimed. The adjectives *imaginative* and *performative* in the last sentence are vital, for they serve as a reminder that the bonds of love established by Christ in baptism are indissoluble, that those whom Christ has joined to himself cannot be sundered from him. "No one will snatch them out of my hand. . . . No one can snatch them out of the Father's hand" (John 10:28–29). Whatever the dynamics whereby any group has arrogated power to themselves, it is neither in their purview nor their power to sever Christ's beloved from him. Nevertheless, while the effects of these actions are limited, they are still real, still affecting those effected by them, harming both those who are excluded and those who exclude them, holding us all back from "the measure of the full stature of Christ" (Eph 4:13).

This recognition sets our considerations on a new terrain, and does so in a few ways. First, it reminds us that the churches' divisions are never absolute, because the church's fundamental theological reality is the union of humanity with God in Christ. Wherever union with Christ obtains, so too, by definition, does some degree of ecclesial unity.[1] On the one hand, this offers a certain balm as we recognize that our divisions are neither definitive nor essential.[2] At the same time, though, given the terrain we've traversed thus far, it actually amplifies the problem. If our divisions are not essential, we are, nevertheless, choosing to live in isolation from each other. If at some essential level we remain in some degree of communion, then our divisions are all the more a refusal of charity, and so all the more a soteriological contradiction.

We shall return to the matter of our agency in the next chapter. For now, we can recognize that the insight of our real though incomplete communion has revolutionized the manner in which the churches view each other and relate to one another, bearing its fullest fruit in what we might call the ecumenical turn of the twentieth century. This turn was one that would take several decades to be realized, and, it would seem, given the reports of an ecumenical winter, it has yet to be fully appropriated. Nevertheless, the ecumenical revolution has launched the churches beyond themselves, calling us out of acquiescence to our divided status quo, and generating creative theological

---

1 Driven home forcefully by Paul D. L. Avis, *Reshaping Ecumenical Theology: The Church Made Whole?* (London: T&T Clark, 2010), 151–55. This perspective also informs, at least to a degree, *LG*, nos. 14–15 [Tanner, 2:860–61]; and *UR*, nos. 3–4, 22 [Tanner, 2:909–12, 919–20].

2 A cogent case for this position may be found in David Bentley Hart, "The Myth of Schism," in *Ecumenism Today: The Universal Church in the 21st Century*, ed. Francesca Aran Murphy and Christopher Asprey (Aldershot, UK: Ashgate, 2008), 95–106.

concepts and bold experiments to account for our newly discerned unity and to enact it more fully.[3]

Second, it calls for a preferential option for the marginalized in both ecumenism and ecclesial mission. This option will take different forms in different arenas. Ecumenically, it will be a matter of prioritizing healing the divisions caused by marginalization, whether those that resulted from oppressed groups striking out on their own to preserve their well-being, or those that resulted from oppressive groups leaving in protest over the affirmation of those whom they wished to exclude. Missionally, it will involve building bridges and penance toward those whom the churches have alienated, who have been led to believe that embracing the gospel would mean rejecting themselves, or that the love of Jesus is not for them, at least not as their most authentic selves.[4] Both of these will require ongoing repentance and deepened conversion from and within the churches. The past cannot be undone, a fact that will concern us quite a bit in the next chapter, but it must still be faced.

Most crucially, our attention to those marginalized within the churches primes us to adapt the ecclesiology of the mystical body of Christ that has informed this theology of the church divided. We must recognize that, due to the historical processes of oppression we have inherited and enacted, the

---

3 The literature on the ecumenical movement and its history is vast. Particularly salient points of gravity include Ruth Rouse, Stephen Neill, and Harold E. Fey, *A History of the Ecumenical Movement*, 2 vols. (Philadelphia: Westminster, 1967); Lukas Vischer and Harding Meyer, *Growth in Agreement: Reports and Agreed Statements of Ecumenical Conversations on a World Level* (New York: Paulist, 1982); Jeffrey Gros, Harding Meyer, and William G. Rusch, eds., *Growth in Agreement II: Reports and Agreed Statements of Ecumenical Conversations on a World Level 1982–1998* (Grand Rapids: Eerdmans, 2000); Jeffrey Gros, Thomas F. Best, and Lorelei F. Fuchs, SA, eds., *Growth in Agreement III: International Dialogue Texts and Agreed Statements, 1998–2005* (Grand Rapids: Eerdmans, 2008); Thomas F. Best, Lorelei F. Fuchs SA et al., eds., *Growth in Agreement IV*, book 1, *International Dialogue Texts and Agreed Statements 2004–2014* (Switzerland: WCC, 2017); Thomas F. Best, Lorelei F. Fuchs SA et al., eds., *Growth in Agreement IV*, book 2, *International Dialogue Texts and Agreed Statements, 2004–2014* (Switzerland: WCC, 2017); Harding Meyer, *That All May Be One: Perceptions and Models of Ecumenicity*, trans. William G. Rusch (Grand Rapids: Eerdmans, 1999); Lorelei F. Fuchs, *Koinonia and the Quest for an Ecumenical Ecclesiology: From Foundations through Dialogue to Symbolic Competence for Communionality* (Grand Rapids: Eerdmans, 2008).

4 Near the end of his life, Robert Doran suggested that the category of "satisfaction" introduced into atonement theory by Anselm could be salvaged if it were reconceived as satisfaction offered to historically oppressed groups, reparations, essentially. *The Trinity in History*, 3:96, 111–12, 115, 161.

charity that binds together the body of Christ must also be expressed as solidarity, a solidarity that will not rest content until justice is done and all of Christ's own take their place at the banquet where the hungry are filled with good things, a work that, by necessity, extends beyond the bounds of the churches into the social structures in which they reside.[5] This, after all, is the church's purpose: to be that community informed by the just and mysterious law of the cross, and at the service of the coming reign of God, as part of the divinely initiated solution to the problem of evil.[6]

This chapter is not about that mandate directly, but it must nevertheless inform our work, for to lose sight of this in the course of constructing a theology of the church is to construct a decadent, decayed ecclesiology, one in which the church's central purpose is ignored, which amounts to allowing the community to continue to live at cross-purposes with its identity and vocation, perpetuating, rather than reversing evils. Keeping this vision before us prevents us from reinscribing a crucifying unity in our attempt to derive a synthetic account of the one church of Christ. It forecloses certain ways of thinking about unity, and in so doing, allows us to chart the course for a positive statement of the nature of unity and its possibility. As we shall see, the unity to which we are called is the unity of all Christians with one another in Christ. We are all incomplete until we are all bound up in a mutual embrace. And far too often, we content ourselves with imagining unity in manners that insulate us from this bracing demand, or from the realization of our incompleteness without each other.

CONCEIVING UNITY: GUIDING ASSUMPTIONS

A notion of church unity that can be intelligently grasped and reasonably affirmed must negotiate between three sometimes tensive poles. On the one hand, it must conform to empirical and historical reality, neither retreating into ideals nor to quasi-mythical historical precedents. At the same time, it must be consonant with the theological core of the church we have articulated. While this core cannot function as an empirically unassailable ideal,

---

5 Copeland, *Enfleshing Freedom*, 92–101, 124–28.

6 Lonergan sketches this in heuristic terms in *Insight*, 718–25, 740–51. It was the career-long preoccupation of Doran to fill out this heuristic structure concretely, *Theology and the Dialectics of History*; *The Trinity in History*.

nevertheless, our notion of the church and its unity must cohere with this core in order to be an ecclesiology. Finally, and closely related to the other two poles, our account of unity must be compatible with the churches' self-understanding, including their histories.

Neglecting any of these criteria yields a deficient ecclesiology. Without empirical grounding, our ecclesiology will be a fiction, a description of ideas, but not of any extramental reality. By the same token, if our account of the church does not cohere with ecclesiological doctrine, then whatever reality we are describing must be something other than what the churches mean when they speak about the church. Similarly, if our ecclesiology countervails the churches' self-understanding to the extent that they cannot recognize themselves in it, then it will serve no purpose. (Not that these self-understandings can never be corrected or improved upon, but this correction and improvement must be in continuity with these communities, their understandings, and their histories.) Two key commitments follow from these criteria: the unity of the church must be a visible unity, and it must be a unity of *churches*. We shall consider each in turn.

There is a general consensus among the churches, at least those involved in the ecumenical movement, that the unity we seek must be visibly instantiated, rather than asserted as an invisible reality that obtains despite our visible divisions. While an invisible unity would seem to offer a salve to the sting of division, imagining it as only apparent, perhaps even illusory, such an invisible unity would be purely ideal, empirically isolated and unverifiable (not to mention at odds with the observable fact of church division). One could, perhaps, aver it as a claim of faith, but it would remain a mere assertion. Yet it's also far from clear that anyone is actually making such an assertion, at least not in any serious way.

In addition to the empirical problems, an invisible unity falls short of both the theological meaning of the church and the churches' self-understanding. While a good many Protestant ecclesiologies trade upon a distinction between the church as visible and invisible, the distinction is not intended to subvert a commitment to the visible church or to its unity as something visibly instantiated. A classic statement of the principle is John Calvin's explanation that

> Holy Scripture speaks of the church in two ways. Sometimes by the term "church" it means that which is actually in God's presence, into which no persons are received but those who are children of God by grace of adoption and

true members of Christ by sanctification of the Holy Spirit . . . Often, however, the name "church" designates the whole multitude of men spread over the earth who profess to worship one God and Christ. . . . In this church are mingled many hypocrites who have nothing of Christ but the name and outward appearance. . . . Just as we must believe, therefore, that the former church, invisible to us, is visible to the eyes of God alone, so we are commanded to revere and keep communion with the latter, which is called "church" in respect to men.[7]

Similar sentiments and distinctions are found in the various Protestant confessions, not always with explicit affirmation of an invisible church, though this is implied through contrast by their specific mention of the "visible church."[8]

For his part, Calvin is fairly resolute in his insistence that one must maintain communion with the visible church, even in rather distorted forms, refusing to separate on account of faulty doctrine, moral wickedness, scandal, or other recognition of ecclesial shortcomings.[9] His recourse to invisibility is an attempt to make sense of the reality that the church is spoken of as pure, holy, the company of the redeemed, and yet is observed to be a mixed company with any number of impurities and shortcomings. Similarly, Martin Luther emphasized a "hiddenness" of the church, rather than an invisibility. And subsequent dialogues have demonstrated a general compatibility between the Lutheran emphasis on hiddenness, and a sacramental understanding of the church community.[10] There is more to the church than meets the eye. It cannot be reduced simply to its institutional apparatus, even if some visible institutional reality remains an integral feature.

While the visible-invisible distinction has been a mainstay of Lutheran and Reformed explanations of the church, and while there have been notable

---

7 John Calvin, *Institutes of the Christian Religion*, ed. John T. McNeill (Louisville, KY: Westminster John Knox, 1960), 4.1.7.

8 E.g., Augsburg Confession, articles VII–VIII; Westminster Confession, chapter 25; Thirty-Nine Articles of Religion, articles 19 and 26. The notion is sometimes attributed to Augustine, but recent scholarship by James Lee has demonstrated the inadequacy of this reading of Augustine. Throughout his career, but especially as his thought matured, he insisted on the visibility of the church. *Augustine and the Mystery of the Church* (Minneapolis: Fortress Press, 2017).

9 Calvin, *Institutes*, 4.1.10–16.

10 See the account in Jakob K. Rinderknecht, "The Church: A Body under Law and Gospel," in *Recasting Lutheran Ecclesiology in an Ecumenical Context*, ed. Jonathan Mumme, Richard J. Serina, and Mark W. Birkholz (Lanham, MD: Lexington Books/Fortress Academic, 2019), 171–87.

defenses of its ongoing utility,[11] there is also a general consensus—including among Lutheran and Reformed perspectives—that this is an inadequate understanding of the church, which indicates its theological incoherence and its failure to align with the churches' self-understandings. After all, if the church is the ecclesia, the assembly, then isn't it *precisely* visible? What would an *invisible* assembly even mean? Paul Avis labels the notion of an invisible church "a contradiction in terms,"[12] while Henri de Lubac argued that it amounts to the same thing as "no church at all."[13] While there is more to the church than what can be seen, there remains something fundamental and irreplaceable about its visibility. The visible and invisible elements cannot be separated from or played off each other. Rather, they form one complex whole.[14]

Accordingly, the ecumenical movement has by and large insisted that its goal is full visible unity. Therefore, a merely invisible unity falls short of this mark as well, for it fails to align with the churches' self-understanding, including those churches who distinguish between the visible and invisible/hidden. An invisible unity is little more than a cipher or wishful thinking. As invisible, it makes no demands upon the churches, nor can it be assessed or verified. It is an assertion and nothing more.

Finally, we must note that Jesus's intent in the high priestly prayer depends upon a visible unity. Before his arrest, he prays to his father for the unity of his followers, "So that the world can believe that you have sent me." The strong implication is that the unity of the church will be an empirical reality, one that can be recognized, and which will serve a criterial and indexical function. By recognizing the unity of Christ's followers, the world is able to believe in the gospel message. While there is more to the churches' unity than what is visible, there cannot be less.

Second, whatever else a united church might be, it will certainly be a union *of churches*, each of which is recognized in its own integrity. This is

---

11 John Webster, "On Evangelical Ecclesiology," *Ecclesiology* 1, no. 1 (2004): 9–35; "The Self-Organizing Power of the Gospel of Christ: Episcopacy and Community Formation," *International Journal of Systematic Theology* 3, no. 1 (2001): 69–82; Bradford Littlejohn, "Believing in the Church: Why Ecumenism Needs the Invisibility of the Church," *Religions* 10, no. 2 (2019): 104–104,.

12 Paul D. L. Avis, *The Vocation of Anglicanism* (London: Bloomsbury, 2016), 125.

13 Henri de Lubac, *The Splendor of the Church*, trans. Michael Mason, 2nd ed. (San Francisco: Ignatius, 1999), 84–88.

14 *LG*, no. 8 [Tanner, 2:854].

demanded historically and empirically because the plurality of churches is an undeniable fact going back to the earliest days of the Christian movement. It is consonant with the ecclesiology of communion and the theology of Christ's mystical body, and so meets the theological criterion. Finally, it is exigent from the churches' self-understanding. None of us understand ourselves or our communities to be anything less than church. This does not preclude the idea that some communities more fully embody the reality of church, which is analog, rather than digital. It only rules out any expectation that we understand ourselves as not church.

With this recognition, we rule out any form of an ecumenism of return, whereby there is posited one true church to which all other divided Christians must revert. While the idea of a singular true church may help to soften the blow of division, for it would mean that the apparent divisions of the church are just that—apparent, with the one true church existing in its integral full-ness, and other Christians simply, though perhaps regretfully, cut off from it—such an account of unity is inadequate across the board. Empirically and historically, such a unity and such a church has never existed. From its very foundations, the Christian church has been a pluriform reality. Unity is a decision of the will performed by disparate persons and their communities, not an already out there now real.

Theologically, such a unity would be a betrayal of unity's purpose, for unity must respect and embrace diversity. A unity that does not do so is a crucifying unity. A unity that would recloset LGBTQ folks, or deny their lives and their loves, is not the unity of the law of the cross, but of crucifixion. A unity that demands BIPOC or Asian cultural erasure in favor of white cul-tural normativity is not the unity enacted by Christ, but instead the unity enacted by Roman empire, the unity that crucified Christ. Such unities stand in opposition to the unity of the law of the cross, which embraces the other in love for the sake of that other's flourishing, stopping at nothing to pro-mote that flourishing. Unity is the expression of love. This love is not love of sameness but love of difference. It can even be the love of one's enemies, for in its founding enactment, the charity that informs the church was the love of God's enemies in and by Christ.

Moreover, none of the mainstream Christian churches actually understand unity to work in this way. Even the Catholic Church, which understands itself to have a unique relationship to the one church of Christ (a point to which we shall return in due course), rejects the idea of an ecumenism of return, whereby the churches' divisions are healed by everyone simply becoming

Roman Catholic. Hence, the idea of a singular church is unacceptable historically, because such a church has never existed; theologically, because such a unity could only ever be a crucifying unity; and by the self-understanding of the churches, none of whom believe themselves to be the whole. Nevertheless, it is important to state forthrightly that such an account of unity is a false path and a siren song, for it remains such a tempting notion. It flows from a conceptualism that decides in advance what unity must be, rather than an intellectualism that grasps what unity's meaning is from an intelligent grasp of and reasonable affirmation about the church.

Should the church be reunited, it will be because the churches have entered into a renewed communion with each other. While the precise details would need to be discerned and negotiated by the churches themselves, concretely, no church should have to repudiate itself or its identity. This is not to say that any community can just uncritically assert themselves. We all have much for which to repent, but none of us need to repent for our existence or for being who we are. To suggest otherwise is to suggest yet another crucifying unity. As we shall see in the next chapter, this final criterion, indispensable as it is, also presents the greatest challenge to making any possible unity actual. First, though, we shall sketch an accounting of the nature of such a possible unity.

THE EXTENT OF UNITY

It is one thing for the churches to lament our divisions, quite another to work toward their redress. While we have seen that unity is not an ultimate good, for it cannot, must not be placed above the well-being of the people who are to be united, nevertheless, work toward this unity we must. While there were certainly precursors, some of which we shall visit in due course, the twentieth century bears pride of place for its earnest enthusiasm in this course of action. It was the century of ecumenism.

A full accounting of the efforts Christians have undertaken to restore their sundered unity far exceeds the scope of a book such as this one, or even a book more narrowly focused on that question.[15] I do not attempt here any proposal for church reunification. This is for the churches themselves to discern (and ultimately for God to grant) and not for me, or any other theologian, to

---

15 For example, consider the two lengthy volumes of ecumenical history up until just 1968: Rouse, Neill, and Fey, *A History of the Ecumenical Movement.*

prescribe. Instead, I propose an account of the churches' unity, one drawn in mutual correction from two principal sources: my own Anglican tradition's ecumenical vision, which reached its high point in the 1920 Lambeth Conference, and the Catholic Church's self-understanding that the one church of Christ subsists in its communion.

Immediately, the limited scope of this proposal is apparent, for these traditions are only two within a wider ecumenical reality that outstrips them both, even taken together. Two qualifications then are immediately in order. First, this book essays *a* theology of the church divided, not *the* theology of the church divided. I can only work with the tools at my disposal, and these are the two traditions with which I am in closest contact, the one as my home, the other as the locus of my work. This is the contribution that I can make. It will fall to others, inhabiting other traditions, utilizing the tools afforded by them, to make their own contributions to this task that exceeds the capacity of any one laborer. Second, and, nevertheless, these limitations grant an important specificity, and so avoid a torpid ecclesiology of the lowest common denominator. Moreover, with these tools, I am able to construct a self-transcending account, one that opens itself up to and eagerly awaits its supplementation from these other laborers in the field. This latter claim shall be borne out in due course.

The Anglican Witness: Incompleteness and Provisionality

At its best the Anglican tradition has been guided by two convictions: first, it is an authentic expression of Christ's one, holy, catholic, and apostolic church. Second, it is by no means the entirety of that church, nor the only such expression of that church.[16] In this regard, Anglicans are hardly unique. Surely no one would deny that their church is an expression of the true church, and anyone lacking this conviction would no doubt seek a church that they believed was truly church.[17] Yet, this nonuniqueness is, I think, part of the

---

16 See the fulsome historical accounting of this point of view in Paul Avis, *Anglicanism and the Christian Church: Theological Resources in Historical Perspective* (London: T&T Clark, 2002). See also Stephen Neill, *Anglicanism*, 4th ed. (Oxford: Oxford University Press, 1978); Stephen W. Sykes, *The Integrity of Anglicanism* (New York: Seabury, 1978); *Unashamed Anglicanism* (London: Darton, Longman, & Todd, 1995).

17 Paul Avis, *The Identity of Anglicanism: Essentials of Anglican Ecclesiology* (London: T&T Clark, 2007), 40.

point. Anglicans believe that we have gifts and graces to contribute to the wider ecumenical whole, but we don't believe ourselves to be necessary in the sense that without us that wider whole would be irretrievably lost. Not even in our recognition of our own limitation and provisionality are we utterly unique, though at times we've found it hard to resist making claims to this effect.[18]

This vision is perhaps best encapsulated by Michael Ramsey, who concludes his consideration of the *ecclesia Anglicana* thus:

> For while the Anglican church is vindicated by its place in history, with a strikingly balanced witness to Gospel and Church and sound learning, its greater vindication lies in its pointing through its own history to something of which it is a fragment. Its credentials are its incompleteness, with the tension and the travail in its soul. It is clumsy and untidy, it baffles neatness and logic. For it is sent not to commend itself as "the best type of Christianity," but by its very brokenness to point to the universal Church wherein all have died.[19]

Note that Ramsey's looking beyond Anglicanism toward a wider reality does not come at the expense of effacing Anglicanism. Ours is an estimably catholic and apostolic tradition, a dimension of our identity that ought to be celebrated and maintained. Yet it is a catholicity that cannot rest upon its apostolic laurels, but necessarily reaches beyond itself to something ever greater.

Our goal here is not to give a full account of Anglican ecumenical thought and practice, nor still to set forth a proposal for the reunion of the churches. Any number of interesting avenues must be left to the side, unexplored. Instead, our path is toward articulating what the unity for which the churches strive in their ecumenical quest will involve. Ours is a theology of the church divided, not a recipe for its union. This being the case, there is one particular feature we shall be gleaning from the Anglican tradition. As with the recognition of Anglican provisionality and incompleteness (with which it is integrally related), this contribution is not necessarily unique to Anglicanism. But Anglicanism is my home, and we have articulated it with particular clarity, so I put it forth primarily in Anglican terms.

---

18 There is a whole subgenre of twentieth-century Anglican reverse chauvinism, where we speak in very high-minded terms about our vocation to disappear. Stephen F. Bayne, "Anglicanism—the Contemporary Situation: This Nettle, Anglicanism," *Pan-Anglican* 5 (1954): 39–45; Anthony Tyrrell Hanson, *Beyond Anglicanism* (London: Darton, Longman, & Todd, 1965).

19 Michael Ramsey, *The Gospel and the Catholic Church* (Cambridge: Cowley, 1990), 220.

The modern ecumenical movement was born at the 1910 World Missions Conference in Edinburgh.[20] The churches there gathered recognized that their divisions were a scandal and a hindrance to the work of mission, and so decided to tackle this problem head on.[21] This venture led to the formation of the World Council of Churches in 1948, which in turn, merged with the International Missionary Council in 1961 (due to the growing recognition that mission and unity were inseparable). So, when the bishops of the Anglican Communion gathered for the 1920 Lambeth Conference, the heady theme of ecumenism pervaded the atmosphere. Just the year before, the Orthodox Patriarch of Constantinople had issued an encyclical letter to all the churches of the world, calling for a new venture of cooperation, following upon the devastations of World War I, akin to the political reconfiguration represented by the League of Nations.[22] In part inspired by this, and also convicted that they had something to contribute to the whole, the Conference issued its now famous "Appeal to All Christian People."[23]

Speaking beyond just the Anglican flock, the bishops addressed themselves to all who bear the name Christian, because by virtue of baptism, all Christians share in the membership of Christ's one church.[24] On this basis, they went on to delineate a vision of Christian unity:

---

20 Once more, see Rouse, Neill, and Fey, *A History of the Ecumenical Movement*, for the history.

21 We can and should note the ways in which mission and coloniality were still thoroughly intertwined at this point. Mission was a matter of European Christians bringing a European Christianity to non-Western mission territories. A truly post- and decolonial theology of mission has yet to emerge. See forays toward it in, e.g., Council for World Mission, "Mission in the Context of Empire" (Council for World Mission website, January 30, 2010); WCC, "Together toward Life: Mission and Evangelism in Changing Landscapes," WCC website, September 5, 2012; Eleonora Dorothea Hof, *Reimagining Mission in the Postcolonial Condition: A Theology of Vulnerability and Vocation at the Margins* (Utrecht: Boekencentrum, 2016).

22 Reproduced in "Document: Encyclical Letter, "Unto All the Churches of Christ Wheresoever They Be," *Greek Orthodox Theological Review* 1, no. 1 (1954): 7–9.

23 On the historical background see Charlotte Methuen, "The Making of 'An Appeal to All Christian People' at the 1920 Lambeth Conference," in *The Lambeth Conference: Theology, History, Polity and Purpose*, ed. Paul Avis and Benjamin M. Guyer (London: Bloomsbury, 2017), 107–31; "Mission, Reunion and the Anglican Communion: The 'Appeal to All Christian People' and Approaches to Ecclesial Unity at the 1920 Lambeth Conference," *Ecclesiology* 16, no. 2 (2020): 175–205.

24 1920 Lambeth Conference, "An Appeal to All Christian People," preamble, in *The Six Lambeth Conferences, 1867–1920*, ed. Randall Thomas Davidson and Honor Thomas (London: SPCK, 1929), 26].

God wills fellowship. By God's own act this fellowship was made in and through Jesus Christ, and its life is in his Spirit. We believe that it is God's purpose to manifest this fellowship, so far as this world is concerned, in an outward, visible, and united society, holding one faith, having its own recognized officers, using God-given means of grace, and inspiring all its members to the world-wide service of the Kingdom of God. This is what we mean by the Catholic Church.[25]

With this, the bishops committed themselves to the general goal of the ecumenical movement, the full, visible unity of the church, understood as encompassing all of the baptized.

This commitment to a full visible unity, and to its universal extent led them to articulate their ideal

of a Church, genuinely Catholic, loyal to all truth, and gathering into its fellowship all "who profess and call themselves Christians," within whose visible unity all the treasures of faith and order, bequeathed as a heritage by the past to the present, shall be possessed in common, and made serviceable to the whole Body of Christ. Within this unity Christian Communions now separated from one another would retain much that has long been distinctive in their methods of worship and service. It is through a rich diversity of life and devotion that the unity of the whole fellowship will be fulfilled.[26]

No church, then, is forced to give up its own self-identity, though it is also conceivable that all would be transformed in their convergence.[27] This transformation, though would be that of a mutual enrichment, as each church opens toward a wider horizon and receives gifts from others, even as it gives its own.

One particularly clear instance of this transformative convergence is the formation of the Church of South India through a merger of former Anglicans, Congregationalists, Methodists, and Presbyterians in 1947. We shall return to consider the CSI and other united churches below, calling into question the assumption that self-transcendence requires merger or absorption. For

---

25 1920 Lambeth Conference, "Appeal," I, in Davidson and Thomas, *Six Lambeth Conferences*, 27.

26 1920 Lambeth Conference, "Appeal," IV, in Davidson and Thomas, *Six Lambeth Conferences*, 27–28.

27 I articulate this dynamic more fully in *Sacrificing the Church*, 150–55. See also 1920 Lambeth Conference, Report of the Committee Appointed to Consider Relation to and Reunion with Other Churches, "Part I Report of the Whole Committee," in Davidson and Thomas, *Six Lambeth Conferences*, 137; and especially 1930 Lambeth Conference, "The Unity of the Church," part I, in *The Lambeth Conference, 1930: Encyclical Letter from the Bishops; With Resolutions and Reports* (New York: Society for Promoting Christian Knowledge; Macmillan, 1930), 112–13.

now, we can note this venture as a following through on the ideals sketched by Lambeth 1920, as Anglicans (and others) moved beyond themselves into a wider catholic reality. Such moves evince a conviction that Anglicanism is not an end in itself, but a reality at the service of the catholic whole, one that cannot stop short of that whole.[28]

So much more could be said about the Lambeth appeal, including their specific proposals about the basis of Christian unity and the reunion of the churches. But with these statements we have gained what we need for our purposes. True to that fundamental Anglican conviction with which we began, we find here a church confident that it is genuinely part of a whole, while also convinced that it is only part. The Lambeth appeal is to a unity unwilling to rest content with only a partial realization. The unity to which we are called is the union of all the baptized with one another in Christ.

Such is the only unity consistent with the ecclesiology of the mystical body that we have articulated. If the church is the fruit of a singular redemption by a singular redeemer, then all those who are redeemed must find their place in it. Anything less than this is something less than what is confessed by belief in the one, holy, catholic, and apostolic church. The unity of the church will be a fully inclusive unity, or it will not yet be the unity for which Christ died. In our last chapter we insisted that this unity's embrace must extend across racial, sexual, and gender differences, and must do so in such a way as to fully embrace all those who are so included. A unity that "includes" at the expense of marginalization or erasure is not the sort of unity for which Christ died, but rather the sort of "unity" that killed Jesus. True unity involves solidarity and liberation. So long as any of the baptized remain alienated from this unity, we shall not have met the goal. This is the vision we gain from Lambeth, not that we could only gain it here, but gain it here we have.

And yet the Lambeth Appeal is unable to square its own circle. Its account of the extent of the unity we seek is the only satisfactory account, yet its articulation of this unity remains stultified by the statement, "this united fellowship is not visible in the world today."[29] Thus, while recognizing the

---

28 As the 1930 Lambeth Conference's Report of the Committee on the Anglican Communion put it, "Viewed in its widest relations, the Anglican Communion is seen as in some sense an incident in the history of the Church Universal," no. 2, in *The Lambeth Conference, 1930*, 153.

29 1920 Lambeth Conference, "Appeal," II, in Davidson and Thomas, *Six Lambeth Conferences*, 27.

necessarily visible character of the churches' unity, the Lambeth appeal is able to affirm this visibility only aspirationally, not actually.[30] On the one hand, this claim is understandable: we do not see the unity of all with all in Christ. Yet if this is all with which we are left, then has the church simply been lost in our faithlessness? In our refusals of charity have we undone the redemptive work of Christ? If we have, what hope remains? Our only hope is in that redemption, which, if we can thwart it, remains no hope after all. We are left in the position of crucifying again the Son of God to our shame (Heb 6:6), and with no succor. The church *must* not have been simply lost. While the Anglican tradition insists that the church still exists: we are here, there are other churches, and so on, it lacks the resources for coherently articulating the basis for that insistence. So, we have gained something vital from our brief Anglican sojourn, yet we must range more widely yet if we are to make good on our endeavor.

The Catholic Church: Where Unity Subsists

While above we noted that Anglicans have at times been prone to a self-effacing reverse chauvinism, the Catholic Church has not been given to any such modesty, a fact to which the Protestant churches have frequently and scathingly adverted, judging Catholic self-esteem to be pathologically high. As we saw in chapter 2, the development of the papacy, accompanied by an expansive vision of the bishop of Rome's primacy and jurisdiction, was a major contributing factor to the Great Schism of 1054. This trajectory probably reached its high point in Boniface VIII's bull *Unam Sanctam*, which set forth submission to the pope as an absolute requirement for salvation, though others might consider the First Vatican Council's formal definition of papal infallibility and universal jurisdiction to be the apex of the trajectory.[31] None of these precise developments or claims are of central importance at this point,

---

30 Yves Congar is fairly trenchant in pursuing this critique in *Divided Christendom: A Catholic Study of the Problem of Reunion*, trans. M. A. Bousfield (London: Centenary Press, 1939), 168–81.

31 Boniface VIII, "Unam Sanctam," November 18, 1302. First Dogmatic Constitution on the Church of Christ, *Pastor Aeternus* (July 18, 1870) [Tanner, 2:811–16]. In my view, *Unam Sanctam*'s is the stronger claim. *Ex cathedra* infallible teaching has only been exercised twice, and, properly understood, it is a fairly circumscribed doctrine, actually reining in some of the excessive ultramontane views that were advanced in the years leading up to and by certain parties at Vatican I.

though they do establish certain parameters within which the churches must operate, or at least with which they must reckon if they are to achieve union with each other. We shall return to that matter in the next chapter.

For our purposes at this point, what matters is that the Catholic Church has always tended to make fairly strong claims for itself, and has consistently operated with a strong sense of its intrinsic connection to the one church of Jesus Christ. This relationship to *the* church was articulated with particular clarity at the Second Vatican Council, as the Dogmatic Constitution on the Church, *Lumen Gentium* expressed:

> Christ, the one mediator, set up his holy church here on earth as a visible structure, a community of faith, hope and love; and he sustains it unceasingly and through it he pours out grace and truth on everyone. This society, however, equipped with hierarchical structures, and the mystical body of Christ, a visible assembly and a spiritual community, an earthly church and a church enriched with heavenly gifts must not be considered as two things, but as forming one complex reality comprising a human and a divine element . . . This church, set up and organised in this world as a society, subsists in the catholic church, governed by the successor of Peter and the bishops in communion with him, although outside its structure many elements of sanctification and faith are to be found which, as proper gifts to the church of Christ, impel towards catholic unity.[32]

In this lengthy extract three points are particularly pertinent. First, any separation between the mystical body of Christ and the institutional church is disallowed. They are not simply identical, and can be distinguished, but they are nevertheless a unity. Second, the institutional dimension ("this church, set up and organised in this world as a society") of this complex reality is said to "subsist" in the Catholic Church, a point we shall need to develop at length. For now, we can note that a unique relationship between the two is being averred. Finally, this intrinsic connection between Catholic Church and mystical body is not construed in exclusivist terms. Elements related to salvation and gifts belonging to the church are found beyond the structure of the Catholic Church.

On the surface, this self-attestation might seem worlds away from ecumenical promise. However, I believe that, properly understood, it holds not only ecumenical promise, but the condition of possibility for the ecumenical task and for any coherent ecclesiology under the conditions of a divided church. These are strong claims. In order to bear them out I must first make my case for how properly to interpret the claim of subsistence in the Catholic Church.

---

32 *LG*, no. 8 [Tanner, 2:854].

While I acknowledge that my considerations here spring from a theologically motivated stance, I am principally concerned to articulate what I take to be the self-understanding expressed by the Catholic Church in this conciliar statement. In other words, as an Anglican, I have a vested interest in asserting the integrity of my own tradition, and I take the *subsistit in* to provide a means for the Catholic Church to join us in this affirmation (among other gains), but Anglicans do not need the Catholic Church's permission to consider ourselves true churches. So, my principal goal is to understand the Catholic position on its own terms. With that, let us turn to consider the statement's meaning.

Considered historically, Vatican II's claims for the Catholic Church are a move toward greater modesty. In this sense they parallel the treatment of the papacy, which, without walking back in the least from the claims staked out by Vatican I, complement the earlier teachings by setting the ministry of the pope within the context of episcopal collegiality.[33] Earlier statements had tended to construe the relationship between the one church and the Catholic Church as one of simple identity. The church is the Catholic Church, full stop. Even twenty-one years earlier, in Pope Pius XII's encyclical *Mystici Corporis Christi*, the simple copulative *est* had been used: "Mystici Corporis Christi, quod est Ecclesia . . . veracem Christi Ecclesiam—quae sanctā, catholica, apostolica, Romana Ecclesia est [The Mystical Body of Christ, which is the church . . . the true Church of Christ—which is the holy, catholic, apostolic Roman Church]."[34] Hence, the move from *est* to *subsistit in* was a move away from a strict identity, and so away from exclusivity.[35]

---

33 *LG*, nos. 22–27 [Tanner, 2:865–72]. See further Michael J. Buckley, *Papal Primacy and the Episcopate: Towards a Relational Understanding* (New York: Crossroad, 1998); Hermann J. Pottmeyer, *Towards a Papacy in Communion: Perspectives from Vatican Councils I & II* (New York: Herder & Herder, 1998).

34 Pius XII, *Mystici Corporis Christi*, Vatican website, June 29, 1943, nos. 1, 13.

35 While some have argued for a relationship of strict identity, e.g., Karl Becker, "The Church and Vatican II's '*Subsistit in*' Terminology," *Origins* 35, no. 31 (2006): 514–22; Alexandra von Teuffenbach, *Die Bedeutung des subsistit in* (München: Herbert Utz, 2002), the reading I propose here is fairly well-established in the theological community, and supported by the history. See, e.g., Francis Sullivan, "Response to Karl Becker, S.J., on the Meaning of Subsistit In," *TS* 67, no. 2 (2006): 395–409; "Quaestio Disputata the Meaning of Subsistit in as Explained by the Congregation for the Doctrine of the Faith," *TS* 69, no. 1 (2008): 116–24; "Further Thoughts on the Meaning of Subsistit In," *TS* 71, no. 1 (2010): 133–47; Sandra Arenas, *Fading Frontiers? A Historical-Theological Investigation into the Notion of the "Elementa Ecclesiae"* (Leuven: Peeters, 2021); Aloys Grillmeier, "Chapter I: The Mystery of the Church," in *Commentary on the Documents of Vatican II*, ed. Herbert Vorgrimler, 5 vols. (New York: Herder & Herder, 1967–69), 1:146–52.

Such an understanding moves toward a more sacramental understanding of the church. It affirms the visibility of the church but refuses to reduce the church to a perfect society, as if its empirical reality were all it were. At the same time, it also refuses to sidestep that empirical reality. The reality of the church as Christ's mystical body is wider than any visible institutional apparatus, even if it cannot be separated therefrom. The church as a visible community bears a sacramental relation to the spiritual mystical body. Sacraments, vital and instrumental as they may be, remain means to some other end, not ends in themselves.

More recent interventions from the magisterium, most especially the Congregation for the Doctrine of the Faith's 2000 decree *Dominus Iesus*, set forth a more restrictive understanding of the *subsistit in*, insisting that it only describes the Catholic Church, and restricting the degree to which any other communities can be considered church. Not all aspects of this clarification are persuasive, though. *Dominus Iesus* explains,

> With the expression *subsistit in,* the Second Vatican Council sought to harmonize two doctrinal statements: on the one hand, that the Church of Christ, despite the divisions which exist among Christians, continues to exist fully only in the Catholic Church, and on the other hand, that "outside of her structure, many elements can be found of sanctification and truth", that is, in those Churches and ecclesial communities which are not yet in full communion with the Catholic Church.[36]

They go on in a footnote to disallow an interpretation of the phrase "that the one Church of Christ could subsist also in non-Catholic Churches and ecclesial communities" as contrary to the Council's intent.[37]

---

36 CDF, *Dominus Iesus*, Vatican website, August 6, 2000. See further Francis A. Sullivan, "Introduction and Ecclesiological Issues," in *Sic et Non: Encountering* Dominus Iesus, ed. Stephen J. Pope and Charles Hefling (Maryknoll, NY: Orbis, 2002), 47–56; Richard R. Gaillardetz, *The Church in the Making:* Lumen Gentium, Christus Dominus, Orientalium Ecclesiarum (New York: Paulist, 2006); Loe-Joo Tan, "'Things Are Not What They Seem': Dominus Iesus, Ecumenism, and Interreligious Dialogue," *Journal of Ecumenical Studies* 48, no. 4 (2013): 523–34; John D'Arcy May, "Catholic Fundamentalism? Some Implications of Dominus Iesus for Dialogue and Peacemaking," *Horizons* 28, no. 2 (2001): 271–93; Jan-Heiner Tück, "Zur Kritik der 'pluralistischen Ekklesiologie'—Anmerkungen zu *Dominus Iesus* 16 und 17," in *"Dominus Iesus": Anstößige Wahrheit oder anstößige Kirche? Dokumente, Hintergründe, Standpunkte und Folgerungen*, ed. Michael J. Rainer (Münster: LIT, 2001), 229–45.

37 CDF, *Dominus Iesus*, no. 56.

While I do not contest the CDF's claim that a unique relationship to the one church is posited for the Catholic Church, nor do I mean to argue that the church subsists in other communities, nevertheless, the decree appears to be at variance with other conciliar affirmations, most especially those that affirm the Orthodox Churches as churches. While the CDF acknowledges this affirmation in *Dominus Iesus*, it sits oddly with the exclusivity sketched out for the Catholic Church. Just as one cannot be a little pregnant, a community is either a church or it is not. Of course, there are degrees of communion, and, hence, gradations of fullness to a community's ecclesial character. "Church," as we've noted, is an analog concept. Nevertheless, even an analog dial has a threshold where it passes from off to on, and vice versa. The council fathers' use of "ecclesial communities" was not intended to say that such communities are *not* churches. Rather, it was intended to respect the self-understanding of certain Christian communities that did not wish to be identified as churches, while also leaving open the question.[38] Nevertheless, the existence of the Orthodox Churches as churches serves as proof of concept for my claim that the *subsistit in* allows for the recognition of the reality of the church to be found authentically beyond the Catholic Church.

Pronouncements by the CDF are not among the ways the Catholic Church understands itself to teach infallibly. Therefore, *Dominus Iesus* is not a definitive word on the matter. It can be mistaken in its judgment of ecclesial exclusivity—as I contend it is—and it can be revised. The Second Vatican Council has left open the matter of whether other churches beyond the Catholic Church and the Orthodox might truly be churches. Indeed, the language of *Unitatis Redintegratio*, which speaks of "*churches* and ecclesial communities which came to be separated from the apostolic see of Rome in the great upheaval which began in the west at the end of the Middle Ages and in later times too," gestures toward a positive assessment of the question.[39] It is

---

38 This would include groups such as the Salvation Army, and also the Anglican Communion, which, while composed of churches, is not itself a church. On the proper interpretation of the council, see Susan K. Wood, "The Correlation between Ecclesial Communion and the Recognition of Ministry," *One in Christ* 50, no. 2 (2016): 243; Otto Hermann Pesch, *Second Vatican Council: Prehistory—Event—Results—Posthistory*, trans. Deirdre Dempsey (Milwaukee: Marquette University Press, 2014), 212–13; Werner Becker, "History of the Decree [on Ecumenism]," in Vorgrimler, *Commentary on the Documents of Vatican II*, 2:45–46; Johannes Feiner, "Commentary on the Decree [on Ecumenism]," in Vorgrimler, *Commentary on the Documents of Vatican II*, 2:70–71, 76–77, 124–25, 144–47.

39 *UR*, no. 19 [Tanner, 2:918]. Emphasis added. See also Peter Neuner, "Kirchen und kirchliche Gemeinschaften," in Rainer, *Dominus Iesus*, 207.

also possible that some future pope or council might definitively affirm that interpretation offered by the CDF in *Dominus Iesus*, which would render my argument obsolete. But it would also be a decisive step backward in the Catholic Church's ecumenical commitments.

So, what positively, do I take the *subsistit in* to mean? First, it claims that the one church of Christ is indeed found integrally somewhere. This makes a vital contribution to ecumenical endeavor and ecclesiological reflection, for it means that in our divisions we have not simply lost the church. It is not an invisible or illusory reality. Because this is so, we can think and speak coherently about the church, despite the surd of division. Second, it authorizes the recognition of "church" to be extended beyond the Roman communion—minimally to the Orthodox, but, I argue that we must range more widely still. With these two claims, we have the basis for an ecclesiology that speaks of the one church, despite its divisions, and without provincially limiting itself to a single communion. A simple *est* might allow a coherent ecclesiology of that one exclusive church, but would disallow anything further. A recognition of plurality without the affirmation of a subsistence *somewhere* would leave us without succor in face of the surd of division. Further, it deliberately positions the Catholic Church in a penultimate position, ecclesiologically. The ultimate position belongs to the one church that subsists in, but is not identical to the Catholic Church.[40]

Finally, while the *subsistit in* does indeed posit a unique status for the Catholic Church, in view of two other points, I find this unique status unobjectionable. First, the gains are profound, and, in my view worth the cost of affirming the principle. Moreover, the Catholic Church is unique in understanding itself in this way, and so these claims do not directly impinge upon those of any other church.[41] The Orthodox, for instance, simply understand

---

40 The qualifier *ecclesiologically* does important work here. As the opening paragraph of *LG* insists, it is Christ who is the light of the nations, while the church merely reflects his light to the world. Absolutely speaking, God alone is ultimate. But within an ecclesiological frame of reference, the one church of Christ is ultimate, and the Catholic Church penultimate.

41 Relatedly, only the Catholic Church has continued to hold ecumenical councils and to define doctrine after 1054. One could, of course, assess this with opprobrium as hubris. One could also, though, recognize in it the Catholic Church acting according to its own self-understanding, just as the other churches who have *not* done so have acted in accordance with their own. As we shall see in the next chapter, we shall all need to make peace with our various pasts, and merely insisting that others shouldn't have taken the paths they have will not get us very far.

themselves to be the church. Their involvement in the ecumenical movement from its earliest days indicates that they do not necessarily mean to exclude others in so doing. In this self-identification, the Orthodox are not wrong, for they *are* church, even if this is not the whole story. Moreover, in general no Protestant body makes any such unique claim for itself. One or another may proffer themselves as more authentic expressions of church than others, but none make quite so grand a claim as to be the communion wherein the church and its unity subsists. In other words, these other claims and self-understandings can stand, unaffected by the Catholic Church's claim.

The only claims that the Catholic Church makes that do impinge upon those made by other churches would be to deny that other churches are indeed church. For this, repentance is in order. And in this repentance, the Catholic Church would be ushered into an even fuller expression of its life in Christ, a point to which we shall return. But there is nothing inherent in the notion of the *subsistit in* that would require making the further claim of denying ecclesial status to other churches. In other words, the Catholic Church can maintain this self-understanding while the other churches maintain their own. Nothing prevents all of these self-understandings from being honored and affirmed.

And, in fact, while its official policy remains one of nonrecognition, the Catholic Church's performance often tends to recognize the status of other churches. The most famous example would be Pope Paul VI's greeting of then Archbishop of Canterbury Michael Ramsey and giving the Anglican prelate the pope's own episcopal ring. While not an official judgment that this was a fellow bishop of a true church, it indicates at least some recognition that Ramsey was not a cosplaying layperson overseeing a community that was simply *not-church*.

While it may chafe some to hear the Catholic Church self-apply the label, two facts bear consideration: (1) there is an exigency for the church to subsist somewhere, as I've articulated above, and (2) as I've just noted, no other church displays this self-understanding. Is it, then, unthinkable that this necessary feature characterize the one church that actually makes this claim for itself? No particular church is ultimate. The most any can claim for itself is penultimacy. So what if we recognize that penultimacy in Rome, with an antepenultimacy (or some other position) for ourselves? Are we really so insistent on being at the front of the queue?

And yet, with this affirmation, the whole story is not told, for there remains a certain incompleteness to even the Catholic Church in which subsists the one church of Christ. This incompleteness is not a lack of any of the means of salvation or elements of the church. They are found in a unique fullness in the communion of the churches in communion with the see of Peter. Nevertheless, this fullness remains wounded unless and until the full complement of those who belong to Christ are gathered together into one. To the extent that the Catholic Church, or any other church, holds itself back from being gathered together with all the rest, it suffers from self-inflicted wounds.

An Anglican Corrective

Michael Ramsey provides a helpful analogy. In his classic *The Gospel and the Catholic Church*, Ramsey articulates a vision of church order and liturgical and sacramental life as giving expression to and existing at the service of the inner reality of a community that shares in the gospel of Christ's death and resurrection—the law of the cross.[42] It is on these grounds that Ramsey argues, forcefully, that the episcopal office is essential to the church, because it affords expression of this union of all with all in Christ.[43] And yet, this insistence on the episcopacy cannot lead into chauvinism or triumphalism, for when the church is divided, the purpose of the episcopal office is undercut. Even those churches who retain the episcopacy retain it in a "maimed" form, with the result that "all Christians need the restoration of the one Episcopate," even those churches that have retained episcopal government.[44] I want to suggest that the Catholic Church has a stake in recognizing this about itself as well, and that doing so, far from threatening its self-understanding as that communion wherein the church of Christ subsists, is the proper conclusion drawn from that affirmation.

The position that the episcopate gives expression to and facilitates the communion of local churches is a mainstream principle of catholic ecclesiology, shared by Anglicans, Orthodox, and Catholics, and, so, uncontroversial at

---

42 Ramsey, *Gospel and Catholic Church*, 55–67.

43 Ramsey, *Gospel and Catholic Church*, 68–85. See further Rowan Williams, "The Lutheran Catholic," in *Glory Descending: Michael Ramsey and His Writings*, ed. Douglas Dales et al. (Grand Rapids: Eerdmans, 2005), 211–22.

44 Ramsey, *Gospel and Catholic Church*, 223. Douglas Dales, "'One Body'—the Ecclesiology of Michael Ramsey," in Dales et al., *Glory Descending*, 227; Louis Weil, "The Liturgy in Michael Ramsey's Theology," in *Michael Ramsey as Theologian*, ed. Robin Gill and Lorna Kendall (London: Darton, Longman, & Todd, 1995), 146–47.

this juncture.[45] When we consider the facts on the ground, it would seem that Ramsey's further application is also warranted, for even if there is a fullness to the communion of the Catholic Church's episcopal college, in union with its head the bishop of Rome, still there are true particular churches not in communion with this college.[46] Even if the Orthodox churches are the *only* such churches considered to be truly church—a conclusion I do not accept—this nettle remains. In this state of division, the episcopate's purpose is not fully expressed or realized, and not just because the union of all with all in Christ is not realized (though we ought to keep that vision before us), but because true churches are alienated from one another. The church is not whole.

Moving beyond this almost syllogistic analysis, we can note that, up to a point, this understanding is also expressed by the Catholic Church's magisterium. Some of the most striking statements to this effect come from the ordinary papal magisterium of John Paul II, who described the separation of the Eastern and Western as a situation of being bereft of a lung.[47] Just as a person may live with just one of their lungs, the church subsists in the Catholic Church, but such is not a healthy state of affairs. Less viscerally, statements from the extraordinary magisterium, which carry greater weight than such papal pronouncements as these, bear out the basic principle.

Returning to *Lumen Gentium*, several statements move us in this direction. To begin, the claim of a unique subsistence is made in the context and for the sake of affirming the "elements of sanctification and truth," which themselves are "proper gifts to the church of Christ" found beyond the structure of the Catholic Church, and that the presence of these elements of the church "impel towards Catholic unity."[48] While this could be read as if these elements are meant to lead the separated siblings back to the Catholic Church, such a reading is incompatible with other statements from the council, which, it is generally recognized, turned away from an ecumenism of return. Later, in

---

45 The question of the historic episcopate has been an ecumenical stumbling block. Nevertheless, the WCC's landmark document *Baptism, Eucharist and Ministry* (Geneva: WCC, 1982) suggests that its long-established character warrants a particular consideration of its prospects as a means of fostering and expressing unity, even as it gestured towards a wider variation in how *episkopé* might be expressed.

46 CDF, *Dominus Iesus*, no. 17.

47 E.g., John Paul II, Ut Unum Sint: *On Commitment to Ecumenism* (Vatican website, May 25, 1995), no. 54.

48 *LG*, no. 8 [Tanner, 2:854]. The fullest exposition of this theme is Arenas, *Fading Frontiers?*

no. 15, the constitution provides a nonexhaustive account of these elements found in the separated churches and ecclesial communities, recognizing their salvific import, before exhorting the Catholic faithful "to purification and renewal so that the sign of Christ may shine more clearly over the face of the church."[49] Muted as it is, taken in the context of considering divisions and imperfect communion, this call implies that so long as the separated siblings remain separate, the fullness of catholic beauty is not clearly discernible in the life of the Catholic Church.

In the Decree on Ecumenism, the statements become more pointed. While insisting that the unity Christ wills for the church "subsists in the catholic church as something she can never lose," the decree makes a sharp, though undefined, distinction between individuals who enter into full communion with the Catholic Church and the work of ecumenism, thereby explicitly ruling out an ecumenism of return.[50] While entry into the Catholic Church is not opposed to ecumenism, they are distinct precisely because of their telos. The former terminates in the Catholic Church, while the latter is ordered to the wider reality of the one church of Christ, which may subsist in, but is not coextensive with, the Catholic Church. There follow similar statements to those of *Lumen Gentium* to the effect that the Catholic faithful's prime directive is to the renewal of the Catholic Church so that its obscured splendor can more readily be discerned.[51]

In its next movement, though, the decree turns to a consideration of the elements of the church found among the separated Christians. Here, not only are they "acknowledge[d]," but also "esteem[ed]," as something provoking "wonder," and capable of building up the Catholic faithful and "bring[ing] a deeper realization of the mystery of Christ and the church."[52] With these statements, we move beyond the mere concession of *elementa ecclesiæ* to a recognition that they can make a positive and enriching contribution to the life of the Catholic Church. This recognition leads to a final observation:

> The divisions among Christians prevent the church from realizing in practice the fullness of catholicity proper to her, in those of her [children] who, though attached to her by baptism, are yet separated from full communion with her. Furthermore, the church herself finds it more difficult to express in actual life her full catholicity in all its bearings.[53]

---

49 *LG*, no. 15 [Tanner, 2:860–61]
50 *UR*, no. 4 [Tanner, 2:911].
51 *UR*, no. 4 [Tanner, 2:911].
52 *UR*, no. 4 [Tanner, 2:912].
53 *UR*, no. 4 [Tanner, 2:912]. My modification.

Hence, even as the one church of Christ subsists in the Catholic Church, it is held back from a full realization and expression of this subsistent catholicity so long as its communion does not fully include all those who are Christ's own.

In a certain measured sense, then, the perspective afforded by the 1920 Lambeth Conference provides a necessary expansion to the Catholic Church's *subsistit in*. While the Catholic Church lacks nothing that it needs to be church, nevertheless, it suffers and is held back from the full realization of its vocation and mission by virtue of its lack of communion with the other churches. Its catholicity lacks nothing that it needs to be itself, yet also stands in need of enrichment from sibling churches and communities. This impetus is behind Lambeth's vision of the church as the union of all the baptized with one another and Christ. The one church of Christ subsists in the Catholic Church, but not in such a way that it does not need the other churches.

In their divisions, all of the churches have continued to operate according to their self-understandings. We shall return to this in greater force in chapter 5, but at this juncture it bears some consideration. By maintaining their liturgical and sacramental lives, their missionary work, their pastoral care and communion, all the churches have continued to operate according to the understanding that they truly are church. Meanwhile, the Catholic Church has been alone in its continuing to define doctrine, principally through continuing to hold ecumenical councils, but also more recently by *ex cathedra* definitions from the pope. This continuation evinces once more, the self-understanding of the *subsistit in*. And the noncontinuation in other churches, their conviction that they cannot hold ecumenical councils in the present divided state of the church, evinces their own self-understandings. To anticipate the discussion in chapter 5, non-Catholics might protest that the Catholic Church's actions in this regard exhibit hubris and should not be undertaken. But we must still reckon with the fact that the Catholic Church *has* operated in this way. The task is not to try to undo the past, but to find a way forward from where we presently find ourselves. By the same token, the Catholic Church can be invited to recognize that while, according to its self-understanding, it has indeed been able to act in this manner, even without the rest, its decisions and definitions are marked by an incompleteness. Bereft of a lung, it has continued to utter definitive teaching, but it has done so with a wheeze.

Above, I said that Lambeth's perspective is needed as a corrective "in a certain measured sense," because even in this recognition there is a testimony to the reality of the *subsistit in*. As we have seen, in principle, the Catholic Church has all it needs for an affirmation of the doctrine that it stands in relation to a reality wider than itself and, in some sense, in need of all the other churches in order to realize that unity which nevertheless subsists in its communion. Yet, while the Catholic Church lacks nothing that it needs to make this affirmation, in practice it has done so in only muted, tenuous manners, failing to fully enact the faith it professes. And precisely to the extent that the Catholic Church refuses to embrace these estranged sibling churches, or even to recognize their legitimate claim to that embrace, it fails to embody the gospel and stands in need of repentance.

Further Failures to Reckon with Provisionality

Here the complex legacy of the so-called Uniate churches and the more recent formation of personal ordinariates for the reception of groups of Anglicans into full communion with the Catholic Church bear a painful witness to the tenuousness of the Catholic Church's grasp of its own limitation. Our treatment of uniatism and the ordinariates shall be brief because the Catholic Church has disavowed the former as a form of ecumenical engagement and has never intended the latter as such.[54] Nevertheless, both display something of a Rome-centric tendency that the Catholic Church has yet to fully overcome.

---

54 On "Uniatism" see Joint International Commission for Theological Dialogue between the Catholic Church and the Orthodox Church, "Uniatism, Method of Union of the Past, and the Present Search for Full Communion [The Balamand Document]" (Vatican website, June 23, 1993). See further Anton Houtepen, "Uniatism and Models of Unity in the Ecumenical Movement," in *Four Hundred Years Union of Brest (1596–1996): A Critical Re-evaluation; Acta of the Congress Held at Hernen Castle, the Netherlands, in March 1996*, ed. Bert Groen and Wil van den Bercken (Leuven: Peeters, 1998), 239–60; Georgi Zyablitsev, "Uniatism as an Ecclesiological Problem Today," in Groen and Bercken, *Four Hundred Years*, 193–99; Johan Meijer, "Greek Catholics Today: How Does It Feel to Live at the Border between East and West?," in Groen and Bercken, *Four Hundred Years*, 173–82. On the ordinariates, see Benedict XVI, Anglicanorum Coetibus: *Providing for Personal Ordinariates for Anglicans Entering into Full Communion with the Catholic Church* (Vatican website, November 4, 2009); Norman Doe, "The Apostolic Constitution Anglicanorum Coetibus: An Anglican Juridical Perspective," *One in Christ* 44, no. 1 (2010): 23–48; Duane L. C. M. Galles, "Anglicanorum Coetibus—Some Canonical Investigations on the Recent Apostolic Constitution," *Jurist: Studies in Church Order & Ministry* 71, no. 1 (2011): 201–33; J. A. Arnold, "Anglicanorum Coetibus: Generous Offer or Aggressive Attack? A Problem of Ecclesiology," *One in Christ* 44, no. 1 (2010): 56–66; James Bradley, "Increase in Wisdom and Stature: Personal Ordinariates from Benedict XVI to Francis," *Jurist: Studies in Church Order & Ministry* 77, no. 1 (2021): 49–72; Przemysław Jan Kantyka, "Ten Years of Ordinariates for Anglicans—a Few Reflections on the New Ecclesiological Model," *Studia Oecumenica* 19 (2019): 7–18.

"Uniatism"

In chapter 2 we briefly surveyed the division of the eastern and western churches. Over the centuries, several Eastern churches whose communion with the Catholic Church was disrupted have either renewed or reaffirmed their communion with Rome. Some of these churches, like the Chaldean Catholic Church, stemmed from earlier divisions surrounding the fifth-century christological controversies, but most separated from the Western church along with the bulk of the Eastern churches in 1054. Others, like the Maronite Church, are regarded as never having entered schism from Rome and reaffirmed their union in the twelfth century, but for most decisions made at the Council of Florence (1431–1449) and in the Union of Brest (1595) are particular watersheds, where, after centuries of division, renewed communion was enacted.[55] At present some twenty-three Eastern churches are in full communion with the Catholic Church.

On the one hand, those Eastern churches that have entered into full communion with the church of Rome are to be celebrated. Any gathering together of Christians, any realization of unity is the result of divine grace and is to be lauded. Unity shall be found by venturing forward together, not by relitigating the past, which cannot be undone anyway. Moreover, these Eastern churches enrich the liturgical diversity of the Catholic Church, moving it at least somewhat beyond Roman provincialism to a recognition that there is more to the Catholic Church than its Latin heritage.[56] Yet, on the other hand, in actual practice, the Eastern Catholic churches have often not been regarded as full and equal sibling churches. They have been subject to Latinization, faced ritual discrimination, and been regarded as inferior to the Latin rite's churches. Moreover, the entry of these churches into full communion with Rome came at the cost of division from their mother churches, and under

---

55 For the history see Oskar Halecki, *From Florence to Brest (1439–1596)* (New York: Fordham University Press, 1958); Andriy Chirovsky, "The 1596 Union of Brest: How the Ukrainian Church Rejoined the Catholic Communion," *The Australasian Catholic Record* 76, no. 3 (1999): 318–27; Laurent Tatarenko, "La Naissance de l'Union de Brest: La Curie Romaine et Le Tournant de l'année 1595," *Cahiers Du Monde Russe* 46, nos. 1–2 (2005): 345–54.

56 This bore particular fruit at the Second Vatican Council, where the Melkites led the charge in asserting the equal dignity of Eastern Churches; Becker, "History of the Decree [on Ecumenism]," 11–14. This dignity was codified in the Decree on the Eastern Catholic Churches, *Orientalium Ecclesiarum* (November 21, 1964) [Tanner, 2:900–7]. Yet, it was a long, painful road to reach this point.

some measure of political duress, with the carrot of Western aid against encroachments from the Ottoman empire held out as a goad toward union.[57]

Of course, it is easy enough, after a century of ecumenism, to recognize the flaws in how this reunion occurred, as the Catholic Church itself has done (after Vatican II, the dignity of the Eastern Catholic Churches is respected to a far higher degree than it has in the past, even though they are still subject to a certain erasure, so long as "Catholic" is treated as synonymous with "Roman"). So my raising the point is not to scold, nor to call for a change. As we shall see in chapter 5, historical change is irreversible. It's not for us to attempt to undo the past, but rather to endeavor to act faithfully in the present that we've inherited from it. Nevertheless, in this history we can discern tendencies that remain in place even after the Catholic Church's ecumenical turn. The much lamented "ecumenical winter" testifies to something of an impasse. No one, including the Catholic Church, seems willing to give any ground, no matter how much consensus is achieved. The prospect of a radical transformation resulting from a deepened conversion to Christ and resultant convergence of those who belong to him seems not to find many takers.

Ordinariates

Similar tendencies are discernible in the Anglican Ordinariates, by which Pope Benedict XVI, building on precedents established by Pope John Paul II, allowed for groups of Anglicans to enter into communion with the Catholic Church, while retaining certain elements of their cultural and liturgical heritage. Unable to countenance the ordination of women first to the priesthood and then to the episcopate or the growing inclusion of LGBTQ persons and relationships within the Anglican Communion—a theme we surveyed in the last chapter—certain Anglicans appealed to the pope to accommodate their entry into the Catholic Church, a request he obliged.[58] Crucially, this was not an ecumenical overture, but rather a pastoral provision, a fact symbolized by the Ordinariates' being under the oversight of the Congregation for the Doctrine of the Faith and not the Pontifical Council for Promoting Christian Unity.

---

57 Meijer, "Greek Catholics Today: How Does It Feel to Live at the Border Between East and West?"; Michael Hrynchyshyn, "The Current Situation of the Greek Catholic Church in Ukraine," in Groen and Bercken, *Four Hundred Years*, 163–72.

58 Benedict XVI, *Anglicanorum Coetibus*.

As a result, the Ordinariate is marked by several starkly unecumenical features, though to criticize it for this is to miss the point. Ecumenism was not the aim. Former Anglican clergy may serve as Catholic priests, but to do so, they must be reordained, as their former ministries are judged invalid by the Catholic Church at present. And rather tighter control is exercised by the CDF over the ordinariate, which functions not as a particular church, but as an entity "juridically comparable to a diocese."[59] Its ordinary exercises a power that is ordinary, *vicarious*, and personal,[60] as opposed to the power of a bishop, which is "proper, ordinary, and immediate."[61] In all cases, rather than a reunion of particular churches (the Ordinariate proceeds as if Anglican churches are not churches at all), the ordinariate is a matter of the pope's personal discretion and pastoral accommodation within the Latin rite of the Catholic Church. None of this is to find fault with the Ordinariate, nor those who have entered the Catholic Church through it (except to the extent the former trades upon a nonrecognition of Anglicanism's status as church, and the latter at least implicitly join in this repudiation of Anglican ecclesiality). The ecumenical way forward lies along a different path. But the episode illustrates that the gravitational pull of the Catholic Church's self-understanding (as that communion within with the church of Christ subsists) is so strong that escape velocities are rarely reached. Despite knowing better, the Catholic Church's actual policy seems to be consistently one of Roman assimilation.

A Counterexample: United Churches

By way of contrast, consider the phenomenon of the united churches of the early twentieth-century. Examples could be multiplied, but the one I find most inspiring, challenging, and exemplary on this front is the Church of South India, in part because of the risk hazarded and the transformation undergone by all parties in the venture. In 1947, after decades of negotiations and preparations, a new church was formed as the South India United Church (itself the result of a merger between Congregational and Presbyterian churches); dioceses from the Anglican Church of India, Burma, Pakistan, and Ceylon; and the Methodist Church of South India entered into full communion with

---

59 Benedict XVI, *Anglicanorum Coetibus*, I§3.
60 Benedict XVI, *Anglicanorum Coetibus*, V.
61 *LG*, no. 27 [Tanner, 2:871].

each other.[62] The result was a church that was not any of its precursors being absorbed into the others, but the striking out on a new joint venture.

The CSI is governed by the historic episcopate, receiving its succession through the Anglican bishops involved in its founding. Yet it was formed in such a way as to not require the repudiation of the former ministries of its clergy. In other words, all clergy that the CSI ordains are ordained by bishops in apostolic succession, but those clergy who entered it from other churches were not reordained. As a result, while it required a certain patience and forbearance, within a generation, the CSI's ministries were folded into the historic episcopate, a model that has borne fruit elsewhere in ecumenical efforts.[63] All parties underwent transformation in this encounter. This was a merger, but not absorption, nor a return ecumenism.

Christ beckons all the churches forward toward such a transformation, though as chapter 5 will argue, our transformation need not involve mergers. The Catholic Church's self-understanding as that communion in which the one church of Christ subsists is true, yet its promise is only partially realized so long as we remain divided. The Catholic Church does not need the Anglican Communion, nor the Church of South India, nor any other church or ecclesial communion to realize this about itself and to act accordingly. And yet, in practice, it has proven to be a difficult teaching, hard to hear, only haltingly embraced. In contrast to the Catholic Church's performative Roman exclusivism, the witness of the 1920 Lambeth Conference can serve as a goad enabling the it to more fully appropriate its own identity and vocation. In contrast to the unidirectionality of uniatism and ordinariates, the

---

62 See, e.g., Lesslie Newbigin, *The Reunion of the Church: A Defence of the South India Scheme*, rev. ed. (Westport, CT: Greenwood, 1960); Episcopal Church, ed., *Empty Shoes: A Study of the Church of South India* (New York: National Council, Protestant Episcopal Church, 1956); Arthur Michael Hollis, *The Significance of South India* (Richmond, VA: J. Knox, 1966); Dyron B Daughrity, "South India: Ecumenism's One Solid Achievement? Reflections on the History of the Ecumenical Movement," *International Review of Mission* 99, no. 1 (2010): 56–68; Mark T. B. Laing, "The International Impact of the Formation of the Church of South India: Bishop Newbigin versus the Anglican Fathers," *International Bulletin of Missionary Research* 33, no. 1 (2009): 18.

63 Perhaps the most notable instance is formation of the Porvoo Communion, among European Anglicans and Lutherans in 1992. "The Porvoo Statement in English" (Porvoo Communion website, October 9, 1992). Also notable is the intercommunion agreement reached by the Episcopal Church and the Evangelical Lutheran Church of America in 1999. "Agreement of Full Communion—Called to Common Mission" (Episcopal Church website, 1999).

CSI presents an alternative vision of convergence: not by return but by joint venture. Hence, we see the elements of sanctification found in the separated churches belong to and impel toward catholic unity, even if they are resisted.

The only viable form of church unity will affirm the ecclesial reality of the partner churches. While this exigence for recognition and affirmation applies to all churches, the Catholic Church in particular must be called to it, for it has struggled mightily to do so. The unity of the church will be a unity of churches, not merely a unity within the Roman Church. The Lambeth vision calls us beyond any particular church to the whole. And ecumenism calls us to recognize that we are called to unity not as so many individuals but precisely as churches.[64] If the ecumenical partners are not churches, then there is no impetus to unity other than an ecumenism of return. But it is the reconciliation of these communities as communities to which we are called. The alternative would be to resort to a one true church ecclesiology that falters on theological and historical grounds. It falters historically, because as we have seen, such an original pristine unity has never existed. Theologically, it falls short because it fails to reckon with (1) an ecclesiology of communion, wherein the universal church exists in and through the particular churches in their communion with each other; (2) ecclesiology's theological core, the union of all the baptized with Christ, and the recognition that this union with Christ is communally expressed and mediated; and, finally (3) the Catholic Church's own self-understanding as that church wherein the one church subsists, but not the sole expression of church. Our final chapter shall consider the complexity of such communities, with their distinctive patterns of life and historical paths, entering into a mutual embrace.

CONCLUSION: THE WHOLE AND THE FRAGMENTS

To embrace this vision is to live by the law of the cross and, thereby, to live in accordance with the Eucharist. It is an invitation for all churches to kenosis, to recognizing that whatever stature they have is not their own, but is to be

---

64 This also coheres with the logic of *LG*, no. 9: "At all times and in every nation whoever fears God and does what is right is acceptable to God. . . . It has pleased God, however, to sanctify and save [people] individually and without regard to what binds them together, but to set them up as a people who would acknowledge him in truth and serve him in holiness" (Tanner, 2:855). My modification.

put at the service of all (Phil 2:5–11). It is to acquiesce to the gesture of love whereby Christ stretched out his arms in order to embrace all in his own body.

When churches divide, they move themselves further from their vocation to be the church, the community of the gospel. Dividing Christians, through these refusals of love, deform their own communities. While, as we shall see in the next, final chapter, over time, these deformities may heal, for God is faithful, even when we are faithless; nevertheless, the founding schismatic act scarifies the body, leaving its mark, a wound not fully healed.

The Gospel of John, famously, does not include an explicit account of the Eucharist, though Christ's bread of life discourse clearly trades in eucharistic themes and imagery. This discourse, within which Christ announces that his flesh is given as true food and his blood as true drink for the life of the world, that any who eat his flesh and drink his blood will abide in him and be raised up on the last day, is preceded by an account of Jesus feeding five thousand people (John 6:1–14).[65] At the end of that feeding episode, Christ directs the apostles to gather up the fragments so that nothing will be lost (John 6:12).

Any would-be apostolic church must also embody this apostolic vocation and gather together the scattered fragments of Christ's body. Those who would point to their own sense of apostolicity as an excuse for refraining from this gathering—as if they do not need the others, or as if apostolicity is a status, rather than a task, such that they can merely wait for the others to "return"— betray their apostolic identity and vocation. Those who would impatiently "compel them to come in," exchanging the law of the cross's forbearance for the coercion of a crucifying unity, only further rend and scarify the flesh of Christ. Those who doubt that this gathering can occur cast themselves in the role of the doubting apostles, who were persuaded that Jesus's command to give the crowd something to eat could not be fulfilled (John 6:7–9). It is a posture of forgetfulness of to whom we belong, whom we follow, and whose body we are. And yet, in that original episode, the apostles' confusion and doubt did not prevent the Lord from feeding his own.

Chapter 2 ended with a reflection on the eucharistic fraction, whereby the celebrant breaks the host that is Christ's body, both for the purposes of allowing the many to share in this one body, and to underscore the sacrificial overtones of Christ's redemptive act. We noted that while the body of Christ is not actually broken by the fraction, we do indeed rend it by our divisions

---

65 Their seeking after another miraculous feeding seems to be the occasion for Jesus's identifying himself as the true bread (e.g., John 6:26–34).

from one another and our refusals of charity. We can now venture beyond this sobering recognition.

It is customary, after the fraction, for the celebrant to place the fragmented host back together, and elevate it with the chalice. In that elevation, the fissure of the fraction is visible. That the host has been divided is evident. This ritual action serves as its own parable and prolepsis.

Despite everything, the pieces will be gathered. Christ's body will be made whole. The marks and memory of our divisions will not be effaced in this union. The risen Christ still bears the wounds of his passion, but they no longer mar him. These are scars rendered glorious. We too shall be healed and whole, but the wounds of our division shall not be erased, cannot be erased, for history cannot be undone.

When the priest raises the reassembled host, he announces, "Behold the Lamb of God; behold him who takes away the sins of the world. Blessed are those called to the supper of the lamb."

History cannot be undone. But it can be borne, and must be traversed. It will, ultimately, be transcended, and consummated. Here and now the banquet has begun, if we would but have ears to hear the summons, and respond to the one who calls us and bids us be one. Our traversal and bearing of this history in hope of its consummation shall be the topic of our next, final chapter.

CHAPTER FIVE

Divided to the End? Obstacles to Unity

The parents have eaten sour grapes, and the children's teeth are set on edge.

Ezekiel 18:2b

In our sins we have been a long time, and shall we be saved?

Isaiah 64:5 (ESV)

The unity the churches seek is a full, visible unity, one that will embrace all Christian communities in a single, though diverse and differentiated communion. Until that communion is composed of all the baptized, we fall short of the goal at which the ecumenical movement aims, the purpose for which Christ came into the world, the intention for which he prayed. As the churches work toward this all-embracing unity, we face two primary obstacles: ourselves and our histories. This chapter considers each in turn.

AGREEMENT, DISAGREEMENT, AND THE EVASION OF AGENCY

The churches' divisions are the result of human decisions. No impersonal or external law has separated us from each other. Rather, we have. Division is a problem of the will. Our first two chapters established this. Unity is a matter not of agreement but of charity. The original unity of the church, such as it was, was a matter of considerable diversity, and not just of diversity, but of disagreement, even disfunction. The idea of a pristine unity wherein all agreed on Christian belief or practice is a projection, an assumption imposed upon a now-distant past, rather than anything that can actually be affirmed to have existed.

Unity's foundation is in the embrace of Christ, who loved us while we were still at enmity with each other and with God. In this embrace no uniformity or agreement can be discerned. Ontologically, the parties involved are disparate, even infinitely so: God becomes human in order to reconcile humans to God. Morally, we are reconciled not because we conform to, but precisely in our variance from God and the good order of God's universe. Epistemically, we are darkened in our understanding, given to suppressing the truth in unrighteousness (Rom 1:18–21; Eph 4:18). It is not sameness or agreement, but love that makes the church to be one. And this oneness does not lead variance, estrangement, enmity to disappear, as the witness of the New Testament and the data of history attest.

When the church was "united," it was the site of contestation, dispute, and polemic, but the conflicted parties remained bound together within the community. Their variance notwithstanding, they belonged to each other. Divisions occur when conflicted parties decide they are no longer in communion with each other. As we have seen, the presenting causes for division have not been matters that required the division of the church.[1] Retrospective investigations have demonstrated this, as our considerations of the East-West schism and the Reformation divisions have borne out. Divergent understandings of the Holy Spirit's procession, or of the pope's authority and jurisdiction, or of justification can be embraced in the communion of the one church, even if at present they are not. We know this, because for at least *some* time they were. The divisions were actions taken subsequent to contestation over the disagreement. The parties in question first disagreed and then divided, rather than being divided by those disagreements, ipso facto. Moreover, the churches have clarified that their disagreements on these matters are not actually church dividing. Thus, they may have been the presenting occasion for divisions, but they are not, properly speaking, those divisions' causes.

Similarly, more recent divisions over sexuality are by no means required. Christians who embrace their LGTBQ siblings (or their own queer selves) can

---

1 I have consistently placed the boundary of Christian recognition with Nicaea. If this boundary is agreed upon, it means that divisions across the line of Nicene orthodoxy are not divisions of the church. Some may contest this boundary, but in placing it thus, I reason in accordance with my own tradition's Chicago-Lambeth Quadrilateral. See also Fries and Rahner, *Unity of the Churches*.

be in communion with Christians who do not, and vice versa. Intrachurch, the Communion Partners remain within the Episcopal Church. Interchurch, while some provinces of the Anglican Communion that reject same-sex marriage have broken communion with those who practice it, not all have. Hence, such communion must be possible, because it is actual, even if, at times contested and fragile. Even those who lack sympathy for my arguments regarding LGBTQ flourishing in the church must reckon with the fact that the embrace of queer Christians preceded the breaking of communion over this embrace. The division was a matter of decision, not some automatic, impersonal force decoupled from human will and action. Even if contemporary schismatics think they are right to have separated from affirming churches, they must still admit that they have indeed made the decision to act upon this judgment.

Division, then, as I've argued consistently, stems from a refusal of charity. The "reason" we are divided from each other is that we have chosen to be divided. Accordingly, the reason we remain divided is that we have not chosen to end our divisions. As we shall see below, there is considerably more to say than just this. However, unless we reckon with it, we'll continue to misunderstand the problem of division. Human decisions have divided us. Similarly, when divided Christians enter into new communion with each other, they do so through human decisions (assisted by divine grace, no doubt, but human decisions still).[2] Should the Christian churches ever be fully united again, it will be because they have decided to be. Unity is not so much a state as it is an action: the determination to be united.

Hence, no amount of variance can suffice to divide Christians from each other, because the unity of the church has always been a unity encompassing diversity. An ecclesiology of agreement is untenable, not just because it remains ever elusive in the present moment, not just because it could only ever be fragile and tenuous, needing only fresh disagreement to be sundered,[3] but primarily because it misconstrues the nature of the church and its unity. The church's unity has never been thus. And, so, to insist on an agreement-based unity is to insist upon a lost cause, the pursuit of a mirage. So long as we believe that such a notion of unity corresponds to any actual thing and not merely a preconceived ideal, unity will forever elude us.

---

2 See Anne M. Carpenter's discussion of the distinguishable, but inseparable quality of the natural and supernatural in human history. *Nothing Gained Is Eternal: A Theology of Tradition* (Minneapolis: Fortress Press, 2022), 38–67.

3 Radner, *End of the Church*, 170; Jenson, *Unbaptized God*, 1–8.

It will, moreover, serve to conceal our own responsibility and agency. All we need to agree upon to be in communion with each other is that we shall be in communion with each other. Christians are the principal obstacle to the churches' unity, because the only thing keeping us divided is our determination to remain so. Pointing to disagreement obscures this, mendaciously suggesting that we are rendered passive, helpless, and unresponsible and unresponsive by the fact that we disagree, and in this way providing cover for our avoidance of taking action to be unified. This parallels the problems uncovered by Barbara Fields and Karen Fields in their study of race making and racism, wherein race, which is a fiction, serves to conceal the activity of racists. Race does not do anything. It cannot, it is a mere concept, which only functions as real because human agents act as if it is real. Instead, it is these human beings who do things, and their doing is hidden behind the cloak of race: *pay no attention to the man behind the curtain.*[4] In a similar way, our disagreements do nothing, and could never divide the church. Only Christians can do that. And when we decide to do so, we must take ownership of it, not pawning off the blame away from our agency and onto mere concepts. Disagreement is a red herring; agreement a MacGuffin.

THE WEIGHT OF HISTORY

Our divisions are caused by our failures of charity. Such has been this book's consistent refrain. Yet this does not tell the whole story. Though Christians divide from each other through a lack of love, still-divided Christians love each other, yet remain divided. True, our charity remains incomplete, not least because it falls short of an all-encompassing solidarity. Nevertheless, among the fruits of the ecumenical movement is a renewed regard for those siblings in Christ from whom we are divided. However imperfectly, we do love each other across the ecumenical divide. And it is precisely this love that drives us on to seek unity's restoration, for this is charity's function: to bind us to one another as one body in Christ. So, if we do indeed love each other, and yet remain divided, there must be more to consider.

As we shall note repeatedly, there is a difference between dividing Christians and already-divided Christians. At the time of their enactment, our

---

4 Fields and Fields, *Racecraft*, 120–48. See further Carpenter, *Nothing Gained Is Eternal*, 27–29, 72.

divisions were and are a matter of refusing to remain in communion with others. For centuries after their enactment, the churches looked askance at each other, calling into question the fidelity of those from whom they were divided. In general, though, this animosity simply no longer characterizes the churches' views of one another.[5] A certain measure of love has been restored, but this love has not restored unity. To an extent this remains a failure of charity. We love each other, but not enough to cleave to one another in full visible communion. But to leave it at that is to miss a key insight. To risk a tautology, we remain divided because we are divided.

On the one hand, the sole barrier to unity is in the will. We *could* simply decide to embrace each other in the bonds of charity and communion. Yet, despite the truth of this affirmation, it fails to reckon with the weight of history. We remain divided because we are divided. We are divided because we have been divided. In his landmark study on Christian division, Yves Congar observed this, noting that

> the worst thing is that the separations have lasted and that their very persistence has become not only a matter of habit and fact but a new motive for separate life. We have got into the way of living without each other, and in opposition to each other, as parallel lines of Christianity which never meet. . . . The mere fact of not being on terms has become a fresh motive, and often the most prominent one, for remaining apart.[6]

---

5 There are exceptions, of course. For instance, sizable Lutheran denominations have eschewed the *JDDJ*, viewing it as a betrayal of Lutheran conviction, and, so, of the gospel. Examples could be multiplied, but to no purpose. If the 1920 Lambeth Conference–informed vision I'm arguing for here is correct, then *any* Christians who are not united to the rest represent a failure of unity. Nevertheless, I leave these outliers to the side in what follows because they are a distinct issue from the one I am pursuing. The fact remains that even where charity *has* been restored, it has not sufficed to restore unity. The problem of ecumenical outliers lies downstream from the ecumenical mainstream where enmity is more or less put to paid. Conversely, though, note Ephraim Radner's observation that this ecumenical development can serve to blunt the pain of division: "It was generally claimed (and still is) that individual churches in their plurality are defined by what is ecclesially good and obedient, if incomplete or limited, not by what is disobedient and sinful. Everybody gets a prize, for each separated church carries a special 'charism' that complements the others, and hence ecclesial distinctiveness (and to this degree the separations that upheld them) is a good." *A Brutal Unity*, 137. Moving away from enmity is unquestionably a move in the right direction, but pain serves a medically important function, and we must be careful not to apply such balms in such a way as to subvert that function.

6 Congar, *Divided Christendom*, 24.

Since then it has become something of an ecumenical truism to note that disagreements that would not have led to the division of the church are apparently grave enough to maintain those divisions once they are enacted.[7] This, once more, ought to alert us to the need to look beyond our disagreements to ourselves if we would understand the "reason" for our divisions, but here I make a different point. However much we might wish for unity, the fact of division represents its own obstacle, because every Christian living today has inherited a divided church, and in such a state of affairs, the only possible way to be Christian is to be a Christian who is divided from others.[8]

To be in communion with one group, or even to move into a church wherein one would be in communion with *more* Christians, or even to move into a church that one believes more fully approaches the fullness of the church, even to the point that the one church subsists in it, is still to not be in communion with some other Christians. As Ephraim Radner puts it,

> The communion of the church, as we have it in our control, is already broken; it has been broken for many centuries; its fragments are no longer amenable to further breakage. One cannot excommunicate the already excommunicated. The Christian world is populated by the excommunicated. Who is a Christian today, but one who is also an excommunicate? What we today call a communion within the Church, among any set of churches, is really the linkage of what is already broken, the gathering up and holding together of what is already torn apart...If a church, because of communion's long condition of being broken, cannot claim integrity, then it cannot withhold a communion it does not have. A divided church has no communion to withhold. It has no more choices. The fundamental call among churches today, any churches, can only be to abide mutually each other's brokenness.[9]

Put in terms of the theology of history with which we have been working, our actions are constrained by the premotion of our divisions. Synchronically, this is our starting point. When we move to a diachronic outlook, the effects compound.

While division is a matter of the will, we must reckon with how our wills are constrained by our histories of division, which exercise an inertial drag upon the will. It is not that we do not want unity; exceptions notwithstanding,

---

7 Jenson, *Unbaptized God*, 4. Also noted by Rinderknecht, *Mapping the Differentiated Consensus*, 1.

8 Yes, reunion remains a possibility, but its actualization would mean that the state of affairs no longer applies.

9 Radner, *Hope among the Fragments*, 75.

we're all working toward it. Instead, we're not sure how to handle our inherited histories. They exercise claims upon us and cannot simply be laid aside. Though couched in terms of an ecumenism of return, which was par for the Catholic course in the 1930s when he wrote, Yves Congar articulates the point well:

> What chiefly keeps our separated [siblings] from reincorporation with us in unity, over and above historic causes and accumulations of misunderstanding, bitterness and prejudice, is the fear that their religious values, those things which they hold most deeply and in which they realize their union with Christ, must be denied and sacrificed, left, so to speak, outside the door of the Church in which we invite them to reunite with us in God.[10]

In other words, beyond such factors as mutual suspicion, misunderstanding, grievances stemming from our troubled pasts, all of which we could probably classify as negatives, there are also positive values that we find ourselves bound to maintain. These too stem from our divided histories, and actually constitute the greater barrier to reunion. Misunderstandings and prejudice can be cleared up through dialogue. How to be reconciled to each other without betraying our own histories is far more difficult. What the quotation from Congar fails to grapple with is that this applies not just to separated siblings returning to Rome, but rather to all the churches as they move toward a fuller communion with each other. All of our histories must be reckoned with and be reckoned with without betrayal. A brief consideration of the dynamics of tradition can shed greater light and grant greater specificity to this still abstract conception.

Tradition as Indispensable

Each church is a living community, traversing history, and forging its own path along the way. As we saw in chapter 2, communities coalesce around shared meanings, and the church's constitutive meaning is the law of the cross. So, as the churches journey through history, we receive and then hand on (*tradere*) this gospel message, the law of the cross (the basic content of tradition).[11]

---

10 Congar, *Divided Christendom*, 40.

11 The basic theoretical basis I assume here is the one established by Carpenter in *Nothing Gained Is Eternal*. See also the precursors to Carpenter's work in Yves Congar, *Tradition and Traditions: An Historical and a Theological Essay* (New York: Macmillan, 1967); John Henry Newman, *An Essay on the Development of Christian Doctrine*, 6th ed (Notre Dame: University of Notre Dame Press, 1989).

In these histories we also receive and hand on patterns of devotion, of worship, of interpreting Scripture, of theological reasoning, of ordering communal life, all of which are related in varying ways to that gospel message: none of them are simply identical to the gospel, yet apart from such other *tradita*, there is no *tradere* of passing it on. The gospel always comes to us clothed in these other artifacts. They are the means by which we receive it, the means by which we live according to it, the means by which we pass it on.[12]

None of this constitutes a problem yet. These are simply necessary features of community existence, which is not to say that the Christian community couldn't exist without these precise features. True, there is a mainstream consensus that certain elements are indispensable for the church's life. Typically, this list would include the sacraments, especially baptism and the Eucharist; the Scriptures; the basics of the Nicene faith, even if not expressed in credal format; and a ministry of *episkopé*.[13] Churches vary in how they order these dimensions of life, with some insisting more strongly on certain elements than others, or insisting on certain forms of them to the exclusion of others.[14] But there is a widespread consensus that these *tradita*, however variously expressed, are so intwined with the *traditio* of the gospel that they cannot be dispensed with.[15] Not without exception, such *tradita* are construed as matters *de jure divino* (by divine law).

---

12 What I suggest here is closely related to, but still distinct from Congar's account of the "monuments of tradition" in *Tradition and Traditions*, 427–58. Among other things, Congar's account needs further development along the lines of the historically minded, empirical view of culture put forward by Bernard Lonergan, e.g., "The Transition from a Classicist World-View to Historical-Mindedness," 3–10. Such a transition allows us to recognize that "contextual theology" is a misnomer, for all theology is a matter of historical and cultural location. See further Stephan B. Bevans, *Models of Contextual Theology* (Maryknoll, NY: Orbis, 1992); Lamin Sanneh, *Translating the Message: The Missionary Impact on Culture*, 2nd ed. (Maryknoll, NY: Orbis, 2009).

13 So also Yves Congar, *True and False Reform in the Church*, trans. Paul Philibert (Collegeville, MN: Liturgical Press, 2011), 150–51; For a landmark statement of this consensus, see WCC, *Baptism, Eucharist and Ministry*.

14 Hence, certain churches would insist not only on a ministry of *episkopé*, but on the specific ministerial ordering of an episcopacy in historical succession, and some would go so far as to deny that other churches with a similar understanding share in this succession (such is the Catholic understanding of the Anglican episcopate). We shall prescind from this question, though, and note the general consensus that some ministry of *episkopé* is agreed upon.

15 Incidentally, these comprise the basic elements of the Chicago-Lambeth Quadrilateral.

Yet even so, in general, the *tradita* have developed as matters of historical contingency. In fact, it is not impossible for *de jure divino* elements of the church to be historically contingent themselves.[16] An adequate theology of history and of divine providence would allow us to recognize that historically contingent developments can become permanent and irreversible features of ongoing church life. For instance, there was nothing necessary or inevitable about the Arian crisis, which itself gave shape to the way that trinitarian doctrine was defined. Yet, for all the contingency involved, there is no walking back Nicaea. The church makes decisions in its pilgrimage, and while not all of these decisions are irreversible, some are.

To take another example, generally speaking, Christians regard Scripture as indispensable for their common life. Yet this indispensability cannot be absolute, for churches have existed without written Scriptures.[17] The Christian community existed for nearly two decades before any of the New Testament texts were composed, and even after their composition, it took time for them to be circulated to all churches, and still more time for the writings that make up the New Testament canon to be fully attested as such. Analogously, it is not a foregone conclusion that every Christian church had access to the Hebrew Scriptures in the earliest days. Moreover, the composition of all these texts, regardless of one's theology of inspiration, was a matter of historical contingency. Their authors operated within and addressed concrete historical situations; a fact driven home by the occasional nature of most of the writings of the New Testament. Even such indispensable features of church life are not absolutely indispensable. God alone is absolute.

Again, the point is not that the church could not possibly be otherwise, but rather that some such *tradita* must accompany the *tradere* of *traditio*. Shared meanings must be given shared expression.[18] This is a feature, not a bug, still

---

16 Karl Rahner, "Reflection on the Concept of '*Ius Divinum*' in Catholic Thought," in *Theological Investigations*, 23 vols. (Limerick: Centre for Theology, Culture and Values, 2005), 5:219–43; "The Historicity of Theology," in *Theological Investigations*, 9:64–82; Richard Hooker, *Of the Laws of Ecclesiastical Polity*, ed. Michael Russell from John Keble's 1836 ed. (self.-pub., 2004), 7.3–14.

17 See Joseph K. Gordon, *Divine Scripture in Human Understanding: A Systematic Theology of the Christian Bible* (Notre Dame, IN: University of Notre Dame Press, 2019).

18 E.g., Augustine, *doctr. chr.* 2.24.37 (WSA, 1/11:148–49); *c. Faust.* 19.11 (WSA, 1/20:244–45). See further R. A. Markus, *Signs and Meanings: World and Text in Ancient Christianity* (Liverpool: Liverpool University Press, 1996), 105–46. On this point, Friedrich Schleiermacher is agreed. E.g., *On Religion: Speeches to Its Cultured Despisers*, trans. John Oman (Louisville, KY: Westminster John Knox, 1994), 147–80; *The Christian Faith*, trans. H. R. Mackintosh and J. S. Stewart (Edinburgh: T&T Clark, 1999), §6 [pp. 26-31].

less a problem. But, as we have already noted, what the church receives, and what the church passes on is not simply the gospel, but rather the gospel and various other communal and cultural accoutrements, which are not always neatly separable from the gospel. In fact, there is no pure gospel, wholly abstracted from these accoutrements. So our reception and transmission of the gospel is always accompanied by other features. Some of them aid our reception and transmission. Others are simply along for the ride, not necessarily aiding, but also not hindering reception or transmission.

Tradition as Ambiguous

Still other *tradita* operate at variance with the gospel, its reception, and its ongoing transmission. That this is the case, we can conclude from the fact that churches have done harm.[19] The crucifying legacies we surveyed in chapter 3 bear this out. There we considered the early church's unwillingness to challenge and oppose slavery (or perhaps their inability to imagine a world without it), a decision balefully displayed in the prevalent master-slave metaphor for Christian discipleship that litters the New Testament, which served to provide cover for the continued propagation of slavery for centuries. In the end, the churches came to recognize that this acquiescence to slavery undercut and was countermanded by fidelity to the gospel.[20] But this realization was a long time coming, in part due to the churches' limited horizons and incomplete conversion, but also due to the way that the gospel itself had been transmitted through these poisonous metaphors.

The point I am making is perhaps even more clearly discerned through a consideration of Paul's words to the Thessalonians concerning the Jews

> who killed both the Lord Jesus and the prophets and drove us out; they displease God and oppose everyone by hindering us from speaking to the gentiles so that they may be saved. Thus they have constantly been filling up the measure of their sins, but wrath has overtaken them at last. (1 Thess 2:15–16)

Here Paul writes in perhaps understandable human vexation. He finds his way opposed by his fellow Jews. This frustration is given expression in the letter. But these incensed words, recorded in Scripture, now become *tradita*.

---

19 I take it as a given that this harm is at odds with God's intention for the church. If God intended the church for evil, then God would also be evil.

20 See, once more, Noonan, *Church That Can and Cannot Change*.

As the gospel is handed on, so are they, and as they are passed along, they bear the bitter fruit of traditions of blood libel and an anti-Semitism shared among the divided churches that would have appalled the apostle (I hope). And even if the churches have by and large repudiated anti-Semitism, it remains a besetting sin, and the blighted harvest is still reaped from centuries of Christian sowing.[21]

Surely Paul did not intend to inaugurate these traditions of anti-Semitism, nor to give rise to the blood libel. He writes elsewhere about his solidarity with Judaism, his confidence that "all Israel shall be saved," and so forth (see especially Rom 9–11). Still, though, these traditions were inaugurated and fueled by his words, whatever his intent. This bitter root may well lie at the origins of Christian division. We saw in chapter 3 that supersessionism helped fund the theological imagination of race making, and that forgetfulness of the precarity of gentile inclusion corresponds to LGBTQ exclusion. Ephraim Radner has suggested that the churches' inability to negotiate difference among themselves stems from our prior inability to negotiate our difference with Judaism.[22] I cannot speculate about historical paths not taken, but perhaps if we had found the means and the will to live in peaceful, loving coexistence with our Jewish elder siblings, even after the "parting of the ways" led to Christianity and Judaism as two definitively distinct religions, we may have thereby developed the resources to handle our intra-Christian differences in loving unity.

The point, though, is this: as the church engages in tradition, it passes along the gospel and other *tradita*. It is possible for these *tradita* to be harmful, distorted, opposed to and by the gospel. This must be possible because it has been actual. As we noted in chapter 1, it follows logically from the sort of redemption by which we have been redeemed. God elevates our activity, so that we are informed by and perform acts of love, but not in such a way as to remove our capacity to fall short of that love.

---

21 See, e.g., Alan Dundes, ed., *The Blood Libel Legend: A Casebook in Anti-Semitic Folklore* (Madison: University of Wisconsin Press, 1991); Jeremy Cohen, *Living Letters of the Law: Ideas of the Jew in Medieval Christianity* (Berkeley: University of California Press, 1999); Matthew A. Tapie, *Aquinas on Israel and the Church: The Question of Supersessionism in the Theology of Thomas Aquinas* (Cambridge: James Clarke & Co, 2015); Lauren F. Winner, *The Dangers of Christian Practice: On Wayward Gifts, Characteristic Damage, and Sin* (New Haven, CT: Yale University Press, 2018).

22 Radner, *Brutal Unity*, 80–86.

We must first of all, then, acknowledge both the ambiguity and indispensability of tradition as a historical process. Apart from tradition, the church and its gospel are inert, dead, locked away in the past and unable to impinge upon the present. Concretely, the Christian movement *could* never have spread, with the message of Christ dying out with the last of the apostles, or perhaps never even being transmitted as far as them. It is only through tradition that the law of the cross reaches us here and now, so far removed from the originary events. Tradition is indispensable. All the same, we must also disabuse ourselves of

> the notion that the only thing Christians ever carry with confidence through history is Christ. For we also carry the bewildering, staggering vastness of our sin through history. Like a cracked cup, split by a tragic irony and guilt, we spill poison and grace into the world.[23]

As the church hands itself on, it passes along frameworks and horizons in which the law of the cross and the way of crucifixion are intermingled, in which the intelligible and the absurd are alloyed. Distortions enter into the framework and are passed on alongside the gospel. In any number of cases, divisions began with the desire to correct these distortions (no one departs from the church because of how *right* they think it is).

The churches have always recognized the possibility of these distortions, as movements of protest, reform, and contestation, along with the bulk of the New Testament with its epistolary correctives and other records of intra-Christian debate bear witness. Given the shape of redemption and the character of the supernatural order, there is no *preventing* such distortions. No necessity governs them: they need not enter the tradition, but they are possible and frequently actual. The question is not whether there will be deformed *tradita*, but rather how to address them.[24]

The problem, of course, is the very ambiguity of tradition. We receive the gospel and other cultural elements (whether positive, neutral, or harmful), not neatly distinguished, but amalgamated. Just as only the actual planetary orbits that exist, not the linear motion, elliptical loops, and gravitational perturbation that allow us to account for those orbital paths, progress, decline, and supernatural redemptive recovery can be conceptually distinguished, but

---

23 Carpenter, *Nothing Gained Is Eternal*, xix.
24 Though perhaps dated, Congar, *True and False Reform in the Church* remains an incisive examination of the question.

what actually exists within history are the concrete human actions that these heuristic categories allow us to describe.[25] Moreover, because we can only operate within the horizons we inhabit, it is not a foregone conclusion that the distortions are always correctly identified. Sometimes the authentic is mistaken for the deformed (see the Donatist rejection of Catholicism's embrace of penitent *traditores*). Other times deformity is uncritically embraced and passed along, as in the slavery metaphor or supersessionism.

Amid history, it can be unclear which is which. For instance, as we've seen, 'the Christian tradition was inaugurated and has generally operated within cultures that assumed certain understandings of gender and sexuality (viz., male superiority and cisheteronormativity). As the gospel was transmitted and received, so were these understandings. As a result, there is a lengthy track record of restricting priestly and episcopal ordination to men and of rejecting LGBTQ expression within the churches. More recently, new understandings of gender and sexuality have emerged. In contemporary Western societies, any position or role that men can do is also open to women—in theory, if not in practice (patriarchy dies hard). And while not uncontested, LGBTQ identities and expression are generally accepted as within the range of gender and sexual experience.[26]

These emergent understandings raise but do not resolve the question: Are the older assumptions simply *tradita* that have accompanied the handing on of the gospel (perhaps distortions opposed to it), or are they, somehow integrally related to it? Are the new assumptions an authentic development that can enter into our handing on of the gospel, new data that sheds light on our former assumptions, or are they newly emerged distortions? The churches differ on this question. Only time and discernment will tell. While I have staked out my own positions vis-à-vis these questions, and have argued accordingly, I recognize the possibility that my discernment has gone awry and history will show me to have been mistaken, but ours is not to wait for the judgment of history, only to act as faithfully as we can within the circumstances in which we live.

---

25 Lonergan, "Insight Revisited," 271–72.

26 For data-driven affirmations of this reality see, e.g., Jonathan Heaps and Neil Ormerod, "Statistically Ordered: Gender, Sexual Identity, and the Metaphysics of 'Normal,'" *TS* 80, no. 2 (2019): 346–69; Paul J Schutz, "En-gendering Creation Anew: Rethinking Ecclesial Statements on Science, Gender, and Sexuality with William R. Stoeger, SJ," *Horizons* 48, no. 1 (2021): 34–68.

That need for discernment is often perceived as a threat, both by those who reject such new developments and by those who embrace them. Both would have the matter already be considered settled, with no further discernment needed, albeit with different outcomes. But it is inescapable: we remain *in via*, and there is no predetermined path for us to follow.

These cases, though, are not parallel. The woman who acts upon her sense of vocation to the priesthood, or the trans person or lesbian couple venturing forth in self-expression and love, is not in the same position when she or they object to an idea that their lives, loves, and vocations should be kept on hold while others decide whether or not they should be allowed to pursue them as are those who refuse to even consider the question. The former act with what authenticity they are able, at least potentially so. The latter short-circuit authenticity, not in the conclusions they reach, per se, but in the failure of self-transcendence that expresses itself in the refusal of relevant questions. The fact is that any of us can reach conclusions only tentatively. This does not preclude our acting according to our best lights. Instead, it demands we do so, while recognizing that our decisions are always subject to revision as we learn more.[27]

While the material content of these particular assessments is relatively novel, the formal shape is nothing new. It has ever been thus. New data, and with them, new questions emerge, and the church must discern how to faithfully proceed. It is amid this need for assessment and discernment that divisions have generally occurred. Some party will reject as inauthentic some *traditum*, whether received from of old or newly introduced. Perhaps they initially attempt to correct this perceived deformity, but eventually, they determine that the cause is hopeless and that separation is necessary. We must recognize, though, that in all cases, including those where the would-be reformer has correctly assessed the *traditum* in question, the separation is a matter of choice and not neccessity. Only that which puts a community beyond the pale of Christian recognition results in a separation, *eo ipso*. And in such cases, by definition, the church is not divided, for the separated community is not Christian.[28]

---

27 This is articulated rather well by Paul Avis as he considers the question of women's ordination within the Anglican Communion, particularly in the absence of ecumenical consensus. *The Identity of Anglicanism*, 118–51.

28 And in such cases, the love of God still reaches and may still inform such communities, which means that Christian churches should also hold them in love. Love does not depend upon sameness.

While such divisions have occurred in the churches' sojourn, most of our divisions are not of this character, as the historical record examined in chapter 2 bears out. In such relatively rare cases, there is no problem of division to resolve, and so we are not concerned with them. Reforms are often slow in coming. Historical change is incremental, often maddeningly so, and there is a human cost to taking the long view that we must squarely, soberly face.[29] But both reform and change occur, and so division remains a choice (including for those who determine that it is the correct choice).

The Only Path Is Forward

It is, once more, all well and good to observe this, but we are called upon to face reality, not protest ideals in the face of it. Division being a choice rather than a necessity does not change the fact that divisions have occurred. Even if the divisions are, upon examination, indefensible, here we are, divided from each other, and along the way, we've been inheriting and passing along frameworks that constitute a portion of the premotion for our contemporary action. While the past is not destiny—for good or for ill, we can choose anew in the present moment, whether more authentically appropriating the law of the cross and repudiating our deformities, or betraying the gospel in new ways, or some mixture of the two—still it constrains us. Who we are now comes from who we have been. Who we will be is decided by who we now are. The question becomes then, not "Should this division have happened?" but rather, "What are we to do now within the state of affairs that actually exists?"

Divided Christians are in a different situation than are dividing Christians.

Divisions have occurred, and the communities-in-questions' lives have continued, meaning that they continue to receive and pass along *tradita* that include the gospel and also other elements connected to it in various ways. But now these histories and these processes of traditioning diverge and develop independently of each other. As the churches continue their historical sojourns, they develop their own theological commitments and emphases, structures for ordering communal life, patterns of devotion, strategies for interpreting Scripture, and so on. These *tradita* by which Christian faith is

---

29 This should not be read as a denunciation of those who've parted ways from communities that would have demanded their ongoing crucifixion (see chapter 3). Even in cases where we might consider the separation to be justified, it is still the case that it results from a decision.

nourished in the churches now demand some measure of loyalty from the community for that very reason, and to the extent that they are at variance with the *tradita* by which faith is nourished in other churches, they constitute an obstacle to reunion.[30]

Divergent, even incommensurable theological commitments, or structures, or patterns of devotion, or strategies for interpreting Scripture are not themselves a barrier to unity. The theological schools of Alexandria and Antioch were both encompassed within the communion of the same church. Cyprian's theology of baptism and practice of rebaptism differed from Pope Stephen's. Franciscans and Dominicans differed on the immaculate conception of Mary, on the reason for the incarnation, and so on. And, while after the papal definition of the immaculate conception, the former Dominican position is now off limits for Catholics, the point still stands. These two contradictory views were both included within the church's communion for centuries. Theologies of grace differed from Suarez to Banez to Cajetan to Thomas Aquinas, and so on. As Congar puts it, while heretical movements like Jansenism and Baianism seemed to proceed along precisely Augustinian lines, "Augustine himself could only have remained in communion with the Catholic Church in the seventeenth century without ceasing to be Augustinian provided he had not refused to be in communion with Ignatius and Molina."[31]

Thus, diversity, even incommensurability is not a problem. The problem arises from the fact that the churches have sojourned in isolation from each other, developing their own heritages.[32] These legacies that are not always readily assimilable to one another, a feature that is amplified by the way in which many of them have developed in contradistinction from each other, with the explicit purpose of differentiating one community from the other.[33] Protestant commitments to the "solas" (Scripture alone, faith alone, grace alone, Christ alone, to God's glory alone) are designed in self-conscious contradistinction from what the reformers perceived the Catholic Church's teaching to be. Similarly, the notion of an invisible church was meant to allow for differentiation from the institutional apparatus of Rome. Concomitantly, the Catholic Reformation's insistence on a visibility as palpable as the Republic of Venice was its own attempt at a repudiation of the Protestant view. As Yves

---

30 Astutely observed by Congar, *Divided Christendom*, 39.
31 Congar, *Divided Christendom*, 44.
32 Congar, *Divided Christendom*, 24–26.
33 Radner, *End of the Church*, 135–98.

Congar observed, "To have learned one's catechism against someone else is a great misfortune."[34]

Here ministerial order proves a particular challenge. Separated churches' divided ministries serve the purpose of allowing the communities to go their separate ways. In some cases, changes in polity arise for the express purpose of repudiating the structures of another community. Presbyterianism is deliberately incompatible with episcopacy. Congregationalism is deliberately incompatible with both. And within episcopally governed communions, the Anglican insistence on a national church's autonomy stems directly from a rejection of the papacy. Here I leave to the side the question of "validity" for two reasons. First, because of the emergent consensus that this is the wrong category for approaching the question of the mutual recognition of ministries. It locks us into a predetermined conceptualist binary, when we should instead be taking an empirical view that begins with the experience of God's grace within the communities in question.[35] Second, the resolution of such questions is for the churches themselves to discover, negotiate, and enact. For our purposes, it suffices to recognize the reality that these *tradita*, by which communal life in the gospel has been facilitated, then, become barriers to reunion, even when the desire for such union emerges.

What are separated churches that desire communion with one another, yet whose histories have been forged so as to maintain existences separate from one another, to do? The answer cannot lie in self-repudiation. While all of the churches have much for which to repent, and while none of their heritages are free from ambiguity, nevertheless, these are the means by which the faith has been transmitted, by which God has continued her work of gathering people together in Christ by the Holy Spirit. This is not to be repudiated. To do so would be to play God false. This is not to say that churches cannot change their minds about these features of their lives. In many cases this is a viable option, though not always. Some decisions are reversible; others are not.

---

34 Yves Congar, *Dialogue between Christians: Catholic Contributions to Ecumenism* (Westminster: Newman Press, 1966), 138.

35 See Susan K. Wood, "The Correlation between Ecclesial Communion and the Recognition of Ministry," *One in Christ* 50, no. 2 (2016): 238–49. See further Otto Hermann Pesch, *Ecumenical Potential of the Second Vatican Council* (Milwaukee: Marquette University Press, 2006), 44–47; *Second Vatican Council*, 210–14. We can note as well Joseph Ratzinger's affirmation of "the saving presence of the Lord in the Evangelical [i.e., Lutheran] Lord's Supper" (*Pilgrim Fellowship of Faith: The Church as Communion*, ed. Stephan Otto Horn and Vinzenz Pfnur, trans. Henry Taylor [San Francisco: Ignatius, 2005], 248).

All of the churches develop over the course of their historical sojourns. They all make communal decisions that give rise to the situations within which their successors will have to decide. Any future unity of the church must respect these histories, must honor the work of God in them, must not repudiate the churches' experience of themselves as church, even in all the ambiguity involved in these experiences and these histories. Two ecumenically vexing examples will render the challenge concrete.

The Papacy and Women's Ordination

Over the course of its history, the Catholic Church has developed a distinctive understanding of the primacy of the bishop of Rome, one that, over the course of its development, led to estrangement first from the Christian East, and then later in the West, from proto-Protestant groups like the Waldensians to the divisions of the sixteenth century to, eventually, the separation of the Old Catholics in response to the definition of papal infallibility.[36]

Along the way these divisions themselves gave shape to the development of Roman primacy. According to the law of premotion, each inherited state of affairs conditions the decisions made at any current juncture, which in turn give rise to the states of affairs within which subsequent decisions will need to be made. Before the East-West schism, the pentarchy of the patriarchal

---

36 For historical and/or theological overviews, see, e.g., John W. O'Malley, *A History of the Popes: From Peter to the Present* (Lanham, MD: Rowman & Littlefield, 2011); Klaus Schatz, "Historical Considerations Considering the Problem of Primacy," in *Petrine Ministry and the Unity of the Church: "Toward a Patient and Fraternal Dialogue,"* ed. James F. Puglisi (Collegeville, MN: Liturgical Press, 1999), 1–14; Dumitru Popescu, "Papal Primacy in Eastern and Western Patristic Theology: Its Interpretation in the Light of Contemporary Culture," in Puglisi, *Petrine Ministry and the Unity of the Church*, 99–114; John P. Meier, "Petrine Ministry in the New Testament and in the Early Patristic Traditions," in *How Can the Petrine Ministry Be a Service to Unity?*, ed. James F. Puglisi, (Grand Rapids: Eerdmans, 2010), 13–33; Roland Minnerath, "The Petrine Ministry in the Early Patristic Tradition," in Puglisi, *How Can the Petrine Ministry Be a Service?*, 34–48; John Reumann, "The Petrine Ministry in the New Testament and in Early Patristic Tradition," in Puglisi, *How Can the Petrine Ministry Be a Service?*, 49–78; Hermann J. Pottmeyer, *Towards a Papacy in Communion: Perspectives from Vatican Councils I & II* (New York: Herder & Herder, 1998); "Historical Development of Forms of Authority and Jurisdiction: The Papal Ministry—an Ecumenical Approach," in Puglisi, *How Can the Petrine Ministry Be a Service?*, 98–107; "Did Vatican I Intend to Deny Tradition?," in Puglisi, *How Can the Petrine Ministry Be a Service?*, 108–23.

sees of Rome, Constantinople, Antioch, Alexandria, and Jerusalem served as something of a counterbalance to the papacy. After 1054, four of these sees were no longer in communion with Rome, leaving a single patriarchate in the West and accelerating the centralization of Roman primacy.[37] The papacy may have developed rather differently in an undivided church, though we cannot know the precise shape of that development. Nor does it matter how that development would have occurred, for it has not occurred, because the conditions for its occurrence did not themselves occur. History moves in only one direction, and the papacy is what it is (which is not to say that it cannot or should not develop in new directions).

While theologically I regard the papacy as an authentic development—and, therefore, a necessary feature of any future reunited church—even at the level of pure pragmatism, we would probably still have to affirm this necessity. To ask the Catholic Church to repudiate the papacy would be a complete non-starter, to say nothing of theological considerations.[38] Particularly given its dogmatic status, such a request would be tantamount to asking the Catholic Church to surrender and deny its own identity. Ecumenism cannot possibly proceed along such lines. Instead, the task is to find a way for the bishop of Rome to exercise his (or, one day, may it please God, her) primacy that can be embraced by the other churches.[39] The way lies ahead and shall be found through forward movement, not by naïve attempts to arrest or reverse historical processes.

The same consideration, though, applies to the other churches, their histories, their *tradita*. In the course of such churches' lives, these developments have occurred. They cannot be expected simply to repudiate the distinctive ways of life nor the ministries according to which they have received, lived by, and passed along the faith. While, in the end, some of these features may

---

37 E.g., Pottmeyer, *Towards a Papacy in Communion*, 23–35; John Zizioulas, "The Future Exercise of Papal Ministry in the Light of Ecclesiology: An Orthodox Approach," in Puglisi, *How Can the Petrine Ministry Be a Service?*, 174–76.

38 See ARCIC, *The Final Report: Windsor, September 1981* (Cincinnati: Forward Movement Publications, 1982); ARCIC, "The Gift of Authority," 1998; Inter-Anglican Theological and Doctrinal Commission, "The Virginia Report," 1997, 3.52; Robert W. Jenson, *Systematic Theology*, vol. 2, *The Works of God* (New York: Oxford University Press, 1999), 228–49; Zizioulas, "Future Exercise of Papal Ministry."

39 John Paul II, *"Ut Unum Sint*: On Commitment to Ecumenism" (Vatican website, May 25, 1995), no. 95; Fries and Rahner, *Unity of the Churches*, 83–92; ARCIC, "The Gift of Authority," nos. 60–63.

not remain and still others will be transformed in the self-transcending movement of convergence, such self-transcendence is not at all the same as self-repudiation. The one fulfills a trajectory, while the other stultifies it. Once more, this is for the churches to discover and discern as they journey together under the providence of God, so I do not offer prescriptions, only the proscription of self-repudiation.

As one example, we can consider the decision of some churches, including my own, to ordain women to the presbyterate and episcopate. Here, I have no intention of defending the practice, which I support, and take as a given. The fact to be faced is that it has occurred. Not without controversy, but occur it has. This move has led some to depart from the churches in question, and to consternation on the part of our ecumenical partners, particularly the Catholic and Orthodox Churches, a point to which I shall return. In general, though, we have found our churches to be enriched by the ministry of women, judging the development to be authentic.

By contrast, the Catholic Church and Orthodox Churches have not embraced this development, with Pope John Paul II declaring that the Catholic Church lacks the authority to ordain women.[40] At present, the state of the question within Catholic teaching is clouded by ambiguity and so subject to further clarification, even revision.[41] While it is taught authoritatively, such that, at present, women cannot be ordained in the Catholic Church, and while it is asserted to be taught definitively, and, so, be irreversible, the statements by which it has been asserted are not those means by which the

---

40 John Paul II, *Ordinatio Sacerdotalis* (Vatican website, May 22, 1994).

41 While according to Catholic teaching the pope teaches infallibly when he does so *ex cathedra*, John Paul II's prohibition was not taught in this manner. So theologians queried on what basis this prohibition was asserted. In response to these *dubia* raised by theologians as to the basis of John Paul II's authoritative pronouncement, the CDF issued a clarification, stating the pope's position to be taught infallibly by the ordinary universal magisterium. "Responsum Ad Propositum Dubium Concerning the Teaching Contained in 'Ordinatio Sacerdotalis.'" Yet this only leads to further ambiguity, for, while the ordinary universal magisterium can indeed teach definitively, the criteria for assessing this is opaque. The CDF cannot teach infallibly, so it is not a foregone conclusion that the dicastery's judgment that the ordinary universal magisterium definitively prohibits women's ordination is correct. Hence, even according to Catholic principles, they could be wrong in this assessment, as could have been John Paul II, meaning that at some future point the Catholic Church could ordain women without any actual self-contradiction. On the principles involved, see the next note.

Catholic Church understands itself to teach infallibly.[42] Further development in a different direction might be an embarrassment, but, on Catholic principles, it is not an impossibility. That doesn't necessarily matter, though, for I am not arguing that the Catholic Church should ordain women. As a non-Catholic, this is none of my business, though, as someone who has been enriched by the ministries of women, I hope that the Catholic Church will someday be so enriched too.

In any case, though, there is no reason why the Catholic Church's self-understanding that it lacks the authority to ordain women should bind the self-understanding of those churches that believe themselves authorized to act in such ways, and who have acted accordingly. There is, in principle, no reason why a church that ordains women and a church that does not cannot be in communion with one another in a differentiated unity.[43] In reality, the Catholic Church's nonacceptance of women's ordination obscures the more basic problem that they also do not recognize the ordinations of the *men* in most non-Catholic churches![44]

While I have committed to not insisting that the Catholic Church ordain women, it is disinguous for the Catholic Church to protest my church's decision to ordain women while also rejecting all our ordinations out of hand. That judgment could only make sense within the context of an affirmation of our ordained ministry in general. If all our ordinations are already "absolutely null and utterly void," are we to believe that when we ordain women, it's absolutely-er null or utterly-er void?[45] We shall return to the matter of ministerial recognition shortly.

---

42 Richard R. Gaillardetz, *Teaching with Authority: A Theology of the Magisterium in the Church* (Collegeville, MN: Liturgical Press, 1997), 159–223; *By What Authority? Foundations for Understanding Authority in the Church*, 2d ed. (Collegeville, MN: Liturgical Press, 2018), 135–52; Francis A. Sullivan, *Magisterium: Teaching Authority in the Catholic Church* (Eugene, OR: Wipf and Stock, 2002), 119–72; Herman J. Pottmeyer, "Refining the Question about Women's Ordination," *America*, October 26, 1996, 16–18.

43 As a case in point, the original reception of women's ordination within the Anglican Communion was uneven, leading to a differentiated approach articulated by Inter-Anglican Theological and Doctrinal Commission, "The Virginia Report." It is worth noting that the Windsor Report's attempt to forge a similar differentiated unity on the matter of LGBTQ affirmation faltered. See chapter 3.

44 See Avis's observation that in the Church of England, the validity of men's and women's priestly ordination is grounded on precisely the same basis Avis, *Identity of Anglicanism*, 129.

45 My improper grammar here serves to highlight the absurdity of the claim.

WE CAN ONLY START WHERE WE ARE: STAGGERING
FORWARD ALONG TORTUOUS PATHS

No Christian nor Christian church should be expected to repent of anything but sin. So, in those cases where our *tradita* are deformities—anti-Semitism, clericalism, abuse, white supremacy, mutual suspicion or hatred, and other such things—repudiation is indeed in order. But when it comes to our divided histories, while repentance is in order for the divisions themselves—predicated as they were by the refusal of charity—our subsequent histories can be cause for gratitude. As I have noted, divided Christians find themselves in a different situation than do dividing Christians.

Something of this perspective is evident in the Second Vatican Council's Decree on Ecumenism, *Unitatis Redintegratio*, which notes that "often enough, people of both sides were to blame. Those who are now born into these communities and who are brought up in the faith of Christ cannot be accused of the sin involved in the separation, and the catholic church looks on them as [siblings], with respect and love."[46] Hence, there is sin in the division, but not necessarily or per se in the divided history. Our teeth are set on edge by the sour grapes eaten by our forebears, but we do not share in the blame for the situation we've inherited. We are responsible for our acts, but not for the circumstances that constrain them.

In a similar vein, and returning to the question of ministries, Karl Rahner offers a proposal that can be illuminating. In the nineteenth century, Pope Leo XIII issued the bull *Apostolicae Curae*, in which he famously deemed Anglican ordinations to be "absolutely null and utterly void." It should come as no surprise that I, an Anglican, do not share this judgment,[47] but for the time being, let us prescind from that. Anglicans are free to protest that the pope should not have made this judgment, but made it he did, and so it has constrained Catholic approaches to ecumenical relations with Anglicans. While a papal bull like *Apostolicae Curae* is an authoritative teaching, it is not an infallible exercise of the papal magisterium, which is all the more

---

46 *UR*, no. 3 [Tanner, 2:910].

47 See, e.g., the response from Frederick Temple and William Maclagan, Archbishops of Canterbury and York, respectively, *Sæpius Officio* (February 19, 1897), in *Anglican Orders: The Documents in the Debate*, ed. Christopher Hill, Edward Yarnold, and Catholic Church (Norwich, UK: Canterbury Press, 1997), 281–317. Consider also George Tavard's call for a reappraisal from the Catholic side. *A Review of Anglican Orders: The Problem and the Solution* (Collegeville, MN: Liturgical Press, 1990).

relevant, since it was issued some twenty-six years after the formal definition of papal infallibility when teaching *ex cathedra*. Even according to Catholic principles, it could, therefore, be mistaken, and thus subject to revision.[48] That's one path forward. But Rahner offers a different one, one that would not require the repudiation of such prior judgments.

Rahner's argument hinges on the idea that Protestant ordinations (he was focused on Lutheran ordinations, rather than Anglican ones, but the principle is transferable), were deemed invalid because of bad faith (*mala fides*).[49] In determining to separate from the Catholic Church, Protestants acted in bad faith, but in the years, decades, centuries since, they are no longer characterized by this *mala fides*. Their separate existence is due to the inheritance of the past, rather than a settled resolve to be separate. Moreover, Catholics can now recognize the fruits of the Spirit in Protestant communities, including their ministries. With *mala fides* removed, and evidence of the Holy Spirit's work recognized, it would seem that the situation has changed, and so should the judgment.[50]

We should note, of course, as Rahner does, that this is a rather Catholic-specific argument. Protestants would, no doubt, frame matters differently from their side (perhaps locating the bad faith on the Catholic side, or at least insisting that the blame be shared, which would cohere with the quotation from *Unitatis Redintegratio* above), and judge the moves Rahner proposes rather unnecessary, perhaps even condescending.[51] And this is fair enough. But each church is constrained by the need to start where they are, not where their ecumenical partners are, nor still where those ecumenical partners might wish them to be instead. Protestants would need to develop their own manners of making peace with Catholics and their history, for instance regarding the development of the papacy, manners that would probably seem so unnecessary as to verge on condescension to Catholics.

The remainder of Rahner's proposal involves a squaring of the circle of Catholic principles that will allow an affirmation of these ministries, despite apparent breaches in historical continuity, and without a repudiation of the

---

48 See the fine-grained treatment of the papal magisterium in Gaillardetz, *Teaching with Authority*, 177–84, 203–23.

49 Karl Rahner, *An Ecumenical Priesthood: The Spirit of God and the Structure of the Church*, ed. and trans. Jakob Karl Rinderknecht (Minneapolis: Fortress Press, 2022), 41–50.

50 Rahner, *An Ecumenical Priesthood*, 51–57, 65–73.

51 Rahner, *An Ecumenical Priesthood*, 73–77.

historical paths by which we've reached this point. The precise mechanism, radical sanation (a canonical principle that allows a marriage that was evidently invalidly contracted, but whose history demonstrates the fruits of marriage, to be retroactively considered valid), is only incidental to our purposes here. It is one proposal for how the Catholic Church could thread the needle of recognizing Protestant ministries without requiring either the Catholic Church or the Protestants in question to repudiate their own histories. For what it's worth, I think it's an elegant solution. Nevertheless, precisely how the churches negotiate this matter is for them to work out in the dynamics of their own historical sojourns. What does matter is the recognition that history changes things, and that the churches need to be aware of and responsive to such change. The situation of divided Christians who've inherited their divisions is rather different than the situation of dividing Christians enacting them for the first time. Yet, we cannot allow that different valuation to blunt the problem of division. We have inherited these circumstances. We must discern and enact faithfulness within the constraints of the present moment under the weight of history.

Thus far, Rahner's proposal has not been accepted. It has barely been heard. A more successful example can be provided by the Joint Declaration on the Doctrine of Justification. From the sixteenth century onward, Catholics and Lutherans had developed rather distinctive, even mutually incommensurable patterns of thought and speech about justification. Within each community, these *tradita* were passed along from one generation to the next. The *JDDJ* forged a path of allowing the two communions to speak with one voice on the matter in a mutually agreeable manner, while also allowing each party to retain their own distinctive patterns. The Catholics and Lutherans had mutually condemned each other's respective positions at the time of the reformation. Those condemnations were not rescinded by either party, but remained in force as "salutary warnings," even as each party also agreed that the condemnations did not apply to the positions articulated in the *JDDJ*. Thus, both parties were able to move forward, speaking with one differentiated voice, without any self-repudiation.

Famously, though, the *JDDJ* has not sufficed to bring about reunion. The churches involved were able to attain a great deal of convergence, one grounded in their mutual recognition of each other as Christian. But, in the end, the fact of their division remains the obstacle to union. Their divided histories hinder their convergence, for, while the doctrine of justification was the presenting cause of the reformation's divisions, the subsequent history has seen the development of other features of life that preclude union. As the *JDDJ* shows, such obstacles are not insuperable, but still, they are not yet surmounted.

Forging New Paths

To the extent that we demand an ecclesiology of agreement, division will continue to elude us.[52] The ecumenical way forward will necessarily involve an embrace of diversity, even of disagreement. This in itself need not be a scandal. Most traditions exhibit high degrees of internal diversity: opposing theological schools within the Catholic Church are exhibit A. The churches in all their differences will need to embrace each other, precisely in those differences, and only in that way will unity be found, and not even found, per se, but forged as they determine to walk together and make a way.

Here we must think beyond convergence as merger. Communion by merger can occur within a limited geographical territory (e.g., South India), but is unfeasible when we consider the Christian communities dispersed throughout the world. While some churches may discern that a merger is the way in which they shall forge new unity, an ecclesiology of communion could resolve this differently. All that is needed is a mutual recognition of one another as churches, and a determination to be in communion with one another. The formation of a new denomination, or the disappearance of its precursors, is not a requirement.

Here the Chicago-Lambeth Quadrilateral holds promise, particularly in the form proposed at the 1886 General Convention in Chicago, which contains a preambular section that specifies,

> That in all things of human ordering or human choice, relating to modes of worship and discipline, or to traditional customs, this Church is ready in the spirit of love and humility to forego all preferences of her own; . . . [and]

---

52 A fairly neglected contribution of Ephraim Radner's *Brutal Unity* is his calling into question whether there is even such a thing as agreement, per se, a proposal borne out through forays into cognitive theory, language acquisition, the dynamics of marital relationships, and so on (311–47). As I mentioned in chapter 1, understandably, much of the attention this volume garnered centered around Radner's account of religious violence and particularly his engagement with Cavanaugh's *The Myth of Religious Violence*. This has had the unfortunate effect of relegating some of the more constructively generative, and potentially controversial, contributions of Radner's proposal to obscurity.

That this Church does not seek to absorb other Communions, but rather, co-operating with them on the basis of a common Faith and Order, to discountenance schism, to heal the wounds of the Body of Christ, and to promote the charity which is the chief of Christian graces and the visible manifestation of Christ to the world.[53]

If the bishops are taken at their word, then only those essentials specified by the quadrilateral—Scriptures, sacraments, creedal faith, and historic episcopate—are nonnegotiable (and of these, the most controversial, the historic episcopate, is noted to be labile to local adaptation). No other elements of ecclesial distinctiveness or heritage is deemed worth holding onto at the expense of unity. But more importantly for our purposes at this point, the model of unity is not absorption but cooperation through the discountenancing of schism. In other words, by a decision to be united.

Along similar lines, some forty years ago, Heinrich Fries and Karl Rahner put forward a proposal for church unity, which is distilled into eight theses:

No church should be required by any of the others to affirm anything beyond the Nicene Creed.
Within these Nicene bounds, no church will judge the beliefs or practices of another church as utterly opposed to the way of salvation.
The churches can maintain their own distinctive structures and lives, without being assimilated to one another.
Regarding the papacy

---

53 *BCP*, 876–77. When the 1888 Lambeth Conference adopted the quadrilateral, they only adopted the material about the necessary instruments and features of church unity, not the preambular material. This omission leads to the tensions observable in the 1948 Lambeth Conference, where the bishops say, "Reunion of any part of our Communion with other denominations in its own area must make the resulting Church no longer simply Anglican, but something more comprehensive. There would be, in every country where there now exist the Anglican Church and others separated from it, a united Church, Catholic and Evangelical, but no longer in the limiting sense of the word Anglican. The Anglican Communion would be merged in a much larger Communion of National or Regional Churches, in full communion with one another, united in all the terms of what is known as the Lambeth Quadralateral," while also worrying about a premature dissolution of the Anglican Communion (Lambeth Conference [1948], *The Encyclical Letter from the Bishops, Together with Resolutions and Reports* [London: S. P. C. K, 1948], 22–23). Taken with full seriousness, the preamble to the Chicago version of the quadrilateral makes such merging and/or dissolution unnecessary.

The churches will accept the papacy as a focus and guarantor of unity.

The pope will limit the circumstances under which he exercises his *ex cathedra* teaching authority to basically expressing the consensus of all the churches.

The churches will be governed by bishops, who will be in communion with each other, but not necessarily subject to Roman regulations.

The churches will share their lives, histories, and experiences so that all can be enriched.

The churches' past ministries will be accepted as legitimate, but all will commit to episcopal ordination by the laying on of hands going forward.

The churches will share "pulpit and altar fellowship."[54]

The Fries-Rahner proposal is not a far cry from the Chicago-Lambeth Quadrilateral, but has the advantage of grasping the nettle that is the historical paths along which the would-be partner churches have traversed, including the development of the papacy.

Of course, Protestant and Orthodox Churches could insist that the Catholic Church renounce the papacy, and that unless and until this occurs no union would be possible. But even prescinding from any theological convictions, such an insistence would be its own crucifying unity, for it would insist upon a self-repudiation. If we believe that the papacy has led the Catholic Church away from the path of salvation, then we have other, far more fundamental issues to be addressing, not least about the nature of the gospel itself. If we do not believe that the papacy has led the Catholic Church away from salvation, then we must reckon with it as a fact. At the same time, though, the Fries-Rahner proposal calls upon the bishop of Rome to exercise his office in the spirit of the law of the cross, not demanding subjugation or conformity for communion. It allows the papacy to become a gift to be received by the partner churches, one which honors their histories, rather than an imposition upon them, as if their historical paths outside of communion with the Roman See were simply misadventures, thereby avoiding a crucifying unity in the other direction.

---

54 Fries and Rahner, *Unity of the Churches*.

The churches make decisions on their historical sojourns. In some, perhaps many, cases, these decisions can be changed (though they can never be unmade, historically). But some of those decisions are irreversible. One can protest that these decisions should not have been made, or that they should not have been made in such irreversible fashion, but such protestation does not change the facts. We must contend with ecclesial reality as it actually is, not as our ideal projections would have it be. And those who would insist on papal renunciation must ask how they would fare were roles reversed, perhaps on questions like women's ordination, or LGBTQ affirmation. Once we begin demanding that partner churches self-repudiate, what's to stop such a demand from being made of us?[55] To put a finer point on it, a reunited church will include the papacy, female clergy, and the affirmation of LGBTQ identities, expression, and relationships, though all in differentiated fashions, the precise shape of which is not yet apparent. I shall return to this below.[56]

Here is where the realism of the quadrilateral and the Fries-Rahner proposal shines brightest. None of these contested issues need to be resolved. Each partner church would be able to continue with its own life, only now sharing it with the wider whole.[57] No one church would be required to adopt any custom, practice, or belief beyond the Nicene Creed. Nor would they impose anything more upon their partners. We no doubt will be transformed as we journey together, but the self-transcendence called for is not of such a character as to lead to a loss of identity. Grace perfects nature. It does not destroy it.

---

55 To an extent, this demand *is* being made, but to make such demands is precisely to stultify any ecumenical progress.

56 I recognize that my affirmation of the Catholic Church's *subsistit in* results in a certain asymmetry, because, as we observed in chapter 4, the Catholic Church has continued to define doctrine through ecumenical councils and papal declarations *ex cathedra*, while the other churches have not understood themselves as positioned for such definitive decisions. Yet recognizing this asymmetry is not the same as ceding all decision-making authority to the Catholic Church; therein lies the ecumenism of return and of crucifying unities. While the status of decisions made in non-Catholic churches *is* different, even according to their own self-understandings, this does not change the fact that the decisions have been made, must be reckoned with, and cannot simply be rejected out of hand. The churches must take each other as they are and venture forth together if they ever hope to forge the unity to which they are called.

57 Similar sentiments appear in the 1920 Lambeth Conference's "Appeal to All Christian People" (Randall Thomas Davidson and Honor Thomas, eds., *The Six Lambeth Conferences, 1867–1920* [London: SPCK, 1929], no. IV [pp. 27–28]).

Ressourcement: History as Prospective

Our discussion of the churches' need to reckon with their histories would be incomplete without some consideration of *ressourcement*, which has become the predominant mode for theological engagement with the tradition. Originally a movement within French Catholicism, a turn to and recovery of Scripture, patristics, and the liturgy as theological sources, *ressourcement* has undergone expansion and transformation, such that it often functions as a sort of shorthand for any turn to the past, and particularly for projects of retrieval.

Yet to understand *ressourcement* in terms of retrieval or repristination is a debasement of the undertaking. We have already ruled out an ecclesiological primitivism as a viable contemporary stance. A retreat to the past accomplishes nothing but a skirting of our responsibility in the present. The *ressourcement* theologians were united in their conviction that historical change was real. Indeed, it was this realization that motivated the *ressourcement* project, which was not a retreat to an ideal prior state—Make the Church Great Again—and this for two reasons. First, there never was such an ideal state. Every era of the church's history has faced challenges, exhibited infidelities, and passed along the faith as best it could. Second, even if such a pristine prior state had ever existed, we could never recover it, because history only moves in one direction.

Hence, while it is not uncommon for theologians to appeal to the consensus of the "undivided church" as the basis for unity, this is a doubly misguided quest. First, while not all divisions have had the same effect—the situation post-1054 or post–sixteenth century is markedly different than it was during the Donatist or Novatian schisms, or in the fractious situation that led Paul to admonish the Corinthians—the historic "undivided church" is a mirage. But, more crucially, too much time has flowed, too many histories have been forged, for any of us to revert to such a church, even if it ever existed. We cannot turn back the clock, nor untread the paths we've trod. We cannot do this historically. Nor should we do it theologically. Whatever the infidelities and failures of these paths, they have been the paths along which the faith has been transmitted, the paths along which we have followed the Lord and been accompanied by him according to his promise (Matt 28:20). Those elements that are sinful we must repent of, but wholesale repudiation of the path, would turn our *traditio* into a *trahison*, a betrayal.

By the same token, understanding the past, understanding the decisions that were made along the way, can shed light on where we find ourselves today. For instance, Vatican I's definition of the pope's universal jurisdiction and infallibility takes on a different valence when seen against the backdrop of the competing claims of Gallicanism and ultramontanism, the encroachment of secular rulers in the church's affairs, and so forth.[58] Understanding such factors can help us discern what motivated the decisions, and so serves as resources for creatively reimagining their results and the possibilities still open to us in the present time.

The movement of *ressourcement* is a turn to the past, not because it's the past, nor to re-create it, but to discern within its witness the mystery of Christ, the law of the cross. The Scriptures, the patristic witness, the liturgy, the traditional threefold object of *ressourcement* attention, each in their various ways, give witness to this singular mystery, refracting its light in variegated brilliance.[59] And, because our reception of this mystery is always a mixed bag—among the *tradita* are the law of the cross and legacies of crucifixion, the gospel and poison—we must attend to these multifarious witnesses, approaching from a variety of vectors, so that we can more properly ascertain what is our authentic heritage, what needs to be passed along, and what needs to be dropped—including those elements that, while not sinful, no longer serve a life-giving purpose—and what needs to be repudiated.[60] And, yes, sometimes elements of our heritage that have been forgotten, but which may offer creative resources for our present task,[61] can be retrieved.

In this way, *ressourcement* can return us to the heritage we share. It cannot undo the paths we've walked, but the singular mystery of Christ and our redemption in him can be discerned along these paths. As we learn to more deeply inhabit this mystery, as we attend to the witness of our forebears to this mystery, we grow in our ability to recognize its work. Recognizing the law of the cross at work in these diverse sources, who often operated according to rather different frameworks and horizons than we do, can prime us to recognize it at work in those from whom we are presently divided, and who have taken different paths in their following the one Lord. This recognition

---

58 Pottmeyer, "Historical Development"; "Did Vatican I Intend to Deny Tradition?"

59 I develop this at length, with particular reference to Henri de Lubac's thought in *Salvation in Henri de Lubac*, esp. 150–56. Carpenter reaches similar conclusions, largely through interrogation of Charles Péguy, in *Nothing Gained Is Eternal*, 89–104.

60 Pope Francis calls for something very similar in *Evangelii Gaudium*, Vatican website, November 24, 2013, no. 43.

61 See the careful work of Joseph G. Mueller, "Forgetting as a Principle of Continuity in Tradition," *TS* 70, no. 4 (2009): 751–81.

does not in itself overcome disunity. But it is a sine qua non of any reunion.[62] Moreover, as we more deeply appropriate the one mystery, as our own conversions to Christ are deepened, we will be drawn together, for everything that rises must converge.[63]

In some ways, this just rehearses conventional ecumenical wisdom. But its vector of approach differs slightly, and, I hope, generatively. Rather than merely celebrating the diversity of our heritages—which is in order, of course—it also calls upon us to recognize that those heritages, as indispensable as they are, also obstruct the way to unity. We can repent of the fact of our divisions, and especially of the sin that lies at their root, while also giving thanks for the paths we've taken (our own and others'). Moreover, to the degree that we learn to recognize and give thanks for the workings of the law of the cross in the heritages of those from whom we're divided, we will come to realize how inexcusable, how untenable those divisions are, until, finally we realize that we have no choice but to reenter communion with each other, whatever practical difficulties may attend this reunion. For our continual reappropriation of the mystery of redemption, the law of the cross, will remind us precisely wherein unity consists—the embrace of the other in love, even across disagreement, even across enmity. Precisely in these.

This will be found, though, not through an undoing of the paths along which we've come. Instead, the churches as they are (and, so, as they have been) shall need to come together in relationships of full communion, not through assimilation to one another, but by the forging of a new path together. They will all undoubtedly be transformed in that encounter, but the transformation will occur as they venture down a new path together.[64]

---

62 Note the similar affirmation in Congar, *Divided Christendom*, 264–67. See also John Paul II, *Ut Unum Sint*, nos. 21–27.

63 So also Congar, *Divided Christendom*, 264–73. This impulse lies behind the "spiritual ecumenism" so often commended by the Catholic Church. E.g., *UR*, no. 8; John Paul II, *Ut Unum Sint*, nos. 21–27. While I fully affirm this principle, I believe it is also vital to insist that spiritual ecumenism cannot stand alone, but must be accompanied by concrete action toward unity. This insistence is all the more vital given the current ecumenical winter. One cannot live by bread alone, but nor will pure spirit suffice.

64 Crucially, this will also not involve a repudiation of the churches that have followed the paths of uniatism, of adding others by way of ordinariates, or entered into mergers with each other. Those paths also cannot and should not be reversed. We must take ourselves and our ecumenical partners as we are, not as our ecumenical or theological ideals say that we should have been.

Walking in the Way of the Cross

I can only imagine that the foregoing sounds at once nice—for who can object to finding the paths of unity together?—and naïve—for who can miss the very real obstacles presented by our divided histories and presents? For that reason, it is also bound to be frustrating: what are we actually to do? I feel this frustration myself, and yet the conclusions seem inescapable, at least if we are unwilling to revert to an ecumenism of return (whether on the Roman model or some other), or to acquiesce to our divisions. No one communion gets to set the terms of union or exert its hegemony over the others. Nor can we simply throw up our hands in defeat. For related reasons, Ephraim Radner famously ended his paradigm-shifting *The End of the Church* with the observation that the quest for unity is "maddeningly antiprogrammatic." After all, our disunity will only be overcome by repentance, but to repent of division is, also, by definition, to cease our divisions.[65]

The path to unity will, then, involve something of a cross in the churches' lives. The end of Christ's earthly life was marked by perplexity, frustration, and the apparent failure of his mission.[66] And yet in the cross is our life and our salvation. Unity will not be comfortable. The cross was not. Yet the cross of unity must be the way marked by the law of the cross, giving life to and for the beloved (even enemies beloved for God's sake), and not a crucifying unity, which comes at the cost of others' life and flourishing.

Division is the result of lost charity. Union will be forged by embracing each other in all our diversity, in all our disagreement, even in our apparent incompatibility, in love. Once more, our considerations in chapter 3 rule out any construal of this embrace that would allow the abuse or harm that proceeds from weaponized appeals to unity, so I will not rehash those considerations here. As we rediscover the law of the cross at work in our own histories (and as we repent of our crucifying legacies), as we recognize the law of the cross in the histories of others, we can learn to cleave to one another in love.

---

65 Radner, *End of the Church*, 352.

66 Shockingly and poignantly articulated by Hans Urs von Balthasar, *Theo-Drama*, 4:357–61; we might consider also Balthasar's depiction of the church's historical sojourn ending in something of a shipwreck, requiring God's eschatological intervention to bring those who will be saved safely into harbor. *The Glory of the Lord: A Theological Aesthetics*, vol. 7, *The New Covenant*, ed. John Riches, trans. Brian McNeil (San Francisco: Ignatius, 1989), 543.

Here, polity remains the primary practical barrier, for it is through the episcopate that the communion of particular churches is enacted, and some of these heritages are not governed by bishops. Yet, as *Baptism, Eucharist and Ministry* has noted, *episkopé* can be exercised in a variety of ways, and as the Chicago-Lambeth Quadrilateral avers, the historic episcopate can be locally adapted. Who is to say what convergences may be possible were the churches to determine that their future paths must coincide? Episcopally governed churches may well be enriched by the presbyteral conciliarity of the Reformed tradition, even as the others grasp the vitality of a historic episcopate. Nothing beyond the sufficient statement of Nicene orthodoxy and some means of extending and enacting communion between churches (which is the episcopate's function) is *required* for this communion, though.

The mutually incommensurable patterns that have emerged in the churches' histories need not prevent communion. The *JDDJ* shows how these can be maintained within new, emergent understandings that are no longer church dividing. I want to suggest, though, that we need not wait until all of these have been resolved. They can be found in the doing, so long as we recognize one another as Christian and are committed to finding the way forward together.

In all of this our very real differences are not papered over, but they would be relocated into the communion of the one, holy, catholic, and apostolic church. Only united with each other can we discern the way forward. Only united with each other can we assess the developments that have occurred in other traditions, because only then do they also become our developments. Here the matters of women's ordination and LGBTQ affirmation are particularly salient, and the mutual embrace of churches that do and do not accept these developments could lead to radical reconfigurations of the states of the questions. Neither "side" would need to accept anything more about the other beyond their being Christians, and, so to be embraced in charity. This embrace would, no doubt, be bracing for all involved.

Churches on both sides could take something of a Gamaliel approach, waiting to see what God brings about: confident that if they are correct, this will shine through eventually, desirous of correction if they've gotten it wrong, and trusting the Holy Spirit to correct themselves, their Christian siblings, or (more likely) both. This reconfigures the process of discernment and reception. Now LGBTQ couples and women priests are not awaiting the ratification of their identities, vocations, or loves by the whole, but rather engaged in a mission of witness so that the whole can be enriched by them. Those who do not embrace these changes can still embrace these Christians, and view them not as threats, but as beloved, and their communities not as apostate, but as engaged in an experiment in discernment. Such a stance requires a high degree of confidence in divine providence and the guidance of the Holy Spirit, a kenotic relinquishment of power in favor of love, of control in favor of responsibility and persuasion.[67]

The contestation, discernment, and so on needed to assess these developments, would occur within the context of mutual embrace, an embrace that is informed by the same law of the cross by which God, in Christ, has embraced us, in all our difference, even our hostility and wrongness. This very diversity can prevent such a unity from becoming a crucifying unity, for it would not be the case that anyone must surrender themselves, or their histories for the sake of unity. Spaces that embrace identities and preferences that are less welcome elsewhere would exist, whereby safety and flourishing can be found, while the witness of the whole can be a crucible of conversion for any viewpoints that are at odds with the way of Christ.

CONCLUSION: AT THE END OF ALL OUR STRIVINGS

We have all inherited a divided church. None of us now living have ever known a unified church. Perhaps our particular churches have been internally unified, but none of them have encompassed the full membership of Christ's body. Each of them falls short of the theological ideal of the union of all of Christ's own with one another and him. And, while new divisions continue to emerge, and their threat casts a shadow over today's churches, by and large none of us have chosen this situation. The brokenness of Christ's body has been the context of any and all of our Christian lives. It is within these fragmentary splinters that we have been baptized, formed in the faith, fed with Christ's body and blood. Anyone who would be Christian today must

---

67 Such an arrangement would still leave us without the full interchangeability of ministries, though this obstacle would be overcome in time through discernment. While it would represent a pain point, particularly for woman and/or LGBTQ priests and bishops, it still wouldn't be a barrier to full communion between churches, per se. For instance, there is no automatic interchangeability of ministries between different rites of the Catholic Church, even amid the recognition of the validity of all the ordinations in question. The differentiation involved could be construed along analogical lines to this.

be a Christian who is divided from others, for there is no other kind possible so long as the full visible unity of all Christians remains unrealized.

The churches' divided histories make up the premotion for our activity here and now, constraining the possibilities open to us. While unity and division are matters of the will—the only thing keeping us divided is our determination that we remain divided—no amount of wishing we were one will bring it about. Unity must be enacted, but how are we to do so without betraying the paths along which we have known the Lord? While some elements of our pasts may well be left behind in a self-transcending transformation as we venture forth together, their transcendence will not be, must not be, cannot without betrayal be their repudiation.

The way forward must be found together, and must ultimately lead to a convergence within which all the baptized are united in one fellowship. This unity will involve a wide diversity, wider than is typically imagined, a diversity encompassing not just difference but also disagreement, also contestation, even strife. Only in such wise will the churches be able to realistically be together. A unity based in agreement is illusory. It has almost certainly never existed. And even if it ever did, it will forever recede in our pursuit. Every new agreement just pushes the goal posts back. Moreover, even if it were ever achieved, it would be risibly tenuous, needing only some fresh disagreement to be sundered once more.[68]

A unity within which contestation is not exceptional, but expected, normal, welcomed, is a unity that can be enacted and that can perdure. It is, practically speaking, the only sort of unity that's realistic. It is, moreover, the only sort of unity that will allow the authentic exercise of ecclesial discernment, for only when all perspectives are included, only when vociferous debate occurs, can the way forward be found. As we have noted, even if the Catholic Church can still make definitive pronouncements due to the *subsistit in*, since it is missing a lung, it can only do so raspingly.

The church's history has tended to keep debate and deliberation relegated to the episcopacy. And yet, all the baptized possess the *sensus fidei*, and the church as the whole people of God is indefectible and infallible in its believing.[69] The teaching office of the hierarchy is properly located within and an expression of this *sensus fidelium*: the bishops and the pope himself are

---

68 Jenson, *Unbaptized God*, 1–8; Radner, *End of the Church*, 170.
69 *LG*, no. 12 [Tanner, 2:858].

charged with teaching the faith of the church, not the faith of the hierarchy.[70] And in a time when within the churches the faithful feel alienated from their bishops, when the bishops have not listened to the laity, when proposed teachings have not been received by the faithful, and when the churches disagree among themselves, the *sensus fidelium* of the whole church must be attended to. It is not a foregone conclusion that lay resistance to hierarchical intervention means that the laity are right and the clergy wrong. But neither is it a foregone conclusion that the clergy are right and the laity merely rebellious. Mutatis mutandis for disagreements between the churches. Only through discernment and listening shall a way forward be found. In this regard, Pope Francis's recent turn to synodality in the Catholic Church is a step in the direction of a wider consultation with the faithful, but it still falls short, because the listening remains limited.[71] I do not suggest a democratization of the church, only that the fullness of the church is needed in order to properly recognize the church's faith. Only together can we discern the truth in its fullness.

We have all inherited divided churches. And no amount of wishing can undo our histories or repair the damage. For over a century now, concerted efforts have been underway to redress the ruptures in Christ's body. Through ecumenical effort, both bilateral dialogues and faith and order work, a high degree of agreement has emerged, but for all this, Humpty-Dumpty remains un-put-together.[72] In part, this is due to the reasons I've enumerated: an ecclesiology of agreement will always fail. In part, it is due to the weight of history: centuries of divergent traditioning cannot be undone by fiat. The same historical dynamics that led to and perpetuated our divisions must also be followed for our forging of unity.

And even in those cases where some limited unity has been achieved: the "return" of the uniate churches to full communion with Rome, the united churches, full communion agreements among various bodies, still it falls

---

70 *LG*, nos. 12, 25 [Tanner, 2:858, 869–70]; *DV*, no. 10 [Tanner, 2:975]; Ormond Rush, *The Eyes of Faith: The Sense of the Faithful and the Church's Reception of Revelation* (Washington, DC: CUA Press, 2009); Sullivan, *Magisterium*.

71 See, e.g., Francis, "Address at Ceremony Commemorating the 50th Anniversary of the Institution of the Synod of Bishops" (Vatican website, October 17, 2015); International Theological Commission, "Synodality in the Life and Mission of the Church" (Vatican website, March 2, 2018).

72 See the witness of Vischer and Meyer, *Growth in Agreement*; Gros, Meyer, and Rusch, *Growth in Agreement II*; Gros, Best, and Fuchs, *Growth in Agreement III*; Best, Fuchs et al., *Growth in Agreement IV*, book 1; Best, Fuchs et al., *Growth in Agreement IV*, book 2.

short of the full, visible unity toward which we must strive, if only because it does not encompass all the baptized within its communion (and often enough for other reasons as well). Even if some Lutherans and Episcopalians have achieved a full communion agreement, other Lutherans demur. And even if all Lutherans embraced the union, what, then of the Reformed? of the Baptists? What if the travails of the Anglican Communion were resolved, but at the cost of sending LGBTQ Christians back into the closet, thereby placing them back upon their crosses? What if the ARCIC process led to the Catholic Church's recognition of Anglican orders, but only for male priests? All of these achievements, while perhaps genuine movements toward unity, would fall woefully short of our calling and task, which cannot leave anyone out or behind.

The scope of the unity that still eludes us is staggering. It is disproportionate to any of the efforts underway. Yet, the Christian tradition is founded upon a disproportion. It is our stock and trade. At the heart of it all is the law of the cross, God's absolutely supernatural solution to the evils of the human race. The self-transcendence to which it calls us exceeds anything we're capable of by nature, bringing us to share in the very life of God.

Strive for unity we must, but at the end of all our strivings, we'll be able to do no more than hold up the broken, crumbling pieces we've worked so hard to gather, and, as the dust runs through our fingers, plaintively cry, "Sovereign Lord, can these bones live?"

Conclusion

Hoping against Hope

Where have the last chapters, with their meandering path, brought us? To the recognition that we face a task utterly beyond our capacity, and yet one at which we must ceaselessly strive. I have, throughout, avoided proffering my own proposal as to how this task can be accomplished, for a threefold reason: (1) as an achievement beyond our capacity, it is, ultimately, something that God must accomplish among us—though not in a way that precludes our own cooperation with grace; (2) as a matter impinging upon the lives of the churches and their relationships with one another, it is for them to discover and forge, not for any theologian to mandate; and (3) this work is intended as a theology of the divided church, a preliminary stage to any such concrete proposal or agenda for the churches.

Yet through this journey, we have gained insight into the contours of such a unity. When the churches are fully and visibly united—and I am confident that they must and shall be, because for this Christ prayed, for this Christ died, for this Christ rose, for this Christ has given the Holy Spirit, for this Christ sits at the right hand of the divine majesty, this purpose of the triune God shall not ultimately fail—theirs will be a unity that embraces and encompasses *all* those who belong to Christ. We Anglicans have been right to insist that the unity of the church is the unity of all the baptized with one another in Christ.

This, then, will be a unity from which none who are Christ's own will be excluded—certainly not actually, for none can snatch Christ's own from his hand (John 10:28), but also not performatively or conceptually. Of necessity, then, it will be a unity composed of great diversity, a far greater diversity than most Christians have dared to imagine. This will be a unity of the churches in their incommensurable differences, a unity that embraces not just diversity, but contestation, strife, even enmity, because we have been embraced by just such a love in Christ.

To be the church is to be bound together in precisely this love, the love that died for us when we were still enemies of God, the love celebrated and entered into at each eucharistic celebration, a love that does not preclude the refusal of that love. Indeed, this love's fullest economic expression—the crucifixion—was precisely thus. When we refuse this love, when we refuse to maintain communion with other Christians, with all other Christians, we enact the same pattern that crucified Christ, playing out the drama of redemption not from the side of the redeemed, nor from the side of the redeemer, but in the position of Pontius Pilate, or of the unnamed soldiers who carried out the crucifixion. And yet, even for his crucifiers, Christ prays that God forgive them. Even the centurion who oversaw the operation was moved to confess "truly this was the Son of God." Even amid our spurning of divine love, all hope is not lost. We shall return to this hope below, but must not be premature in so doing. The nettle must be grasped before any balm is applied.

Our divisions, whatever other factors they've involved—and it is legitimate enough to attend to those other factors, for while division itself is a surd, lacking all intelligibility, surrounding that surd are all sorts of intelligible factors that can and should be made sense of to the extent that we're able—stem from the refusal of charity. They are performative rejections of the gospel, of the saving union of humanity with and in Christ. Sometimes the failure of charity is on the part of those who depart—for example, the Donatists or their contemporary heirs, who insist upon a pure church. Sometimes it is reciprocated—for example, Augustine's "compel them to come in," or the Episcopal Church's lawsuits against departing schismatics. Sometimes, the refusal of charity is on the part of the larger body from which others find they must depart for the sake of their own survival and dignity. A church that constructs itself as white, male, heterosexual, and so on, refuses to embrace in love significant portions of its membership. (And a condescending, paternalistic, patronizing love is not the charity that informed Christ's sacrifice, nor that which is given in the Holy Spirit. It is, at best, a parody of that love.) Not all BIPOC or API or female or LGBTQ Christians have felt they needed to strike out on their own, but those who have do not bear the culpability for the division.

A crucifying unity makes mockery of the cross of Christ and the unity of the church, and must be refused at all costs. This theology has examined crucifying logics in the guise of unities that come at the expense of BIPOC and LGBTQ well-being, but any unity that would efface diversity and difference, which would require assimilation to anything other than the Nicene faith, reproduces the same pattern. We are called upon to embrace one another *in our actuality*, not in some ostensible ideal form within which particularity and distinctive identity is lost. As we move toward one another, we reject nothing of ourselves but our sin, and we expect our ecumenical partners to do the same.

This leaves open the question of whether certain sins simply exclude from the church's communion. And it is particularly fraught, given my insistence that the churches embrace and promote the well-being of their queer members. After all, not a few major traditions regard sexual expression outside of heterosexual marriage to be sinful. Once more, I will not engage in an apologetic for queer affirmation, though I do not accept the premise that LGBTQ identity and expression are necessarily sinful. And once more I caution that we must not construe this as a matter of a heterosexual church deigning to include LGBTQ folks. It is, rather, a matter of recognizing their membership in the church and repenting of pretending that they weren't already Christ's body all along. Nevertheless, a few points are in order: first I reiterate that any support in the New Testament for exclusion from the church on the basis of sin is applied to individuals and not to churches as such, as well as aiming toward restoration, not exclusion per se. Second, since we are operating at the level of communities, not individuals, it is probably best for the churches to focus upon the planks in their own eyes, rather than worrying about what splinters might be in others'. Third, after all, none of us, either as individuals or communities, are redeemed in such a way as to totally remove all sin. It is arbitrary to insist that some particular sin, even if correctly identified, excludes an ecumenical partner from our embrace. Fourth, reconceiving the unity of the church as a unity of diverse churches, embracing even disagreement, can afford a way forward on such matters. Being in communion with a church does not imply an endorsement of all that they say, do, or stand for. Instead, it is a recognition that they, too, are

Christians, and so we're stuck together. It moves our disagreements, including over moral matters, into the arena of the churches' communion, rather than outside it. If we think that our sibling churches are wrong, we can continue to debate the matter, while holding each other fast in love. Imaginations can be shifted, so that nonaffirming churches can look upon affirming churches not as faithlessly endorsing sin, but as undertaking an experiment in discernment on behalf of the whole. If we are wrong, time will tell. Meanwhile, diverse churches in communion with each other means that there will be safe spaces for queer folks.

Further, and more to the point: We must ask ourselves seriously, when we consider refusing communion to another Christian community on the basis of some sin, even assuming we are right (and the cross should disrupt any such assumptions regarding our moral valuation), do we really think that sin should be a cause for exclusion from the community of salvation? Are we so sure that we would not find ourselves shut out? If Christ embraces them, then so must we. Once more, how this would work is for the churches to discover together. All I can do is point to the fundamental reality in which church unity consists and warn us against departing from it.

Far from being a laissez-faire indifferentism, such a unity calls for *far more* from those who would enact it. It's easy enough to hold fast to those with whom you share some basic likeness and broad-based agreement. To embrace the other, to embrace one whom one regards as an enemy is far more bracing.

As we do so, we must be on guard against allowing this union of enemies to devolve into a crucifying unity. The call to embrace is not a call to allow others to carry out harm. Affirming Christians must hold fast to heterosexist Christians. But they must not allow homophobia, transphobia, or the like to harm queer Christians. Antiracist Christians must hold fast to and embrace their racist siblings in Christ (never assuming that they themselves are free from the white supremacy that so pervasively pollutes the air we breathe), but must not stand idly by while BIPOC, API or any other racial grouping is harmed.

THE WIDTH, BREADTH, HEIGHT, AND DEPTH OF LOVE

How far does this embrace extend, then? As far as the "distance" between the infinite God and finite creatures. As far as the "distance" between the infinitely holy one and the most depraved of human sinfulness. As far as the utter extremities of godlessness, for there is nowhere so far from God, so alienated, so godforsaken that the Son of God has not been their first, filling it with the embrace of divine love. And, so, in a crucial sense, the answer to this question is *always*: farther still.

As an ecclesiology, my argument stops at the boundary of Christian recognition, for we are concerned with the Christian church. The solidarity of the entire human family is vital, and not unrelated to ecclesiology, but it is, nevertheless, distinct. To cast the line further, beyond Christian recognition, is its own act of violence, one that does not respect the integrity of non-Christian conscience or experience, a colonizing act, no matter how inclusively-minded we might think it is. Following my own tradition, I have conceived this boundary as Nicene orthodoxy. Others might place it elsewhere, and might do so for good reasons. Some may view my insistence on Nicaea as the sole boundary of Christian recognition as too loose, others as too restrictive. But here I stand.

Yet, while as an ecclesiology, we must stop here, our concern cannot. Love cannot stop there. By the impetus of the Christian faith, by the reality in which the church consists, we are led beyond the boundaries of the church, beyond the boundaries of Christian faith, to the embrace of all. This embrace is not ecclesial communion, per se. Yet, we must stand in solidarity with the whole human family. Our love must extend to all that God loves, else it is a betrayal of that love. This love knows no bounds. Neither must our solidarity and embrace.

In particular, we must reckon with the supersessionism that has pervaded so much of the Christian tradition. Lurking behind so many of our failures of charity, behind so many of our divisions, perhaps behind them all, is our failure to honor, love, and embrace our Jewish elder siblings. We must not forget that Paul's ideal unified ecclesiology is articulated in the context of insisting upon reconciliation of Jews and gentiles to one another in Christ. Only in the mutual embrace of Jew and gentile can an authentic ecclesial unity be forged. And this not necessarily in the sense of an influx of Jews into the now-predominantly gentile church. Some Jews become Christians, but no Christian should insist upon this. Instead, the church must be purged of its antisemitism, its anti-Judaism (the two are distinct), and its supersessionism.

So long as we forget that we are gentiles, with no claim to God, God's people, or God's covenants, we shall also tend to draw the lines of inclusion too tightly. So long as we imagine that those whom God has called with gifts and callings that are irrevocable are replaceable, we will be unable to enact the embrace that unity demands. Precisely what this nonsupersessionist Christianity might be, we cannot yet say, for it will be a matter of learning new ways to be Christian and unlearning vast portions of the ways we have been Christian. The path we have taken through history is littered with anti-Semitism. That path cannot be undone, but a new one can be trod. And tread it we must, for until we've dealt with this foundational evil, we cannot hope for a better outcome.

IN THE END, LOVE

The churches' paths through history are littered with broken fragments, littered with legacies of harm. As we sojourn through time, celebrating the Eucharist, we have at once been bound to one another, and seen bitter fruit borne. The crumbs strewn along the road are Christ's body, but also the contaminants we have introduced: our rivalries, dissensions, divisions, exclusions; the law of the cross and our crucifying logics. This is the history of our brokenness, and not just a brokenness, but of our breaking, the body of Christ's rupture is not passive, but something that has been actively undertaken within and by the churches. No one but us has broken this body. Our history is one of our own making. And yet, this is also none other than the history of our redemption.

That the churches are divided is an evil. That the churches exist is a good. Through us, in all our brokenness, all our rupture, God continues the work of redemption. Human beings are still brought into saving communion with her through these flawed, fragmented, ambiguous, death-dealing, life-giving communities. That there is still a Christian writing this. That there will (hopefully) be Christians reading it, testifies to the fact that our failures do not thwart this divine purpose. While our divisions stem from failures of charity, refusals of love, ultimately, it is not our love, but the love of God that binds together the church. Their love is a love that surpasses even our bitterest failures, a love so infinite that it can never be exhausted.

Hence, the last word belongs not to our failures or infidelities, but to God's mercy and grace. The word of divine mercy, the Word eternally spoken by, with, and as God is the decisive one. God has spoken in the Son (Heb 1:1).

This word is perpetually valid and shall never be abrogated. It reverberates through the forlorn halls of our unfaithful history, calling us to new life, calling us to one another. It rushes to us from a future we cannot yet anticipate, but which must surely come, for this word cannot be broken. We hear this word not as a present possession, but in expectant, penitent hope.

Behold, I am making all things new.

Bibliography

Althaus-Reid, Marcella. *Indecent Theology: Theological Perversions in Sex, Gender and Politics.* London: Routledge, 2000.

———. *The Queer God.* London: Routledge, 2003.

Anatolios, Khaled. *Retrieving Nicaea: The Development and Meaning of Trinitarian Doctrine.* Grand Rapids: Baker, 2011.

Anglican-Roman Catholic International Commission. *The Final Report: Windsor, September 1981.* Cincinnati: Forward Movement Publications, 1982.

———. "The Gift of Authority." 1998.

Arenas, Sandra. *Fading Frontiers? A Historical-Theological Investigation into the Notion of the "Elementa Ecclesiae."* Leuven: Peeters, 2021.

Arnold, J. A. "Anglicanorum Coetibus: Generous Offer or Aggressive Attack? A Problem of Ecclesiology." *One in Christ* 44, no. 1 (2010): 56–66.

Augustine. *Answer to Faustus, a Manichean.* Edited by Boniface Ramsey. Translated by Rolland Teske. The Works of Saint Augustine: A Translation for the 21st Century 1/20. Hyde Park, NY: New City Press, 2007.

———. *The City of God (I–X).* Edited by Boniface Ramsey. Translated by William Babcock. The Works of Saint Augustine: A Translation for the 21st Century 1/6. Hyde Park, NY: New City Press, 2012.

———. *The City of God (XI–XXII).* Edited by Boniface Ramsey. Translated by William Babcock. The Works of Saint Augustine: A Translation for the 21st Century 1/7. Hyde Park, NY: New City Press, 2013.

———. *The Donatist Controversy I.* Edited by David Hunter. Translated by Boniface Ramsey. The Works of Saint Augustine: A Translation for the 21st Century 1/21. Hyde Park, NY: New City Press, 2019.

———. *Homilies on the Gospel of John (1–40).* Edited by Allan D. Fitzgerald. Translated by Edmund Hill. The Works of Saint Augustine: A Translation for the 21st Century 3/12. Hyde Park, NY: New City Press, 2009.

———. *Letters 1-99.* Edited by John E. Rotelle. Translated by Roland Teske. The Works of Saint Augustine: A Translation for the 21st Century 2/1. Hyde Park, NY: New City Press, 1997.

———. *Teaching Christianity.* Edited by John E. Rotelle. Translated by Edmund Hill. The Works of Saint Augustine: A Translation for the 21st Century 1/11. Hyde Park, NY: New City Press, 1996.

Avis, Paul. *Anglicanism and the Christian Church: Theological Resources in Historical Perspective.* London: T&T Clark, 2002.

———. *The Identity of Anglicanism: Essentials of Anglican Ecclesiology.* London: T&T Clark, 2007.

———. *Reconciling Theology.* London: SCM Press, 2022.

———. *Reshaping Ecumenical Theology: The Church Made Whole?* London: T&T Clark, 2010.

———. *The Vocation of Anglicanism.* London: Bloomsbury, 2016.

Ayres, Lewis. *Augustine and the Trinity.* Cambridge: Cambridge University Press, 2010.

———. *Nicaea and Its Legacy: An Approach to Fourth-Century Trinitarian Theology.* Oxford: Oxford University Press, 2004.

Baldwin, James. "Going to Meet the Man." In *Going to Meet the Man,* 227–49. New York: Dial Press, 1965.

Balthasar, Hans Urs von. *The Glory of the Lord: A Theological Aesthetics.* Volume 7, *The New Covenant.* Edited by John Riches. Translated by Brian McNeil. San Francisco: Ignatius, 1989.

———. *Theo-Drama: Theological Dramatic Theory.* Volume 4, *The Action.* Translated by Graham Harrison. San Francisco: Ignatius, 1994.

Barnes, Michel R. "Augustine in Contemporary Trinitarian Theology." *Theological Studies* 56, no. 2 (1995): 237–50.

———. "De Régnon Reconsidered." *Augustinian Studies* 26 (1995): 51–79.

Bartel, Timothy W. "Adiaphora: The Achilles Heel of the Windsor Report." *Anglican Theological Review* 89, no. 3 (2007): 401–19.

Bates, Stephen. *A Church at War: Anglicans and Homosexuality.* London: Hodder & Stoughton, 2005.

Bavel, Tarcisius van. "The 'Christus Totus' Idea: A Forgotten Aspect of Augustine's Spirituality." In *Studies in Patristic Christology,* edited by Thomas Finan and Vincent Twomey, 84–94. Portland, OR: Four Courts Press, 1998.

Bayne, Stephen F. "Anglicanism—the Contemporary Situation: This Nettle, Anglicanism." *Pan-Anglican* 5 (1954): 39–45.

Beach, Foley. "A North American Perspective: Neo-Pagan Anglicanism." In *The Future of Orthodox Anglicanism,* edited by Gerald R. McDermott, 81–102. Wheaton, IL: Crossway, 2020.

Becker, Karl. "The Church and Vatican II's '*Subsistit in*' Terminology." *Origins* 35, no. 31 (2006): 514–22.

Becker, Werner. "History of the Decree [on Ecumenism]." In *Commentary on the Documents of Vatican II,* edited by Herbert Vorgrimler, translated by R. A. Wilson, 2:1–56. New York: Herder and Herder, 1968.

Benedict XVI. "Anglicanorum Coetibus: Providing for Personal Ordinariates for Anglicans Entering into Full Communion with the Catholic Church." Vatican Website, November 4, 2009. https://tinyurl.com/8fwmv252.

Best, Thomas F., Lorelei F. Fuchs, SA, John Gibaut, Jeffrey Gros, FSC, and Despina Prassas, eds. *Growth in Agreement IV.* Book 2, *International Dialogue Texts and Agreed Statements, 2004–2014.* Switzerland: World Council of Churches, 2017.

Best, Thomas F., Lorelei F. Fuchs SA, John Gibaut, Jeffrey Gros FSC, and Despina Prassas, eds. *Growth in Agreement IV.* Book 1, *International Dialogue Texts and Agreed Statements 2004–2014.* Switzerland: World Council of Churches, 2017.

Bevans, Stephan B. *Models of Contextual Theology.* Maryknoll, NY: Orbis, 1992.

Boniface VIII. "Unam Sanctam," November 18, 1302. https://tinyurl.com/5fczhxf3.

The Book of Common Prayer. New York: Church Hymnal Corporation, 1979.

Bradford Littlejohn. "Believing in the Church: Why Ecumenism Needs the Invisibility of the Church." *Religions* 10, no. 2 (2019): 104–18.

Bradley, James. "Increase in Wisdom and Stature: Personal Ordinariates from Benedict XVI to Francis." *Jurist: Studies in Church Order & Ministry* 77, no. 1 (2021): 49–72.

Brittain, Christopher Craig. *A Plague on Both Their Houses: Liberal vs. Conservative Christians and the Divorce of the Episcopal Church USA.* London: Bloomsbury, 2015.

Brittain, Christopher Craig, and Andrew McKinnon. *The Anglican Communion at a Crossroads: The Crises of a Global Church.* University Park: The Pennsylvania State University Press, 2018.

Brock, Rita Nakashima, and Rebecca Ann Parker. *Proverbs of Ashes: Violence, Redemptive Suffering, and the Search for What Saves Us.* Boston: Beacon, 2001.

Brown, Joanne Carlson, and Carole R. Bohn, eds. *Christianity, Patriarchy, and Abuse: A Feminist Critique.* New York: Pilgrim Press, 1989.

Buckley, Michael J. *Papal Primacy and the Episcopate: Towards a Relational Understanding.* New York: Crossroad, 1998.

Calvin, John. *Institutes of the Christian Religion.* Edited by John T. McNeill. Louisville, KY: Westminster John Knox, 1960.

Carpenter, Anne M. *Nothing Gained Is Eternal: A Theology of Tradition.* Minneapolis: Fortress Press, 2022.

Carter, J. Kameron. *Race: A Theological Account.* Oxford: Oxford University Press, 2008.

Cavanaugh, William T. *The Myth of Religious Violence: Secular Ideology and the Roots of Modern Conflict.* Oxford: Oxford University Press, 2009.

Chauvet, Louis-Marie. "Le pain rompu comme figure théologique de la présence eucharistique." *Questions Liturgiques* 82, no. 1 (2001): 9–33.

Cheng, Patrick S. *Radical Love: Introduction to Queer Theology.* New York: Seabury, 2011.

———. *Rainbow Theology: Bridging Race, Sexuality, and Spirit.* New York: Seabury, 2013.

Chirovsky, Andriy. "The 1596 Union of Brest: How the Ukrainian Church Rejoined the Catholic Communion." *The Australasian Catholic Record* 76, no. 3 (1999): 318–27.

Coakley, Sarah. *The New Asceticism.* London: Bloomsbury, 2015.

———. "Sacrifice Regained: Evolution, Cooperation and God." Gifford Lectures, University of Aberdeen, 2012. https://tinyurl.com/nhhyp9r9.

Cohen, Jeremy. *Living Letters of the Law: Ideas of the Jew in Medieval Christianity.* Berkeley: University of California Press, 1999.

Colin E. Gunton. *Father, Son, and Holy Spirit: Toward a Fully Trinitarian Theology.* London: T&T Clark, 2003.

Cone, James H. *Black Theology and Black Power.* Maryknoll, NY: Orbis, 2019.

———. *A Black Theology of Liberation.* Maryknoll, NY: Orbis, 2020.

———. *The Cross and the Lynching Tree.* Maryknoll, NY: Orbis, 2013.

———. *God of the Oppressed.* Maryknoll, NY: Orbis, 1997.

Congar, Yves. *Dialogue between Christians: Catholic Contributions to Ecumenism.* Westminster: Newman Press, 1966.

———. *Divided Christendom: A Catholic Study of the Problem of Reunion.* Translated by M. A. Bousfield. London: Centenary Press, 1939.

———. *Tradition and Traditions: An Historical and a Theological Essay.* New York: Macmillan, 1967.

———. *True and False Reform in the Church*. Translated by Paul Philibert. Collegeville, MN: Liturgical Press, 2011.

Congregation of the Doctrine of the Faith. "Dominus Iesus." Vatican website, August 6, 2000. https://tinyurl.com/y8p5af2n.

———. "Responsum Ad Propositum Dubium Concerning the Teaching Contained in 'Ordinatio Sacerdotalis.'" Vatican website, October 28, 1995. https://tinyurl.com/52dhahez. .

Copeland, M. Shawn. *Enfleshing Freedom: Body, Race, and Being*. Minneapolis: Fortress Press, 2009.

———. *Knowing Christ Crucified: The Witness of African American Religious Experience*. Maryknoll, NY: Orbis, 2018.

Cornwall, Susannah. *Controversies in Queer Theology*. London: SCM, 2011.

Council for World Mission. "Mission in the Context of Empire." Council for World Mission Website, January 30, 2010. https://tinyurl.com/jyh5ju4s.

Coutsoumpos, Panayotis. *Paul and the Lord's Supper: A Socio-historical Investigation*. New York: Peter Lang, 2005.

Crowley, Paul. *Unwanted Wisdom: Suffering, The Cross, And Hope*. New York: Continuum, 2005.

Dales, Douglas. "'One Body'—the Ecclesiology of Michael Ramsey." In *Glory Descending: Michael Ramsey and His Writings*, edited by Douglas Dales, John Habgood, Geoffrey Rowell, and Rowan Williams, 223–38. Grand Rapids: Eerdmans, 2005.

Dalwood, Charlotte. "Orthodoxy and the Politics of Christian Subjectivity: A Case Study of the Global Anglican Future Conference (GAFCON)." *Journal of Anglican Studies* 18, no. 2 (2020): 235–50.

Daly, Robert J. *Christian Sacrifice: The Judaeo-Christian Background before Origen*. Washington, DC: Catholic University of America, 1978.

———. *Sacrifice Unveiled: The True Meaning of Christian Sacrifice*. London: T&T Clark, 2009.

Daniélou, Jean. "Les orientations présentes de la pensée religieuse." *Études* 249 (1946): 5–21.

Daughrity, Dyron B. "South India: Ecumenism's One Solid Achievement? Reflections on the History of the Ecumenical Movement." *International Review of Mission* 99, no. 1 (2010): 56–68.

Davidson, Randall Thomas, and Honor Thomas, eds. *The Six Lambeth Conferences, 1867–1920*. London: SPCK, 1929.

Doe, Michael. "From Colonialism to Communion." *Journal of Anglican Studies* 7, no. 2 (2009): 213–20.

Doe, Norman. "The Apostolic Constitution Anglicanorum Coetibus: An Anglican Juridical Perspective." *One in Christ* 44, no. 1 (2010): 23–48.

Doran, Robert M. *Theology and the Dialectics of History*. Toronto: University of Toronto Press, 2001.

———. *The Trinity in History: A Theology of the Divine Missions*. Volume 1, *Missions and Processions*. Toronto: University of Toronto Press, 2013.

———. *The Trinity in History: A Theology of the Divine Missions*. Volume 2, *Missions and Relations*. Toronto: University of Toronto Press, 2019.

———. *The Trinity in History: A Theology of the Divine Missions*. Volume 3, *Redeeming History*. Edited by Joseph Ogbannaya. Milwaukee: Marquette University Press, 2022.

Dostoyevsky, Fyodor. *The Brothers Karamazov.* Translated by David Magarshack. New York: Penguin, 1958.

Douglas, Ian T. "An American Reflects on the Windsor Report." *Journal of Anglican Studies* 3, no. 2 (2005): 155–79.

Douglas, Kelly Brown. *The Black Christ.* Maryknoll, NY: Orbis, 1993.

——. *Sexuality and the Black Church: A Womanist Perspective.* Maryknoll, NY: Orbis, 1999.

——. *What's Faith Got to Do with It? Black Bodies/Christian Souls.* Maryknoll, NY: Orbis, 2005.

Driver, Jeffrey. "Beyond Lambeth 2008 and ACC14: Tuning a Polity of Persuasion to the Twenty-First Century." *Journal of Anglican Studies* 7, no. 2 (2009): 195–211.

Duggan, Joseph F. "Postcolonial Anglicanism: One Global Identity or Many Contextual Identities?" *Anglican Theological Review* 90, no. 2 (2008): 353–67.

——. "The Postcolonial Paradox: Becoming Less Than Whole(s) Producing Parts That Exclude Other Parts." *Journal of Anglican Studies* 7, no. 1 (2009): 67–77.

Dundes, Alan, ed. *The Blood Libel Legend: A Casebook in Anti-Semitic Folklore.* Madison: University of Wisconsin Press, 1991.

Eiesland, Nancy L. *The Disabled God: Toward a Liberatory Theology of Disability.* Nashville: Abingdon, 1994.

Ellacuría, Ignacio. *Freedom Made Flesh: The Mission of Christ and His Church.* Translated by John Drury. Maryknoll, NY: Orbis, 1976.

Episcopal Church, ed. *Empty Shoes: A Study of the Church of South India.* New York: National Council, Protestant Episcopal Church, 1956.

Episcopal Church and the Evangelical Lutheran Church of America. "Agreement of Full Communion—Called to Common Mission." Episcopal Church website, 1999. https://tinyurl.com/2s42frka.

Fanon, Frantz. *Black Skin, White Masks.* Translated by Charles Lam Markmann. New York: Grove Press, 1991.

Feiner, Johannes. "Commentary on the Decree [on Ecumenism]." In *Commentary on the Documents of Vatican II,* edited by Herbert Vorgrimler, translated by R. A. Wilson, 2:57–164. New York: Herder and Herder, 1968.

Fields, Barbara J., and Karen E. Fields. *Racecraft: The Soul of Inequality in American Life.* New York: Verso, 2022.

Flipper, Joseph J. "White Ecclesiology: The Identity of the Church in the Statements on Racism by United States Catholic Bishops." *Theological Studies* 82, no. 3 (2021): 418–39.

Flynn, Gabriel, and Paul D. Murray. *Ressourcement: A Movement For Renewal in Twentieth-Century Catholic Theology.* Oxford: Oxford University Press, 2014.

Ford, David F. "A Wisdom for Anglican Life: Lambeth 1998 to Lambeth 2008 and Beyond." *Journal of Anglican Studies* 4, no. 2 (2006): 137–56.

Francis. "Address at Ceremony Commemorating the 50th Anniversary of the Institution of the Synod of Bishops." Vatican website, October 17, 2015. https://tinyurl.com/yc2fh7tb.

——. *Evangelii Gaudium.* Vatican website, November 24, 2013. https://tinyurl.com/3abf2aaa.

Frend, W. H. C. *The Donatist Church: A Movement of Protest in Roman North Africa.* Oxford: Clarendon Press, 1952.

Fries, Heinrich, and Karl Rahner. *Unity of the Churches—an Actual Possibility*. Philadelphia: Fortress Press, 1985.

Fuchs, Lorelei F. *Koinonia and the Quest for an Ecumenical Ecclesiology: From Foundations through Dialogue to Symbolic Competence for Communionality*. Grand Rapids: Eerdmans, 2008.

GAFCON. "GAFCON Response to Archbishop of Canterbury." GAFCON website, June 14, 2023. https://tinyurl.com/mryuh8a4.

———. "The Kigali Commitment." GAFCON website, April 21, 2023. https://tinyurl.com/399d4r6h.

Gaillardetz, Richard R. *By What Authority? Foundations for Understanding Authority in the Church*. 2nd ed. Collegeville, MN: Liturgical Press, 2018.

———. *The Church in the Making*: Lumen Gentium, Christus Dominus, Orientalium Ecclesiarum. New York: Paulist, 2006.

———. *Teaching with Authority: A Theology of the Magisterium in the Church*. Collegeville, MN: Liturgical Press, 1997.

Galles, Duane L. C. M. "Anglicanorum Coetibus—Some Canonical Investigations on the Recent Apostolic Constitution." *Jurist: Studies in Church Order & Ministry* 71, no. 1 (2011): 201–33.

Global South Fellowship of Anglican Churches. "Ash Wednesday Statement of GSFA Primates on the Church of England's Decision Regarding the Blessing of Same Sex Unions." GSFA Website, February 20, 2023. https://tinyurl.com/4nyv4du5.

———. "Press Release." Global South Fellowship of Anglican Churches website, July 29, 2022. https://tinyurl.com/8ecwe8kk.

Good, Deirdre J., Willis J. Jenkins, Cynthia B. Kittredge, and Eugene F. Rogers. "A Theology of Marriage Including Same-Sex Couples: A View from the Liberals." *Anglican Theological Review* 93, no. 1 (2011): 51–87.

Gordon, Joseph K. *Divine Scripture in Human Understanding: A Systematic Theology of the Christian Bible*. Notre Dame, IN: University of Notre Dame Press, 2019.

Grillmeier, Aloys. "Chapter I: The Mystery of the Church." In *Commentary on the Documents of Vatican II*, edited by Herbert Vorgrimler, translated by Kevin Smyth, 1:138–52. New York: Herder & Herder, 1967.

Grimes, Katie Walker. *Fugitive Saints: Catholicism and the Politics of Slavery*. Minneapolis: Fortress Press, 2017.

Gros, Jeffrey, Thomas F. Best, and Lorelei F. Fuchs, SA, eds. *Growth in Agreement III: International Dialogue Texts and Agreed Statements, 1998–2005*. Grand Rapids: Eerdmans, 2008.

Gros, Jeffrey, Harding Meyer, and William G. Rusch, eds. *Growth in Agreement II: Reports and Agreed Statements of Ecumenical Conversations on a World Level 1982–1998*. Grand Rapids: Eerdmans, 2000.

Gutiérrez, Gustavo. *A Theology of Liberation: History, Politics, Salvation*. Translated by Caridad Inda and John Eagleson. Maryknoll, NY: Orbis, 1988.

Hadley, Christopher M. *A Symphony of Distances: Patristic, Modern, and Gendered Dimensions of Balthasar's Trinitarian Theology*. Washington, DC: The Catholic University of America Press, 2022.

Halecki, Oskar. *From Florence to Brest (1439–1596)*. New York: Fordham University Press, 1958.

Hanson, Anthony Tyrrell. *Beyond Anglicanism*. London: Darton, Longman, & Todd, 1965.

Hart, David Bentley. "A Gift Exceeding Every Debt: An Eastern Orthodox Appreciation of Anselm's Cur Deus Homo." *Pro Ecclesia* 7, no. 3 (1998): 333–49.

———. "The Myth of Schism." In *Ecumenism Today: The Universal Church in the 21st Century*, edited by Francesca Aran Murphy and Christopher Asprey, 95–106. Aldershot, UK: Ashgate, 2008.

Hassett, Miranda Katherine. *Anglican Communion in Crisis: How Episcopal Dissidents and Their African Allies Are Reshaping Anglicanism*. Princeton, NJ: Princeton University Press, 2007.

Heaney, Robert S. "Coloniality and Theological Method in Africa." *Journal of Anglican Studies* 7, no. 1 (2009): 55–65.

Heaps, Jonathan, and Neil Ormerod. "Statistically Ordered: Gender, Sexual Identity, and the Metaphysics of 'Normal.'" *Theological Studies* 80, no. 2 (2019): 346–69.

Hill, Christopher, Edward Yarnold, and Catholic Church, eds. *Anglican Orders: The Documents in the Debate*. Norwich, UK: Canterbury Press, 1997.

Hof, Eleonora Dorothea. *Reimagining Mission in the Postcolonial Condition: A Theology of Vulnerability and Vocation at the Margins*. Utrecht: Boekencentrum, 2016.

Hollis, Arthur Michael. *The Significance of South India*. Richmond, VA: J. Knox, 1966.

Holmes, Michael W., ed. *The Apostolic Fathers: Greek Texts and English Translations*. 3rd ed. Grand Rapids: Baker, 2007.

Holy Synod, Ecumenical Patriarchate of Constantinople and New Rome. "Document: Encyclical Letter, 'Unto All the Churches of Christ Wheresoever They Be.'" *Greek Orthodox Theological Review* 1, no. 1 (1954): 7–9.

Hooker, Richard. *Of the Laws of Ecclesiastical Polity*. Edited by Michael Russel from John Keble's 1836 edition. Self-published, 2004.

Houtepen, Anton. "Uniatism and Models of Unity in the Ecumenical Movement." In *Four Hundred Years Union of Brest (1596–1996): A Critical Re-evaluation; Acta of the Congress Held at Hernen Castle, the Netherlands, in March 1996*, edited by Bert Groen and Wil van den Bercken, 239–60. Leuven: Peeters, 1998.

Hrynchyshyn, Michael. "The Current Situation of the Greek Catholic Church in Ukraine." In *Four Hundred Years Union of Brest (1596–1996): A Critical Re-evaluation; Acta of the Congress Held at Hernen Castle, the Netherlands, in March 1996*, edited by Bert Groen and Wil van den Bercken, 163–72. Leuven: Peeters, 1998.

Inter-Anglican Theological and Doctrinal Commission. "The Virginia Report," 1997.

International Theological Commission. "Synodality in the Life and Mission of the Church." Vatican Website, March 2, 2018.

James Baldwin: The Price of the Ticket. Maysles Films; PBS American Masters, 1989.

Jennings, Willie James. *After Whiteness: An Education in Belonging*. Grand Rapids: Eerdmans, 2020.

———. *The Christian Imagination: Theology and the Origins of Race*. New Haven, CT: Yale University Press, 2011.

Jenson, Robert W. *Systematic Theology*. Volume 2, *The Works of God*. New York: Oxford University Press, 1999.

———. *Unbaptized God: The Basic Flaw in Ecumenical Theology*. Minneapolis: Fortress Press, 1992.

John Paul II. *Ordinatio Sacerdotalis*. Vatican Website, May 22, 1994. https://tinyurl.com/nhh9vc9k.

———. *Ut Unum Sint: On Commitment to Ecumenism*. Vatican website, May 25, 1995. https://tinyurl.com/27rtdbbv.

Johnson, Elizabeth A. *Creation and the Cross: The Mercy of God for a Planet in Peril*. Maryknoll, NY: Orbis, 2019.

Joint Declaration on the Doctrine of Justification. Vatican website, October 31, 1999. https://tinyurl.com/4j2ps5r2.

Joint International Commission for Theological Dialogue between the Catholic Church and the Orthodox Church. "Uniatism, Method of Union of the Past, and the Present Search for Full Communion [The Balamand Document]." Vatican website, June 23, 1993. https://tinyurl.com/2hfyjp9b.

Kane, Ross. "Tragedies of Communion: Seeking Reconciliation amid Colonial Legacies." *Anglican Theological Review* 97, no. 3 (2015): 391–412.

Kantyka, Przemysław Jan. "Ten Years of Ordinariates for Anglicans—a Few Reflections on the New Ecclesiological Model." *Studia Oecumenica* 19 (2019): 7–18.

Keen, Karen R. *Scripture, Ethics, and the Possibility of Same-Sex Relationships.* Grand Rapids: Eerdmans, 2018.

Keleher, James P. *Saint Augustine's Notion of Schism in the Donatist Controversy.* Mundelein, IL: Saint Mary of the Lake Seminary, 1961.

Kendi, Ibram X. *How to Be an Antiracist.* New York: One World, 2019.

———. *Stamped from the Beginning: The Definitive History of Racist Ideas in America.* New York: Nation Books, 2016.

Kilmartin, Edward J. *The Eucharist in the West: History and Theology.* Edited by Robert J. Daly. Collegeville, MN: Liturgical Press, 1998.

Kim, Yung Suk. *Christ's Body in Corinth: The Politics of a Metaphor.* Minneapolis: Fortress Press, 2014.

King, Martin Luther. "Letter from Birmingham Jail." African Studies Center–University of Pennsylvania, 1963. https://tinyurl.com/2mt4w567.

Klinghardt, Matthias. *Gemeinschaftsmahl und Mahlgemeinschaft: Soziologie und Liturgie frühchristlicher Mahlfeiern.* Tübingen: Francke, 1996.

Klinghardt, Matthias, and Hal Taussig, eds. *Mahl Und Religiöse Identität Im Frühen Christentum = Meals and Religious Identity in Early Christianity.* Tübingen: Francke, 2012.

Kwok, Pui-Lan. "The Legacy of Cultural Hegemony in the Anglican Church." In *Beyond Colonial Anglicanism: The Anglican Communion in the Twenty-First Century,* edited by Ian T. Douglas and Kwok Pui-Lan, 47–70. New York: Church Publishing, 2001.

———. *Postcolonial Imagination and Feminist Theology.* Louisville, KY: Westminster John Knox, 2005.

LaCugna, Catherine Mowry. *God for Us: The Trinity and Christian Life.* San Francisco: HarperSanFrancisco, 1991.

Laing, Mark T. B. "The International Impact of the Formation of the Church of South India: Bishop Newbigin versus the Anglican Fathers." *International Bulletin of Missionary Research* 33, no. 1 (2009): 18.

Lambeth Commission on Communion. "The Windsor Report." Anglican Communion Office, 2004. https://tinyurl.com/9fer295h.

The Lambeth Conference, 1930: Encyclical Letter from the Bishops: With Resolutions and Reports. London : New York: SPCK, 1930.

Lambeth Conference (1948). *The Encyclical Letter from the Bishops, Together with Resolutions and Reports.* London: SPCK, 1948.

The Lambeth Conferences (1867–1930): The Reports of the 1920 and 1930 Conferences, with Selected Resolutions from the Conferences of 1867, 1878, 1888, 1897, and 1908. London: SPCK, 1948.

Lee, James K. *Augustine and the Mystery of the Church.* Minneapolis: Fortress Press, 2017.

Lee, Peter John. "Indaba as Obedience: A Post Lambeth 2008 Assessment 'If Someone Offends You, Talk to Him'." *Journal of Anglican Studies* 7, no. 2 (2009): 147–61.

Living in Love and Faith: Christian Teaching and Learning about Identity, Sexuality, Relationships and Marriage. New York: Church House, 2020.

Lonergan, Bernard J.F. "Christology Today: Methodological Considerations." In *A Third Collection*, edited by Robert M. Doran and John D. Dadosky, 70–93. Collected Works of Bernard Lonergan 16. Toronto: University of Toronto Press, 2017.

———. "Dimensions of Meaning." In *Collection*, edited by Frederick E. Crowe and Robert M. Doran, 232–45. Collected Works of Bernard Lonergan 4. Toronto: University of Toronto Press, 1988.

———. "God's Knowledge and Will." In *Early Latin Theology*, edited by Robert M. Doran and H. Daniel Monsour, translated by Michael G. Shields, 257–411. Collected Works of Bernard Lonergan 19. Toronto: University of Toronto Press, 2011.

———. *The Incarnate Word.* Edited by Robert M. Doran and Jeremy D. Wilkins. Translated by Charles Hefling. Collected Works of Bernard Lonergan 8. Toronto: University of Toronto Press, 2016.

———. *Insight: A Study of Human Understanding.* Edited by Frederick E. Crowe and Robert M. Doran. Collected Works of Bernard Lonergan 3. Toronto: University of Toronto Press, 1992.

———. "Insight Revisited." In *A Second Collection*, edited by Robert M. Doran and John D. Dadosky, 221–33. Collected Works of Bernard Lonergan 13. Toronto: University of Toronto Press, 2016.

———. *Method in Theology.* Edited by Robert Doran, SJ, and John Dadosky. Collected Works of Bernard Lonergan 14. Toronto: University of Toronto Press, 2017.

———. "The Notion of Sacrifice." In *Early Latin Theology*, edited by Robert M. Doran and H. Daniel Monsour, translated by Michael G. Shields, 2–51. Collected Works of Bernard Lonergan 19. Toronto: University of Toronto Press, 2011.

———. *The Ontological and Psychological Constitution of Christ.* Edited by Michael Shields, Frederick Crowe, SJ, and Robert Doran, SJ. Collected Works of Bernard Lonergan 7. Toronto: University of Toronto Press, 2002.

———. "The Origins of Christian Realism." In *A Second Collection*, edited by Robert M. Doran and John D. Dadosky, 202–20. Collected Works of Bernard Lonergan 13. Toronto: University of Toronto Press, 2016.

———. *The Redemption.* Edited by Robert M. Doran, Jeremy Wilkins, and H. Daniel Monsour. Translated by Michael G. Shields. Collected Works of Bernard Lonergan 9. Toronto: University of Toronto Press, 2018.

———. "The Supernatural Order." In *Early Latin Theology*, edited by Robert M. Doran and H. Daniel Monsour, translated by Michael G. Shields, 52–255. Collected Works of Bernard Lonergan 19. Toronto: University of Toronto Press, 2011.

———. "Supplementary Notes on Sanctifying Grace." In *Early Latin Theology*, edited by Robert M. Doran and H. Daniel Monsour, translated by Michael G. Shields, 562–665. Collected Works of Bernard Lonergan 19. Toronto: University of Toronto Press, 2011.

———. "The Transition from a Classicist World-View to Historical-Mindedness." In *A Second Collection*, edited by Robert M. Doran and John D. Dadosky, 3–10. Collected Works of Bernard Lonergan 13. Toronto: University of Toronto Press, 2016.

———. *The Triune God. Doctrines.* Edited by Robert M. Doran and H. Daniel Monsour. Translated by Michael G. Shields. Collected Works of Bernard Lonergan 11. Toronto: University of Toronto Press, 2009.

——. *The Triune God: Systematics*. Edited by Robert M. Doran and H. Daniel Monsour. Translated by Michael G. Shields. Collected Works of Bernard Lonergan 12. Toronto: University of Toronto Press, 2007.

——. *Verbum: Word and Idea in Aquinas*. Edited by Frederick E. Crowe and Robert M. Doran. Collected Works of Bernard Lonergan 2. Toronto: University of Toronto Press, 1997.

Long, D. Stephen. *The Perfectly Simple Triune God: Aquinas and His Legacy*. Minneapolis: Fortress Press, 2016.

Long, David P. "Eucharistic Ecclesiology and Excommunication: A Critical Investigation of the Meaning and Praxis of Exclusion from the Sacrament of the Eucharist." *Ecclesiology* 10, no. 2 (2014): 205–28.

Louth, Andrew. "Should the WCC Expel Patriarch Kirill?" *Public Orthodoxy* (blog), August 26, 2022. https://tinyurl.com/4whr4uw6.

Lubac, Henri de. *Augustinianism and Modern Theology*. Translated by Lancelot Sheppard. New York: Herder & Herder, 2000.

——. *A Brief Catechesis on Nature and Grace*. Translated by Richard Arnandez. San Francisco: Ignatius, 1984.

——. *Catholicism: Christ and the Common Destiny of Man*. Translated by Lancelot C. Sheppard and Elizabeth Englund. San Francisco: Ignatius Press, 1998.

——. *Corpus Mysticum: The Eucharist and the Church in the Middle Ages*. Edited by Laurence Paul Hemming and Susan Frank Parsons. Translated by Gemma Simmonds, Richard Price, and Christopher Stephens. Notre Dame, IN: University of Notre Dame Press, 2007.

——. *History and Spirit: The Understanding of Scripture According to Origen*. Translated by Anne Englund Nash. San Francisco: Ignatius, 2007.

——. *Medieval Exegesis: The Four Senses of Scripture*. 3 vols. Grand Rapids: Eerdmans, 1998.

——. *The Motherhood of the Church Followed by Particular Churches in the Universal Church and an Interview Conducted by Gwendoline Jarczyk*. Translated by Sergia Englund. San Francisco: Ignatius, 1982.

——. *The Mystery of the Supernatural*. Translated by Rosemary Sheed. New York: Herder & Herder, 2012.

——. *The Splendor of the Church*. Translated by Michael Mason. 2nd ed. San Francisco: Ignatius Press, 1999.

——. *Surnaturel : Études Historiques*. Edited by Michel Sales. Collection Théologie. Paris: Desclée de Brouwer, 1991.

Marks, Darren C. "The Windsor Report: A Theological Commentary." *Journal of Anglican Studies* 4, no. 2 (2006): 157–76.

Markus, R. A., ed. "Augustine: A Defence of Christian Mediocrity." In *The End of Ancient Christianity*, 45–62. Cambridge: Cambridge University Press, 1991.

——. *Signs and Meanings: World and Text in Ancient Christianity*. Liverpool: Liverpool University Press, 1996.

Massingale, Bryan N. *Racial Justice and the Catholic Church*. Maryknoll, NY: Orbis, 2010.

Maximus the Confessor. *On the Cosmic Mystery of Jesus Christ*. Translated by Paul M. Blowers and Robert Louis Wilken. Crestwood, NY: St. Vladimir's Seminary Press, 2003.

May, John D'Arcy. "Catholic Fundamentalism? Some Implications of Dominus Iesus for Dialogue and Peacemaking." *Horizons* 28, no. 2 (2001): 271–93.

Mbembe, Achille. *Critique of Black Reason*. Translated by Laurent Dubois. Durham, NC: Duke University Press, 2017.

———. *On the Postcolony*. Berkeley: University of California Press, 2001.

McGowan, Andrew. *Ancient Christian Worship: Early Church Practices in Social, Historical, and Theological Perspective*. Grand Rapids: Baker, 2014.

———. *Ascetic Eucharists: Food and Drink in Early Christian Ritual Meals*. Oxford: Clarendon, 1999.

Meier, John P. "Petrine Ministry in the New Testament and in the Early Patristic Traditions." In *How Can the Petrine Ministry Be a Service to the Unity of the Universal Church?*, edited by James F. Puglisi, 13–33. Grand Rapids: Eerdmans, 2010.

Meijer, Johan. "Greek Catholics Today: How Does It Feel to Live at the Border between East and West?" In *Four Hundred Years Union of Brest (1596–1996): A Critical Re-evaluation; Acta of the Congress Held at Hernen Castle, the Netherlands, in March 1996*, edited by Bert Groen and Wil van den Bercken, 173–82. Leuven: Peeters, 1998.

Methuen, Charlotte. "The Making of 'An Appeal to All Christian People' at the 1920 Lambeth Conference." In *The Lambeth Conference: Theology, History, Polity and Purpose*, edited by Paul Avis and Benjamin M. Guyer, 107–31. London: Bloomsbury, 2017.

———. "Mission, Reunion and the Anglican Communion: The 'Appeal to All Christian People' and Approaches to Ecclesial Unity at the 1920 Lambeth Conference." *Ecclesiology* 16, no. 2 (2020): 175–205.

Meyer, Harding. *That All May Be One: Perceptions and Models of Ecumenicity*. Translated by William G. Rusch. Grand Rapids: Eerdmans, 1999.

Mignolo, Walter D. *The Darker Side of Western Modernity: Global Futures, Decolonial Options*. Durham, NC: Duke University Press, 2011.

Minnerath, Roland. "The Petrine Ministry in the Early Patristic Tradition." In *How Can the Petrine Ministry Be a Service to the Unity of the Universal Church?*, edited by James F. Puglisi, 34–48. Grand Rapids: Eerdmans, 2010.

Moffitt, David M. *Atonement and the Logic of Resurrection in the Epistle to the Hebrews*. London: Brill, 2011.

———. "Blood, Life, and Atonement: Reassessing Hebrews' Christological Appropriation of Yom Kippur." In *The Day of Atonement: Its Interpretation in Early Jewish and Christian Traditions*, edited by Thomas Hieke and Tobias Nicklas, 211–24. Leiden: Brill, 2012.

Mombo, Esther. "The Windsor Report: A Paradigm Shift for Anglicanism." *Anglican Theological Review* 89, no. 1 (2007): 69–78.

Moore, Celia A. "Dealing with Desegregation: Black and White Responses to the Desegregation of the Diocese of Raleigh, North Carolina, 1953." In *Uncommon Faithfulness: The Black Catholic Experience*, edited by M. Shawn Copeland, 63–77. Maryknoll, NY: Orbis, 2009.

Mudd, Joseph C. *Eucharist as Meaning: Critical Metaphysics and Contemporary Sacramental Theology*. Collegeville, MN: Liturgical Press, 2014.

Mueller, Joseph G. "Forgetting as a Principle of Continuity in Tradition." *Theological Studies* 70, no. 4 (2009): 751–81.

Neill, Stephen. *Anglicanism*. 4th ed. Oxford: Oxford University Press, 1978.

Neuner, Peter. "Kirchen und kirchliche Gemeinschaften." In *"Dominus Iesus": Anstößige Wahrheit oder anstößige Kirche? Dokumente, Hintergründe, Standpunkte und Folgerungen*, edited by Michael J. Rainer, 196–211. Münster: LIT, 2001.

Newbigin, Lesslie. *The Reunion of the Church: A Defence of the South India Scheme.* Westport, CT: Greenwood Press, 1960.

Newman, John Henry. *An Essay on the Development of Christian Doctrine.* 6th ed. Notre Dame, IN: University of Notre Dame Press, 1989.

Nichols, Aidan. *Rome and the Eastern Churches: A Study in Schism.* Collegeville, MN: Liturgical Press, 1992.

Noonan, John T. *A Church That Can and Cannot Change: The Development of Catholic Moral Teaching.* Notre Dame, IN: University of Notre Dame Press, 2005.

Nowak, Martin A., and Sarah Coakley, eds. *Evolution, Games, and God: The Principle of Cooperation.* Cambridge, MA: Harvard University Press, 2013.

O'Donovan, Oliver. *Church in Crisis: The Gay Controversy and the Anglican Communion.* Eugene, OR: Cascade, 2008.

O'Malley, John W. *A History of the Popes: From Peter to the Present.* Lanham, MD: Rowman & Littlefield, 2011.

Pesch, Otto Hermann. *Ecumenical Potential of the Second Vatican Council.* Milwaukee: Marquette University Press, 2006.

———. *Second Vatican Council: Prehistory—Event—Results—Posthistory.* Translated by Deirdre Dempsey. Milwaukee: Marquette University Press, 2014.

Pius XII. *Mystici Corporis Christi.* Vatican website, June 29, 1943. https://tinyurl.com/56aja2f8.

Popescu, Dumitru. "Papal Primacy in Eastern and Western Patristic Theology: Its Interpretation in the Light of Contemporary Culture." In *Petrine Ministry and the Unity of the Church: "Toward a Patient and Fraternal Dialogue,"* edited by James F. Puglisi, 99–114. Collegeville, MN: Liturgical Press, 1999.

Porvoo Communion. "The Porvoo Statement in English." Porvoo Communion Website, October 9, 1992. https://tinyurl.com/2p8xswex.

Pottmeyer, Herman J. "Did Vatican I Intend to Deny Tradition?" In *How Can the Petrine Ministry Be a Service to the Unity of the Universal Church?,* edited by James F. Puglisi, 108–23. Grand Rapids: Eerdmans, 2010.

———. "Historical Development of Forms of Authority and Jurisdiction: The Papal Ministry—an Ecumenical Approach." In *How Can the Petrine Ministry Be a Service to the Unity of the Universal Church?,* edited by James F. Puglisi, 98–107. Grand Rapids: Eerdmans, 2010.

———. "Refining the Question about Women's Ordination." *America,* October 26, 1996, 16–18.

———. *Towards a Papacy in Communion: Perspectives from Vatican Councils I & II.* First American edition. New York: Herder & Herder, 1998.

Przywara, Erich. *Analogia Entis: Metaphysics: Universal Structure and Universal Rhythm.* Translated by John R. Betz and David Bentley Hart. Grand Rapids: Eerdmans, 2014.

Raboteau, Albert J. "Relating Race and Religion: Four Historical Models." In *Uncommon Faithfulness: The Black Catholic Experience,* edited by M. Shawn Copeland, 9–25. Maryknoll, NY: Orbis, 2009.

Radner, Ephraim. *A Brutal Unity: The Spiritual Politics of the Christian Church.* Waco, TX: Baylor University Press, 2012.

———. *The End of the Church: A Pneumatology of Christian Division in the West.* Grand Rapids: Eerdmans, 1998.

———. *Hope among the Fragments: The Broken Church and Its Engagement with Scripture.* Grand Rapids: Brazos, 2004.

———. *A Profound Ignorance: Modern Pneumatology and Its Anti-Modern Redemption.* Waco, TX: Baylor University Press, 2019.

Rahner, Karl. "Christology within an Evolutionary View of the World." In *Theological Investigations,* Electronic Centenary Edition, 5:157–92. Limerick: Centre for Theology, Culture and Values, 2005.

———. *An Ecumenical Priesthood: The Spirit of God and the Structure of the Church.* Edited and translated by Jakob Karl Rinderknecht. Minneapolis: Fortress, 2022.

———. "The Historicity of Theology." In *Theological Investigations,* 9:64–82. Limerick: Centre for Theology, Culture and Values, 2005.

———. "Reflection on the Concept of '*Ius Divinum*' in Catholic Thought." In *Theological Investigations,* 5:219–43. Limerick: Centre for Theology, Culture and Values, 2005.

———. *The Trinity.* New York: Continuum, 2001.

Ramsey, Michael. *The Gospel and the Catholic Church.* Cambridge: Cowley, 1990.

Ratzinger, Joseph. *Pilgrim Fellowship of Faith: The Church as Communion.* Edited by Stephan Otto Horn and Vinzenz Pfnur. Translated by Henry Taylor. San Francisco: Ignatius, 2005.

Régnon, Théodore de. *Études de théologie positive sur la Sainte Trinité.* 3 vols. Paris: Retaux, 1892.

Reumann, John. "The Petrine Ministry in the New Testament and in Early Patristic Tradition." In *How Can the Petrine Ministry Be a Service to the Unity of the Universal Church?,* edited by James F. Puglisi, 49–78. Grand Rapids: Eerdmans, 2010.

Rinderknecht, Jakob K. "The Church: A Body under Law and Gospel." In *Recasting Lutheran Ecclesiology in an Ecumenical Context,* edited by Jonathan Mumme, Richard J. Serina, and Mark W. Birkholz, 171–87. Lanham, MD: Lexington Books/Fortress Academic, 2019.

———. *Mapping the Differentiated Consensus of the Joint Declaration.* New York: Palgrave Macmillan, 2016.

Rogers, Eugene F. *After the Spirit: A Constructive Pneumatology from Resources outside the Modern West.* Grand Rapids: Eerdmans, 2005.

———. *Blood Theology: Seeing Red in Body- and God-Talk.* Cambridge: Cambridge University Press, 2021.

———. *Sexuality and the Christian Body: Their Way into the Triune God.* Oxford: Blackwell, 1999.

Rouse, Ruth, Stephen Neill, and Harold E. Fey. *A History of the Ecumenical Movement.* 2 vols. Philadelphia: Westminster, 1967.

Rush, Ormond. *The Eyes of Faith: The Sense of the Faithful and the Church's Reception of Revelation.* Washington, DC: Catholic University of America Press, 2009.

Sanneh, Lamin. *Translating the Message: The Missionary Impact on Culture.* 2nd ed. Maryknoll, NY: Orbis, 2009.

Schatz, Klaus. "Historical Considerations Considering the Problem of Primacy." In *Petrine Ministry and the Unity of the Church: "Toward a Patient and Fraternal Dialogue,"* edited by James F. Puglisi, 1–14. Collegeville, MN: Liturgical Press, 1999.

Schleiermacher, Friedrich. *The Christian Faith.* Translated by H. R. Mackintosh and J. S. Stewart. Edinburgh: T&T Clark, 1999.

———. *On Religion: Speeches to Its Cultured Despisers.* Translated by John Oman. Louisville, KY: Westminster John Knox, 1994.

Schlesinger, Eugene R. "Eucharistic Sacrifice as Anti-violent Pedagogy." *Theological Studies* 80, no. 3 (2019): 653–72.

——. "Opus Dei, Opus Hominum: The Trinity, the Four-Point Hypothesis, and the Eucharist." *Irish Theological Quarterly* 88, no. 1 (2022): 56–75.

——. "The Sacrificial Ecclesiology of *City of God* 10." *Augustinian Studies* 47, no. 2 (2016): 137–55.

——. *Sacrificing the Church: Mass, Mission, and Ecumenism.* Lanham, MD: Lexington Books/Fortress Academic, 2019.

——. *Salvation in Henri de Lubac: Divine Grace, Human Nature, and the Mystery of the Cross.* Notre Dame, IN: University of Notre Dame Press, 2023.

Schutz, Paul J. "En-gendering Creation Anew: Rethinking Ecclesial Statements on Science, Gender, and Sexuality with William R. Stoeger, SJ." *Horizons* 48, no. 1 (2021): 34–68.

Schwiebert, Jonathan. *Knowledge and the Coming Kingdom: The Didache's Meal Ritual and Its Place in Early Christianity.* New York: Bloombury, 2008.

Sergius Bulgakov. *The Comforter.* Translated by Boris Jakim. Grand Rapids: Eerdmans, 2004.

Sherrard, Philip. *Church, Papacy, and Schism: A Theological Enquiry.* London: SPCK, 1978.

Sobrino, Jon. *The Eye of the Needle: No Salvation outside the Poor; a Utopian-Prophetic Essay.* London: Darton, Longman, & Todd, 2008.

——. *Jesus the Liberator: A Historical Theological Reading of Jesus of Nazareth.* Translated by Paul Burns and Francis McDonagh. Maryknoll, NY: Orbis, 1994.

Sokolowski, Robert. *The God of Faith and Reason: Foundations of Christian Theology.* CUA Press, 1995.

Sonderegger, Katherine. *Systematic Theology.* 2 vols. Minneapolis: Fortress Press, 2015–2020.

Song, Robert. *Covenant and Calling: Towards a Theology of Same-Sex Relationships.* London: SCM, 2014.

Stewart, Alistair C. *The Original Bishops: Office and Order in the First Christian Communities.* Grand Rapids: Baker, 2014.

Sullivan, Francis A. "Further Thoughts on the Meaning of Subsistit In." *Theological Studies* 71, no. 1 (2010): 133–47.

——. "Introduction and Ecclesiological Issues." In *Sic et Non: Encountering Dominus Iesus,* edited by Stephen J. Pope and Charles Hefling, 47–56. Maryknoll, NY: Orbis, 2002.

——. *Magisterium: Teaching Authority in the Catholic Church.* Eugene, OR: Wipf and Stock, 2002.

——. "Quaestio Disputata the Meaning of Subsistit in as Explained by the Congregation for the Doctrine of the Faith." *Theological Studies* 69, no. 1 (2008): 116–24.

——. "Response to Karl Becker, S.J., on the Meaning of Subsistit In." *Theological Studies* 67, no. 2 (2006): 395–409.

Sykes, Stephen. *The Integrity of Anglicanism.* New York: Seabury, 1978.

——. *Unashamed Anglicanism.* London: Darton, Longman, & Todd, 1995.

Tan, Loe-Joo. "'Things Are Not What They Seem': Dominus Iesus, Ecumenism, and Interreligious Dialogue." *Journal of Ecumenical Studies* 48, no. 4 (2013): 523–34.

Tanner, Kathryn. *God and Creation in Christian Theology: Tyranny or Empowerment?* Minneapolis: Fortress, 2005.

Tapie, Matthew A. *Aquinas on Israel and the Church: The Question of Supersessionism in the Theology of Thomas Aquinas.* Cambridge: James Clarke & Co, 2015.

Tatarenko, Laurent. "La Naissance de l'Union de Brest: La Curie Romaine et Le Tournant de l'année 1595." *Cahiers Du Monde Russe* 46, nos. 1–2 (January 1, 2005): 345–54.

Tavard, George H. *A Review of Anglican Orders: The Problem and the Solution.* Collegeville, MN: Liturgical Press, 1990.

Teuffenbach, Alexandra von. *Die Bedeutung des subsistit in.* München: Herbert Utz Verlag, 2002.

The Trevor Project. "Facts about LGBTQ Youth Suicide." Accessed August 19, 2022. https://tinyurl.com/493butky.

Tillard, Jean-Marie R. *Church of Churches: The Ecclesiology of Communion.* Translated by R. C. de Peaux. Collegeville, MN: Liturgical Press, 1992.

———. *Flesh of the Church, Flesh of Christ: At the Source of the Ecclesiology of Communion.* Translated by Madeleine Beaumont. Collegeville, MN: Liturgical Press, 2001.

———. *L'Église locale: Ecclésiologie de communion et catholicité.* Paris: Les Éditions du Cerf, 1995.

Tilley, Maureen A. *The Bible in Christian North Africa: The Donatist World.* Minneapolis: Fortress Press, 1997.

Tonstad, Linn Marie. *God and Difference: The Trinity, Sexuality, and the Transformation of Finitude.* London: Routledge, 2017.

Tück, Jan-Heiner. "Zur Kritik der 'pluralistischen Ekklesiologie'—Anmerkungen zu *Dominus Iesus* 16 und 17." In *"Dominus Iesus": Anstößige Wahrheit oder anstößige Kirche? Dokumente, Hintergründe, Standpunkte und Folgerungen*, edited by Michael J. Rainer, 229–45. Münster: LIT, 2001.

Vischer, Lukas, and Harding Meyer. *Growth in Agreement: Reports and Agreed Statements of Ecumenical Conversations on a World Level.* New York: Paulist, 1982.

Wainwright, Geoffrey. *Eucharist and Eschatology.* New York: Oxford University Press, 1981.

Ware, Timothy. *The Orthodox Church: An Introduction to Eastern Christianity.* 3rd ed. London: Penguin, 2015.

Webster, John. "On Evangelical Ecclesiology." *Ecclesiology* 1, no. 1 (2004): 9–35.

———. "The Self-Organizing Power of the Gospel of Christ: Episcopacy and Community Formation." *International Journal of Systematic Theology* 3, no. 1 (2001): 69–82.

Weil, Louis. "The Liturgy in Michael Ramsey's Theology." In *Michael Ramsey as Theologian*, edited by Robin Gill and Lorna Kendall, 141–58. London: Darton, Longman, & Todd, 1995.

Welby, Justin. "Archbishop of Canterbury's Statement Following a Meeting with the Archbishop, Bishops and Senior Clergy of the Anglican Church of Ghana." Archbishop of Canterbury website, November 21, 2021. https://tinyurl.com/2v43nnn8.

———. "Archbishop of Canterbury's Statement on Ghana's Anti-LGBTQ+ Bill." Archbishop of Canterbury website, October 26, 2021. https://tinyurl.com/yrwkbdt8.

———. "Archbishop of Canterbury's Statement on the Church of Uganda." Archbishop of Canterbury website, June 9, 2023. https://tinyurl.com/yu8nnyyu.

Wilder, Courtney. *Disability, Faith, and the Church: Inclusion and Accommodation in Contemporary Congregations.* Santa Barbara, CA: Praeger, 2016.

Williams, Delores S. *Sisters in the Wilderness: The Challenge of Womanist God-Talk.* Maryknoll, NY: Orbis, 1993.

Williams, Rowan. *Arius: Heresy and Tradition.* Grand Rapids: Eerdmans, 2002.

———. "The Body's Grace." In *Theology and Sexuality: Classic and Contemporary Readings*, edited by Eugene F. Rogers, 309–21. Oxford: Blackwell, 2002.

———. "The Lutheran Catholic." In *Glory Descending: Michael Ramsey and His Writings*, edited by Douglas Dales, John Habgood, Geoffrey Rowell, and Rowan Williams, 211–22. Grand Rapids: Eerdmans, 2005.

———. "One Holy Catholic and Apostolic Church: Archbishop's Address to the 3rd Global South to South Encounter Ain al Sukhna, Egypt." Archbishop of Canterbury website, October 28, 2005. https://tinyurl.com/yr4a36ka.

Winner, Lauren F. *The Dangers of Christian Practice: On Wayward Gifts, Characteristic Damage, and Sin.* New Haven, CT: Yale University Press, 2018.

Wood, Susan K. "The Correlation between Ecclesial Communion and the Recognition of Ministry." *One in Christ* 50, no. 2 (July 2016): 238–49.

Woolverton, John F. "The Chicago-Lambeth Quadrilateral and the Lambeth Conferences." *Historical Magazine of the Protestant Episcopal Church* 53, no. 2 (1984): 95–109.

World Council of Churches. *Baptism, Eucharist and Ministry.* Geneva: World Council of Churches, 1982.

———. "Together towards Life: Mission and Evangelism in Changing Landscapes." WCC website, September 5, 2012. https://tinyurl.com/3pk8u3xf.

Zizioulas, John D. *Being as Communion: Studies in Personhood and the Church.* Crestwood: St. Vladimir's Seminary Press, 1997.

———. "The Future Exercise of Papal Ministry in the Light of Ecclesiology: An Orthodox Approach." In *How Can the Petrine Ministry Be a Service to the Unity of the Universal Church?*, edited by James F. Puglisi, 169–79. Grand Rapids: Eerdmans, 2010.

Zyablitsev, Georgi. "Uniatism as an Ecclesiological Problem Today." In *Four Hundred Years Union of Brest (1596–1996): A Critical Re-evaluation; Acta of the Congress Held at Hernen Castle, the Netherlands, in March 1996*, edited by Bert Groen and Wil van den Bercken, 193–99. Leuven: Peeters, 1998.

Index